Torture, Truth and Justice

This book highlights how, and why, torture is such a compelling tool for states and other powerful actors. While torture has a short-term use value for perpetrators, it also creates a devastating legacy for victims, their families, and communities. In exposing such repercussions, this book addresses the questions 'What might torture victims need to move forward from their violation?' and 'How can official responses provide truth or justice for torture victims?'

Building on observations, documentary analysis, and over 70 interviews with both torture victims and transitional justice workers this book explores how torture was used, suffered, and resisted in Timor-Leste. The author investigates the extent to which transitional justice institutions have provided justice for torture victims. She illustrates how truth commissions and international courts operate together and reflects on their successes and weaknesses with reference to wider social, political, and economic conditions. Stanley also details victims' experiences of torture and highlights how they experience life in the newly built state of Timor-Leste.

Tracking the past, present and future of human rights, truth and justice for victims in Timor-Leste, *Torture, Truth and Justice* will be of interest to students, professionals, and scholars of Asian studies, international studies, human rights, criminology, and social policy.

Elizabeth Stanley is Senior Lecturer in Criminology at the Victoria University of Wellington. She is the author of a number of book chapters and articles on torture, truth commissions, and social justice.

Politics in Asia series

Formerly edited by Michael Leifer
London School of Economics

*ASEAN and the Security of
South-East Asia*
Michael Leifer

**China's Policy Towards Territorial
Disputes**
The Case of the South China Sea
Islands
Chi-kin Lo

India and Southeast Asia
Indian Perceptions and Policies
Mohammed Ayoob

Gorbachev and Southeast Asia
Leszek Buszynski

Indonesian Politics under Suharto
Order, Development and Pressure
for Change
Michael R. J. Vatikiotis

**The State and Ethnic Politics in
Southeast Asia**
David Brown

**The Politics of Nation Building and
Citizenship in Singapore**
Michael Hill and Lian Kwen Fee

Politics in Indonesia
Democracy, Islam and the Ideology
of Tolerance
Douglas E. Ramage

**Communitarian Ideology and
Democracy in Singapore**
Beng-Huat Chua

**The Challenge of Democracy
in Nepal**
Louise Brown

Japan's Asia Policy
Wolf Mendl

**The International Politics of the
Asia-Pacific, 1945–95**
Michael Yahuda

**Political Change in Southeast
Asia**
Trimming the Banyan Tree
Michael R. J. Vatikiotis

Hong Kong
China's Challenge
Michael Yahuda

Korea versus Korea
A Case of Contested Legitimacy
B. K. Gills

Taiwan and Chinese Nationalism
National Identity and Status in
International Society
Christopher Hughes

Torture, Truth and Justice

The Case of Timor-Leste

Elizabeth Stanley

Routledge
Taylor & Francis Group

LONDON AND NEW YORK

First published 2009
by Routledge
2 Park Square, Milton Park, Abingdon, Oxon, OX14 4RN

Simultaneously published in the USA and Canada
by Routledge
711 Third Avenue, New York, NY 10017

Routledge is an imprint of the Taylor & Francis Group, an informa business

First issued in paperback 2011

Typeset in Times New Roman
by Taylor & Francis Books

British Library Cataloguing in Publication Data
A catalogue record for this book is available from the British Library

Library of Congress Cataloging in Publication Data
Stanley, Elizabeth, 1972-
    Torture, truth and justice : the case of Timor-Leste / Elizabeth Stanley.
        p. cm. – (Politics in Asia)
    1. Torture victims–East Timor. 2. Torture–East Timor. 3. East Timor–
Social conditions. I. Title.
    HV8599.E27S83 2008
    364.6'7–dc22
    2008021886

ISBN10: 0-415-47807-3 (hbk)
ISBN10: 0-415-66673-2 (pbk)
ISBN10: 0-203-41659-7 (ebk)

ISBN13: 978-0-415-47807-6 (hbk)
ISBN13: 978-0-415-66673-2 (pbk)
ISBN13: 978-0-203-41659-4 (ebk)

This book is dedicated to my late grandmother,
Ann Stanley.

Contents

Acknowledgements

This book would not have been possible without the participation of Timorese victims who shared their stories of pain and hope. These individuals, their families and friends have inspired, looked after, and provoked me in so many ways. Workers within transitional justice and non-governmental bodies also regularly gave their time, skills, and support despite intense work pressures.

I particularly thank all those at the Judicial System Monitoring Programme and the International Catholic Migration Commission in Dili – their encouragement and links made this book a much happier endeavour. Amnesty International freely provided hard copies of their extensive back catalogue on Timor-Leste. A number of people including Aida, Casimiro, and Helder gave much needed interpretation and translation services, and Scott and Virginia provided vital transcription and research services. Peter Guinness was also particularly supportive and his offer of accommodation during my first visit to Timor-Leste was very welcome. Thank you all.

Sections of this book have been aired in various guises: observations from Stanley (2004, 2007a) form a backdrop for Chapter 1; Stanley (2008b) is a shortened version of Chapter 2; the ideas in Chapter 3 have developed from the analysis in Stanley (2005b); the thoughts for Chapter 4 began in Stanley (2002); ideas from Stanley (2008a) assisted in the writing of Chapters 6 and 7; and, the arguments in Chapter 8 found exposure in Stanley (2007c). I would like to thank all the lovely, supportive editors who enhanced these arguments. All omissions and analytical weaknesses are, of course, my own. The Federation Press granted me permission to use part of a chapter previously published in Anthony & Cunneen (eds), *The Critical Criminology Companion*, Hawkins Press (an imprint of The Federation Press), PO Box 45, Annandale NSW 2038, Australia. © The Federation Press Pty Ltd. The journal *Social Justice* also granted me permission to use material earlier published as 'Transnational Crime and State-Building'.

So many fellow critical thinkers have stimulated and supported me throughout my studies. Their names are too numerous to list here – although I must make mention of Roberta Bacic, Penny Green, Patrick Hayden, Fiona Hutton, Jan Jordan, Jude McCulloch, John Pratt, Bill Rolston, Phil

Scraton, and Tony Ward, who have each provided enthusiasm as well as critical feedback on earlier versions of this book. My ex-colleagues at the Centre for Studies in Crime and Social Justice, UK, nurtured my academic development. My co-workers at the Institute of Criminology, the Crime and Justice Research Centre and the School of Social and Cultural Studies have also provided much-needed encouragement. This, together with the financial assistance provided by Victoria University of Wellington (through the University Research Fund and FHSS grants), made this work possible.

I would also like to thank other friends, their partners and growing families, who have made this project happier – you know who you are, thank you! I have also enjoyed years of support and love from all my family – special thanks to Mammy Kath, Nick, Sue, and Bill. Finally, last but not least, to Acky – thank you for your love, enthusiasm, rallying, and patience, and for encouraging much appreciated diversions.

Abbreviations and Other Terms

ABRI	Indonesian Armed Forces
Apodeti	Timorese Popular Democratic Association
babinsa	village guidance officer
Bahasa Indonesia	Main language spoken in Indonesia
biti	traditional mat used in conflict resolution
Brimob	Indonesian paramilitary police (Mobile Brigade)
CAVR	Commission on Reception, Truth and Reconciliation
CEP	Community Empowerment and Social Governance Project
CIA	Central Intelligence Agency
CMATS	Certain Maritime Agreements in the Timor Sea
CNRT	National Congress for the Reconstruction of East Timor
CRA	Community Reconciliation Act
CRP	Community Reconciliation Process
CTF	Commission on Truth and Friendship
DLU	Defence Lawyers Unit
Falintil	Armed Forces for the National Liberation of East Timor
F-FDTL	*Falintil Forças de Defensa de Timor-Leste* (new Timorese army)
Fretilin	East Timorese pro-independence group
GSS	General Security Services [Israel]
ICC	International Criminal Court
ICJ	International Court of Justice
IMF	International Monetary Fund
Intel	Intelligence Task Force (informants)
INTERFET	International Force in East Timor
JSMP	Judicial System Monitoring Programme
Kodahankam Timor	East Timor Regional Defence and Security Command
Kodim	district military commands
Komnas Ham	Indonesian National Commission on Human Rights

Kopassus	elite counter-insurgency forces
Koramil	sub-district military commands
KOTA	*Klibur oan Timor Asuwain*
NGO	non-governmental organization
PASC	Pilot Agricultural Service Centres
PKI	Communist Party of Indonesia
PNTL	National Police of Timor-Leste
POLRI	Republic of Indonesia Police
PRADET	Psychosocial Recovery and Development in East Timor
Renal	*Fretilin* Rehabilitation Centre
RPKAD	Special Unit Kopassanda
SCU	Serious Crimes Unit
SPSC	Special Panels for Serious Crimes
STP-CAVR	Post-CAVR Technical Secretariat
suco	village
tais	textiles
Tetum	language spoken in East Timor
TFET	Trust Fund for Timor-Leste
TNI	Indonesian National Military
UDT	Timorese Democratic Union
UN	United Nations
UNDP	United Nations Development Programme
UNAMET	UN Assistance Mission in East Timor
UNMISET	UN Mission in East Timor
UNMIT	UN Integrated Mission in Timor-Leste
UNOTIL	UN Office in Timor-Leste
UNTAET	UN Transitional Administration in East Timor

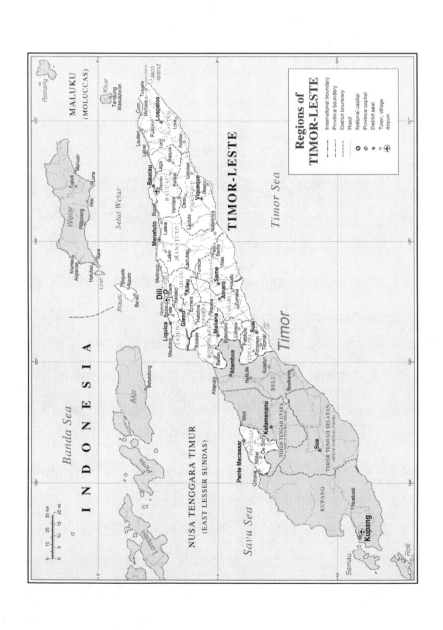

1 Introduction

Timor-Leste (East Timor) is a small country located off the north-west coast of Australia, around 400 miles from Darwin. People from Melanesia and continental Asia inhabited the region from at least 20,000 BC and, from the fourteenth century, international traders began to use the sandalwood-rich island as a trading post. In 1702, Timor was officially established as a Portuguese colony (Jardine 1997).[1] The island was divided into two parts, East and West, by the International Court in 1913. From this time, West Timor was governed by the Dutch (becoming part of Indonesia in 1949) and Timor-Leste (that includes the enclave of Oecusse in the West as well as the islands of Ataúro and Jaco) was retained by the Portuguese (ibid.; Taylor 2003).

The Portuguese control of Timor-Leste continued, uninterrupted, until World War II when Allied Dutch and Australian troops landed in the territory to block Japan's advance to the south. They were not successful as by January 1943, after over a year of fighting, Japan controlled the whole island. Having supporting the allies, an estimated 40,000 to 60,000 East Timorese lost their lives during this period (Gault-Williams 1990), many women were forced into sexual slavery, and local infrastructure was badly damaged. With Japan's defeat in 1945, the Portuguese returned to their colonial post.

Throughout its administration, Portugal did not invest in the country. By the early 1970s, for instance, 93 per cent of the population remained illiterate (Simons 2000). Aside from services for senior officials, the capital Dili had no electricity, water supply, or telephone services. There were few paved roads and while an indigenous elite existed, within both urban and rural areas, most Timorese were relatively untouched by colonial powers (ibid.). Accordingly, while East Timorese people spoke Portuguese, practised Catholicism, and experienced state structures that reflected European traditions, most retained their agricultural, self-sufficient existence in small mountain villages controlled by traditional rulers (ibid.).

This situation completely altered following an April 1974 coup[2] in Portugal. Immediately, Portugal began to withdraw from its colonies in Africa and Asia, leaving a power vacuum in Timor-Leste (Taylor 2003).

Three main parties, *Fretilin* (Front for an Independent East Timor), UDT (Timorese Democratic Union) and *Apodeti* (Timorese Popular Democratic Association), emerged and following a short civil war, Fretilin surfaced as the leading party (ibid.).[3] The resulting period of peace was limited as for various reasons (including a desire to attain strategic claims on regional archipelago islands; to provide a lesson to other areas claiming independence; to benefit from oil reserves in the Timor Sea; and to fight alleged communism) the Indonesian government proposed that an independent Timor-Leste could not exist (Amnesty International 1977; Nairn 1997; Stanley 2008a; J. Taylor 2003).

Commencing a campaign of destabilization – named *Operasi Komodo* (Operation Komodo) – Indonesian forces staged military attacks on towns bordering West Timor, they began to solicit international support for Timor's integration into Indonesia, they gathered intelligence, and they encouraged UDT leaders to undertake a coup (J. Taylor 1991). The subsequent attempted UDT-led uprising against *Fretilin* was not successful and, as shown below, this action led to long-term antagonism and violence between these two groups and their supporters. During this period of unrest and uncertainty, Portuguese officials removed themselves from the region and refused to participate in any decolonization processes. In some despair, and sensing that they were on their own, Fretilin leaders declared the independence of Timor-Leste at the United Nations (UN) on 28 November 1975. Just nine days later, and with the acquiescence of Western powers, the Indonesian government launched a sustained attack.[4] The subsequent occupation lasted almost a quarter of a century.

The recently completed Commission for Reception, Truth and Reconciliation estimates that over 102,800 people, over an eighth of the population, were killed during this occupation (CAVR 2005). People died in *ad hoc* killing sprees, planned massacres, bombing raids, and 'disappearances'; others died in military operations,[5] such as the 'fence of legs' operation that used Timorese civilians as human shields when Indonesian troops went to search for *Fretilin* armed resisters. Tens of thousands were forcibly removed from their homes and land in the mountains, and slowly starved to death in low-lying, unfertile and malaria infested 'resettlement camps' established by the Indonesian military (Nairn 1997). Individuals thought to be sympathetic to Fretilin, and their military wing *Falintil*, were similarly exiled on the island of Ataúro where they suffered illness and starvation. In addition to these killings, other Timorese people were routinely raped, ill-treated, detained without trial, and tortured.

More generally, Timorese people suffered all kinds of controls; for instance, restrictions were placed on the gathering of groups, individuals had to obtain permits to travel beyond their immediate neighbourhood, they experienced periodic curfews and house-to-house searches, their mail was checked, and cultural events were monitored (Amnesty International 1985, 1993). These restrictions on movement and residence were part of a strategy to control the population; however, they also marked military attempts to 'resocialize' the people into willing workers (J. Taylor 2003: 175). The Indonesian officials coerced villagers into work and the Timorese were directed to provide labour for the Indonesian infrastructure and for cash crops (Nairn 1997). In particular, the Indonesian military took control of coffee plantations and used the revenues to offset their costs (D. Jenkins 1980).

Compared to the Portuguese administration, Indonesia did spend time and funds on the development of Timor-Leste. During occupation, schools were opened, roads were built, health services were implemented, and farming procedures were modernized (Sherlock 1996). However, the main beneficiaries of these 'improvements' were the new Indonesian immigrants who were given favoured status (International Commission of Jurists 1992). Educated East Timorese struggled to attain work, even in unskilled professions, and had to prove their loyalty by acquiring Indonesian citizenship for government positions (CAVR 2005). These experiences created antagonism between young East Timorese and the Indonesian regime, and they contributed to the emergence of a new wave of resistance from the early 1990s (Sherlock 1996). Added to that, East Timorese were deeply suspicious of the new services provided and saw many provisions as an extension of the control apparatus. As Martinho explained:

> The schools were used to try to change us into 'good Indonesians', the clinics were used to sterilize us, the roads were used to transport us from one prison to another. We had no jobs, they took our land. And, we were supposed to be happy.

So, despite developmental 'sweeteners', the independence movement in Timor-Leste thrived and a network of fighters and supporters countered the occupation (Jardine 1999). This fight ran throughout the 1970s and 1980s; however it was not until the 1990s that the situation in Timor-Leste received significant international attention. The Santa Cruz massacre of 12 November 1991, in particular, was a significant turning point. International journalists secretly filmed, and later broadcast, this brutal event in which approximately 270 people were shot or beaten to death by Indonesian soldiers in a Dili cemetery. Following these recorded killings the campaign for self-determination gained a momentum that eventually could not be stopped and, in January 1999, the Indonesian government announced that the Timorese people could choose between autonomy and independence in a referendum. Despite the increased violence that was used against the population to 'encourage' votes in support of Indonesia, 78.5 per cent voted for independence on 30 August 1999.

The Indonesian retribution was brutal. In just a few weeks, over 1,400 individuals were killed, thousands were beaten or raped, over three-quarters of all buildings and infrastructure were destroyed and burnt, and three-quarters of the population fled their homes to hide in the mountains or crossed the border into West Timor (Robinson 2002). UN staff, evacuated after being held under siege, returned on 20 September 1999 with a UN multinational military force. Over the following months, a fragile peace was established and, in May 2002, the country finally joined the United Nations as a sovereign state (Stanley 2008a).

The international context

From the start of the occupation, the Indonesian government found ready support from other powerful allies. *Time* magazine noted that General Suharto's seizure of power in Indonesia was the 'West's best news for years in Asia' (Pilger 1998) as unlike his predecessor, President Sukarno, Suharto was viewed as being pro-US and anti-communist. Accordingly, the US Embassy was 'generally sympathetic with and admiring of what the army was doing' in the region (Jardine 1997: 22). This position was reiterated by US, UK, and Australian politicians on the basis that an independent Timor-Leste would be both unviable and a potential communist threat (Monk 2001; J. Taylor 2003).

Therefore, notwithstanding numerous UN Security Council Resolutions that called for Indonesia's immediate withdrawal, violations were denied and no action was taken to stop Indonesia or to support *Fretilin* (Kiernan 2002; Robinson 2002). During UN debates on Timor-Leste, powerful states would encourage others to fall in line. For example, in 1982 the Vanuatu representative to the UN was 'quietly informed by the Australian delegate that his government might curtail its aid to Vanuatu unless its prime minister took a less supportive stance on self-determination for East Timor' (J. Taylor 2003: 180). As a result of such activities, most UN members failed to support Timor-Leste and either abstained or voted against relevant resolutions (Stanley 2007a).

While Indonesia held geographic, ideological, and political interests for powerful states it also presented strategic, economic opportunities. US-based multinational companies such as Goodyear, General Electric, Caltex, and AT&T had strong interests in Indonesia's national resources and market opportunities (Jardine 1997). These major investors lobbied to support Suharto when the Dili massacre attracted international condemnation (Nairn 1997; Stanley 2007a). In the same way, the Australian government gave full recognition to Indonesia's claim over Timor-Leste in a bid to access oil and mineral reserves in the Timor Sea. In 1989, Australia signed the Timor Gap Treaty with Indonesia, which gave 'possession' of an estimated seven billion barrels of oil belonging to Timor-Leste (Pilger 1998); as is detailed in Chapter 8, this remains a central economic issue for the Timorese people.

The international support for Indonesia also yielded significant economic opportunities for military sales and training. Australia's military training only helped, as the Australian Foreign Minister from 1988 to 1996, Gareth

Evans, admitted (in Robinson 2002: 164), to professionalize swathes of human rights abusers. Yet, the 'arming up' of Indonesian forces brought significant business for supporting states (Stanley 2007a). The US and UK, for instance, provided 'ground attack aircraft, helicopters, missiles, frigates, battlefield communication systems, [and] armoured vehicles' to Indonesia (J. Taylor 2003: 178). Some 90 per cent of the Indonesian weaponry used during the initial invasion of Timor-Leste was supplied by US companies (Jardine 1997; Kohen 1981) and throughout the occupation the US administration approved over US$1 billion of weapons sales (Chomsky 2000). When grassroots pressure eventually led to the US Congress voting to block weapons delivery, Britain became Indonesia's largest arms provider (Phythian 2000). Despite the growing international pressure for Indonesia to withdraw from Timor-Leste, British arms sales to Indonesia grew throughout the 1990s. In 1996, when New Labour came to power, sales were valued at £438 million (ibid.). Throughout this period, British politicians accepted Indonesian government guarantees that supplies would not be used for internal suppression (Chomsky 2000). As Alan Clark, the British Defence Minister responsible for the sale of Hawk aircraft to Indonesia, remarked: 'My responsibility is to my own people. I don't really fill my mind much with what one set of foreigners is doing to another' (Pilger 1994: 18).

Powerful states and transnational bodies continued, therefore, to ignore the plight of the Timorese people and, in many cases, directly assisted the Indonesian government to implement repressive policies. The World Bank channeled approximately US$30 billion to the Suharto regime. Despite issues of corruption, false accounting, and the militaristic appropriation of funds, the World Bank accepted that Indonesia pursued 'good governance' (Bello and Guttall 2006). Indonesia applied these monies to the Timorese people – for example, poverty alleviation budgets were used in Indonesia's 'socialization' campaign of terror to deter people from voting for independence (La'o Hamutuk 2000).

This supportive stance was assisted by limited media coverage of events. Those few journalists who attempted to subvert Indonesian attempts to stop any reporting in the region faced surveillance, controls, and (as in the case of the 'Balibo Five'[6]) sometimes death. Even when the territory was said to be 'open', Indonesian officials regularly blocked visits from humanitarian groups, human rights workers, and journalists (Amnesty International 1985). The distressing experiences of the East Timorese were generally not of interest to Western newspaper editors or TV programmers (Martinkus 2001; Nairn 1997). Moreover, newspapers minimized their coverage during periods of mass repression. For example, between August and December 1975, the *Los Angeles Times* ran 16 articles on Timor-Leste. Yet, from March 1976 to November 1979, when killings were occurring indiscriminately, 'there was not a single mention' of the country in the paper (Jardine 1997: 23).

This position was not unusual, and when the situation in Timor-Leste was reported in the mainstream media, it relied heavily on Indonesian misrepresentations (Chomsky 1996; Klaehn 2002). Indonesia sustained a solid propaganda effort in the face of criticisms. Before and during the occupation, media sources were heavily censored and influenced to present the Indonesian point of view (Cabral 2000). Articles were regularly planted in the press, media events were staged, and international journalists and politicians, as well as Timorese people, were encouraged to present material in favour of Indonesian policies. This propaganda had a number of recurrent themes: the denigration of communism, a paternalistic attitude to the Timorese population, a focus on the developmental 'good' provided by the Indonesian government, a focus on the potential division of Indonesia, and a disregard for foreign, notably non-governmental organization, intervention (ibid.: 73–75; see also McRae 2002). Perhaps the true terror in Timor-Leste was not illustrated in international, mainstream reporting because this would undermine the political and economic benefits of retaining friendships with Indonesia. As Herman (1982: 143) argues, 'there was certainly no political advantage to be gained from focusing on the abuses'.

Of course, alternative reporting did illuminate the East Timorese situation – this is precisely why Bishop Belo and José Ramos Horta were awarded the Nobel Peace Prize in 1996 and it is why human rights activists destroyed British Aerospace Hawk Jets, to prevent genocide, in the same year (Pilger 1998).[7] These kinds of international acts underpinned an ideological shift in the political and media realms of once supportive countries. While the eventual referendum for Timor-Leste can certainly be attributed to Indonesian political change in May 1998, when President Suharto was replaced by President B. J. Habibie (the latter being a character who wanted to portray himself as a reformer, distant from corruption and economic instability), it can also be linked to the activities of powerful international interests that began to withdraw cooperation from Indonesia (Davidson 2001). As examples: President Clinton broke US Administration ties with the Indonesian military; the International Monetary Fund suspended talks on economic recovery; the World Bank froze US$300 million destined for Indonesia; the Paris club of creditors delayed their decision making; the British Foreign Secretary announced suspension of arms exports; and a general international agreement emerged that Indonesia must implement the results of the referendum (Robinson 2002). While, as J. Taylor (2003: 185) proposes, 'It seemed that a unique set of events, within Indonesia and internationally, had combined to produce a brief period in which self-determination could be exercised', these acts also illustrate that the crimes in Timor-Leste might have been previously stopped by the withdrawal of international support for Indonesian policies on Timor-Leste (Chomsky 1996).

Many states, corporations, and transnational bodies ignored human rights standards in pursuit of their own strategic, economic, and ideological goals. While the Indonesian state was central to repression in Timor-Leste, it could not act on its own and it appears that Indonesia would probably have retreated from the region if other external actors had intervened. As will be seen in the following chapters, these contextual global networks of power underpinned the creation and sustenance of local violence – led by Indonesian officials, but involving the East Timorese themselves.

Book overview

Against this backdrop, this book tracks the experiences of one group of human rights victims – torture victims[8] – during and in the aftermath of this Indonesian occupation of Timor-Leste. In particular, the original primary research in this book pursues three main themes: (i) how torture has been used, suffered, and resisted; (ii) the extent to which transitional justice institutions – specifically courts and truth commissions – might provide truth and justice for torture victims; and, (iii) how torture victims experience life in the wake of their violation. This book evaluates, therefore, the past, present, and future of human rights, truth, and justice for torture victims.

The decision to focus on torture victims has been, at times, questioned by onlookers – after all, as has already been indicated, the people of Timor-Leste have suffered a multitude of violations. In this light, why concentrate on such a specific group? This focus emerged as a consequence of previous work, on truth commissions in Chile and South Africa (Stanley 2001, 2004). During this research two major issues became evident. First, that torture victims (along with victims of sexual violence and rape) endure the most serious violation that the victim can survive. As shown in Chapter 2, torture victims suffer the most violent and grotesque atrocities, and they endure numerous physical and psychological repercussions. Second, despite these violations and sequelae, torture victims are frequently excluded from those institutions established to provide truth and justice. Truth commissions and court proceedings regularly confine their attention to violations that culminate in death and often leave thousands of living victims without recourse to official acknowledgement or redress. In the same way, the debates on transitional justice have brought limited attention to the issue of torture. This book attempts to fill this gap.

The book aims to expose the repercussions of violence and transitional justice suffered by victims. It details their experiences and highlights their needs for future considerations of truth and justice. This stance is also relatively unusual in the literature on transitional justice which tends to focus on the laws, philosophies, and policies of 'dealing with the past' rather than on considering the experiences of victims. In these respects, the following case study on Timor-Leste is significant on a much wider canvas. In highlighting the 'view from below' in this one country, this book presents an analysis about the potential and limits of transitional justice more generally. Certainly, the new research in this book raises significant questions about how transitional justice institutions are implemented as '*ex post facto* face-savers for the international community' in situations when the 'international community' have not offered any previous protection for civilians, and how the discourse of transitional justice – that stands for something profound, desirable, and always beneficial – can be applied as a legitimizing cover for practices that are ultimately harmful or distressing to victims (Bell *et al.* 2007: 156).

In addition, the ensuing analysis of transitional justice is set against the realities in which people live. The reason for this is that, during interviews, victims deeply reflected on the continuing violence that they endure. As shown in future chapters, victims do not necessarily separate continuing structural violence from the violence that they suffered during torture. For them, human rights violations are bundled together. When talking about torture or transitional justice, victims consistently refer to their living conditions and to broader activities in the region. Transitional justice mechanisms – such as courts or truth commissions – never operate in a vacuum and victims rarely view these institutions in isolation or disconnected from broader economic, political, or social decision-making. Rather, for most victims, the success or failure of these institutions depend – very much – on what changes they see around them.

This book is concerned, therefore, with context. In this focus, it seeks to reflect on the ways in which courts and truth commissions are experienced by the very individuals (the victims) that they are meant to serve. This approach also ensures that transitional justice bodies can be observed in terms of how they are grafted onto, and perform, particular relations of power. In doing so, it is hoped that we might consider and improve how we do justice in ways that are relevant and meaningful to victims of human rights violations. Thus, while the book focuses on the case of Timor-Leste and torture victims specifically, it has a deeper resonance with debates on human rights and transitional justice across the world.

The research context

This book is also based on a critical approach to researching human rights violations. This method requires some explanation. Thus, this section outlines some broad reflections on critical methodology; these are followed by an exploration of the difficulties in communicating about torture, the usefulness of 'storytelling', the reasons why victims chose to contribute to this book, and details on who contributed.

Taking a critical approach to human rights research

The production of human rights knowledge over the last decade or so has been phenomenal; '*the* normative political language' (S. Cohen 1993: 99) of our time has dramatically infused media reporting, political commentaries, non-governmental organizations' reports, academic publications, legal transcripts, and so on. Needless to say, this growth has not been reflected in positive changes that sustain human rights values as violations almost appear to have increased in their scale and intensity during the same period and most violators continue to 'get away with it'. The knowledge developed on rights has not dovetailed with more benign behaviour (Farmer 2003). From the outset then, this author is mindful of the limitations and weaknesses of producing yet another rights-based publication.

At the same time, this book is based on a personal belief that human suffering in all its forms should be acknowledged and, preferably, responded to in ways that will alleviate its causes and conditions. As S. Cohen (2001: 296) makes clear:

> The choice is between 'troubling recognitions' that are escapable (we can live with them) and those that are inescapable. This is not the 'positive freedom' of liberation, but the negative freedom of being given this choice. This means making *more* troubling information available to more people. Informed choice requires more raw material: statistics, reports, atlases, dictionaries, documentaries, chronicles, censuses, research, lists. Someone has to inform us *exactly* how many children in the world (and just *where* and *why*) are still dying of measles, are conscripted as twelve-year-olds into killer militias, are sold by their families into child prostitution, are beaten to death by their parents. This information should be regular and accessible: rolling in front of our eyes like the news headlines on the screens in Times Square.

Put simply, we need to gather and disseminate information so that we might recognize and respond to suffering. Critical analysis of violations may assist towards breaking down the 'cultures of denial' that surround acts of violence (S. Cohen 2001). In the current climate of the 'war on terror', where the methods and calibration of torture are commonly discussed as if the potential victims do not humanly exist and as if there is no terror or pain (Feitlowitz 1998), such work on torture might have a practical use. It might offer a way to understand the dynamic nature of power, and how it is played out through legitimized state violence as well as within the everyday fear experienced by those who sense themselves as targets (Sim 2003). With these aspirations, this author has sought to write '*against* rather than simply *about*' human rights violations (ibid.: 247).

Critical academics (Alasuutari 1998; Berrington *et al.* 2003; Sim *et al.* 1987) have exposed the need for research that emphasizes 'the view from below', and this work is no exception in its desire to provide a small space for those who are regularly silenced or neutralized through popular and official channels. In addition, this book focuses on the ideological frames through which the experiences of victims have been variously ignored and misinterpreted. This approach has significance as victims of human rights violations are frequently denied their victimhood by state officials. It is commonplace that victims are depicted as deserving of their treatment as they are constructed as occupying denigrated positions – as 'terrorists', as 'subversives', as 'dangerous prisoners', and so on (Huggins *et al.* 2002; Stanley 2004). This research establishes that these ideological boundaries are unhelpful, at the very least, and that there is a need to 'dig beneath the surface of historically specific, oppressive, social structures' (Harvey 1990: 1) to illustrate violations and victims for what they are.

This work is not about making the sufferings of victims viewable or 'bearable to others' (Chandler 1999: 144); rather, in many ways, this book seeks to make connections between people who live distinctly different lives. It attempts to reinforce the idea that, at a global level, our lives are connected; we are each 'implicated in the lives of others' (Butler 2004: 7). This stance is one of identification – breaking the negation that gives rise to: violations; or a lack of empathy or loss for those who are killed or harmed; or an identification with perpetrators (Butler 2004) – and is an attempt to make real the commonalities between those who experience or stand at the side of victimizations. Such a recognition-based approach aims to 'instigate a transformation' (ibid.: 44) by exposing how victims of torture are so firmly linked to 'us' in their aspirations, needs, and humanity. Accordingly, it is hoped that this work may foster 'a banality of virtue' (S. Cohen 2001: 264) in which we are left with no choice but to act to make things better.

The personal basis of this research does not however stand alone. To progress a tactic of 'deep' recognition, there is a need to penetrate the everydayness of brutality and to ensure that the stories of individual suffering are not insulated from broader social or structural processes and practices. The fact that awful events happened 'long ago to other people' (Chandler 1999: 111) does not necessarily indicate that the conditions that gave rise to those events have evaporated. Consequently, within this critical approach it is apparent that torture as a gross human rights violation cannot be examined separately from other forms of 'structural violence' or 'pathologies of power' that underline and obscure violations; as Farmer (2003: 219) notes: 'Social inequalities based on race or ethnicity, gender, religious creed, and – above all – social class are the motor force behind most human rights violations.' As a result, individualized forms of violence, like torture, tend to be 'embedded in entrenched structural violence' (ibid.) and, in the aftermath of gross human rights violations, victims regularly struggle against the daily grind of inequalities.

For instance, consider the experiences of one research interviewee, Maria (cited in Stanley 2007a: 171). Throughout the occupation, Maria suffered horrific human rights violations – she was illegally detained; state officials would not give her family any information about her arrest or detention; over years, she endured numerous tortures including sexual assaults, the extraction of her fingernails, electroshock, beatings, cuttings and food deprivation. Such experiences are certainly classified as gross human rights violations. However, speaking from her one-room home, Maria explained that her violations went beyond physical torture:

These scars are from years ago ... there must be justice in a country which has law and order ... but look at my situation now [here, she gestured to her surroundings and dress], this is about violence and rights. The economic situation of this country is important too. We have nothing, not even a monument for those who died. My family needs support.

For Maria, violence has progressed on a continuum. There have been times of intense pain and suffering, inflicted by Indonesian military or security officials, yet her main concern is how she is going to survive the seemingly endless, everyday violations that pervade her life.

From this example, the value of a contextualizing, critical approach to research is made apparent. It is not necessarily useful to address Maria's situation with reference to the 'evil nature' of individual military officers who engaged in torture. Instead, an analysis that demonstrates how social structures frame, direct, and manage violence is required; it is this latter approach that is taken in this book. Demonstrating the power dynamics that sustain multiple forms of violations against groups and populations is a fundamental aspect of this work.

With these methods, this research resolutely stands 'on the side' of those who have suffered violations. It establishes the historical basis of events that have harmed not just torture victims, but the whole population in Timor-Leste. However, it also sets out to examine the transitional justice mechanisms that have been pursued in the aftermath of the occupation. In research that contextualizes judicial and truth-seeking mechanisms within an analysis of the global dynamics of power, this book seeks to demonstrate how certain groups are able to 'operate beyond public scrutiny and thus accountability' (Tombs and Whyte 2003: 4, emphasis in original removed). Further, this critical approach is concerned with how these transitional justice mechanisms might lead to a discourse that actually legitimates some knowledges over others (Berrington *et al.* 2003). The analysis undertakes, then, a critical look at how transitional justice is being conducted within an era that is, undoubtedly, globally inegalitarian (Farmer 2003). It is an attempt to counter the taken-for-granted attitudes about gross human rights violations, truth, and justice.

Communicating the pain of torture

In previous work, the author has detailed how and why torture victims remain silent about their experiences (Stanley 2004). There are many reasons for this lack of 'talk', including how victims react to their devalued social identities, the desire of individuals to protect themselves or others, as well as feelings of complicity in the act of torture itself. Alongside these explanations, however, victims are faced with the fundamental difficulty of communicating their experience and pain to others. This latter issue is worthy of further examination as it raises significant methodological questions for this project.

It must be remembered that torture is often an attempt by state officials to get individuals to use their voice against themselves and against others. While, as shown in the following chapter, torture is regularly used to humiliate, spread fear, and control specific groups or individuals, the common understanding is that it operates to get information out of individuals. In this event, the 'voice' of the tortured is simultaneously directed and destroyed by the torturer. Through the application of pain, humiliation, and fear, torturers seek to control who says what, when, and how. As Elaine Scarry (1985: 54) details:

> ... torturers ... mime the work of pain by temporarily breaking off the voice, making it their own, making it speak their words, making it cry out when they want it to cry, be silent when they want its silence, turning it on and off ...

For the torturer, making victims talk 'is about power, about imposing one's will on another' (Crelinsten 1995: 37). For the tortured, 'to be silent or to speak may constitute the difference between life and death' (Agger and Buus Jensen 1996: 82), but the voice may be the only thing to control. Silence can be a chosen form of resistance to violations (Rivera-Fuentes and Birke 2001; Ross 2003a). Torturers may also aim to instil silence among their victims by making them fearful of the repercussions of speaking out.[9] However, this is arguably not intended to be a total silence as regimes want to keep some 'memory of fear alive'; instead, torturers seek to 'control ... the spaces of speech and silence' (Trumper 1999: 27).

Still, Scarry (1985) details how torture wipes out the 'voice' completely. As she remarks, the 'goal of the torturer is to make ... the body, emphatically and crushingly *present* by destroying it, and to make ... the voice, *absent* by destroying it' (ibid.: 49). The experience of violence is such that speech becomes useless to provide an insight into pain, and known language cannot adequately represent trauma. Stories of torture are 'inhabited by the impossibility of telling' (Laub 1992: 79).

The 'impossibility of telling' represents, at first glance, a personal perspective in which individual victims faced with a stifling experience can find no way to explain their position. Yet the language to explain torture only really exists 'within a collectivity' (de Saussure 1974: 14). As others (Das 1997; Rejali 2003) have argued, the failure to communicate about torture is representative not just of the destruction of the 'voice' or knowledge of the victim, but of a 'failure in spirit' of the listeners. That is, stories of torture are subject to silence as victims sense that listeners cannot take in their account of what happened. The silence of torture could be attributed to the way in which audiences shut out or do not hear difficult stories; it perhaps 'comes much more from the others' need to forget and to not have to deal with the pain involved in encountering survivors of violence' (Rosenthal 2003: 926). The understanding that stories of torture will not be understood can represent a further burden to victims and may contribute to increased feelings of 'alienation and not belonging' (ibid.: 925).

Communicating the pain of torture can be seen in terms of personal struggles to find the language to reflect experiences of violence, but it can also be linked to the wider societal and institutional reticence to hear painful or chaotic stories that challenge common-sense notions of state protection. Certainly, victims may be discouraged from speaking out when there is little outlook for prosecutions, commissions, or other change (Huggins *et al.* 2002). Furthermore, the public desire to make testimonies easily digestible leaves victims in an isolated position in which silence is often the easier option (Humphrey 2000; Sironi and Branche 2002). Silence becomes a form of communication. In a situation where experiences cannot be easily replayed into words, it can be a 'legitimate discourse on pain' (Ross 2001: 272).

In these circumstances, what should be the role of research? After all, there is, as Chandler (1999: 111) notes, 'something unsettling about "fine writing" about pain'. In describing agony and emotions, writers struggle to depict torture for what it is. Perhaps this is to be expected given the conditions detailed above. In this context, the role of critical research may be just that of 'bearing witness', a simple issue of 'rehumanizing' victims or generating association between victims and bystanders (ibid.). The concern, from a critical perspective, is one of 'breaking the silence and calling ... atrocities ... by the name they deserve' (Becker 2005: 9).

A related challenging issue is whether research and subsequent writing on torture actually serves to insulate bystanders 'from what really happened to the mind and bodies of the victim' (ibid.). Any discourse on torture may have 'the effect of softening and cleaning what went on' (Chandler 1999: 144). In the wake of evidence of torture at Abu Ghraib, for instance, it is clear that the exposure of torture has not readily equated to onlooker association with victims. Instead, the discourse has been dominated by politicians, military officials, legal personnel, academics, corporate workers, and the few highlighted perpetrators. The main discussions have been of aberrational activities, the limited training of deviant officers, and the merits of torture and 'torture lite' in the face of threats to national security. Little has been reported from the victims' perspectives and the identification has been with the perpetrators (Butler 2004) – this is seen, for example, in the websites that allow individuals to post photographs of themselves in poses similar to those taken by torturers (specifically referred to as 'doing a Lynndie'[10]). The perpetrator perspective has also been apparent in much recent academic literature (Bagaric and Clarke 2005; Dershowitz 2002; Ignatieff 2004) that has been directed towards the legitimization and promotion of torture (under certain conditions and with certain limits of course!). With such cultural resources, the distance has perhaps widened between onlookers and victims. This book attempts to work against this recent progression.

Breaking silence through stories

Given the issues of silence and dissociation that pervade torture, it seems reasonable that a methodological approach that provides a means for victims to speak, and to be listened to, would be appropriate for this research. Yet providing testimony may not necessarily always be a solution to feelings of exclusion and pain for victims. In fact, if done carelessly, the experience may well contribute to the victim's sense of inequality and alienation. With this in mind, this section examines the value of storytelling to this book and details some of the reasons why individuals chose to participate, and why others did not.

Storytelling is foundational to human interaction. The stories people tell about themselves and their lives both constitute and interpret those lives (Ewick and Silbey 1995). Storytelling has the capacity to reveal truths that have previously been silenced or denied. In many instances, these truths have been 'right before our eyes and therefore simply taken for granted'; however they occupy spaces that have been 'hitherto unrecognized' (Scheper-Hughes 1996: 889). Taken together, 'multiple stories which have been buried, silenced or obscured … have the capacity to undermine the illusion of an objective, naturalised world which so often sustains inequality and powerlessness' (Ewick and Silbey 1995: 198–99).

Like Rolston's (2000: xv) research on state killings in Northern Ireland, the underlying premise of this book is that 'stories are important … because they … reveal how far the state degraded the ideal of human rights … and how some people struggled to uphold that ideal in the most hostile of environments'. With the transition to democratic rule in Timor-Leste, this is something of a 'good news story' in its illustration of how Timorese people undertook a sustained resistance against Indonesian occupation over almost 25 years. The stories that Timorese people tell show their coping and survival strategies; they illustrate the possibilities of resistance. Yet a key focus of the research is on the aftermath of this self-determination struggle and, in many ways, it is evident that the fight for human rights is far from over. As exemplified later in this book, torture victims have faced numerous challenges in having their experiences heard and dealt with by the truth and justice mechanisms established in the wake of transition. Further, it is evident that torture continues to be used by police officers; under the new democratic regime, rights are still degraded (Stanley 2005a). The stories of torture that are told in this book reflect, then, the present as well as the past.

In relating the past, storytelling also looks to the future – what people say, how they say it, and who to, is often dependent on emotive, political, legal, or moral expectations. The process of storytelling becomes a social practice itself, demonstrating cultural values, power relations, and aspirations (Ewick and Sibley 1995). In response to a question on why they agreed to participate in this research, many individuals detailed that they hoped that more people, across the world, would hear about the Timorese experience and, from that, choose to take action. In most situations, individuals connected the wider acknowledgement of their stories with social change. Thus, Joao commented:

> If your country knows the truth about what happened, then perhaps they might see fit to provide money so that we can have a memorial, in Dili, for the Santa Cruz massacre.

While Thomas argued:

> I want your people to hear about what happened and to help us establish an international tribunal.

In these instances, stories were not given over for personal benefit or pleasure, but in an attempt to motivate others to provide measures for remembrance, truth, and justice. In other examples, victims detailed that they wanted the 'Western world' to comprehend their role in the atrocities. As Fransisco proposed:

> I want to tell you what your country, Britain, did. Your country made a lot of money out of suffering and they have shown little care for that. You must hear that, and you must make others hear it.

In the same meeting, Fransisco remarked that my education had probably been paid from monies derived from defence sales. My status, as an academic born and educated in the UK, might have been linked to the suffering of the Timorese people. Really, I could not refute this suggestion as that may have been possible. Fransisco's story, like many others, was used to share wider values. It was used to 'express – and indeed enact – the social conditions of power and influence in everyday life' (Coffey and Atkinson 1996: 76). His story was a performance in response to the values and meanings he attributed to me, as a white, British, academic female.

While victims' views of my history and status certainly had implications for the research process, their decisions about my own personal demeanour also played a part. Two victims (Alberto and Emilia) commented that my 'nice eyes' and 'open face' convinced them that they could relate their experiences. However, this surface-level stance belay deeper considerations. The opportunity to tell a story, for this pair, also reflected their need to receive respect and validation from another person (Becker 2005). Further, they reiterated the damage that had been caused to them (Ross 2003a), and each spoke strongly about the value of speaking out in order to break their feelings of isolation and to build their self-identity (Lawler 2002).

In other circumstances, the chance to tell a story was taken by the interviewee to be an opportunity to make open political statements. So, while most stories would be related in private, individuals might also use their narrative to send messages. For example, Antonio agreed to be interviewed on the proviso that it was to take place in the yard outside his office. The actual story was then related not just to myself and the interpreter, but to approximately 20 other individuals, as well as numerous animals. As Antonio told his story, the audience would listen, sometimes nod, and occasionally add further comment. Politically attuned, Antonio viewed his storytelling as an opportunity to progress social debate and under-standing. He turned his story into a direct public narrative, a way of expressing opinion to others in his environment (Lawler 2002). This experi-ence demonstrated how stories can lack impartiality or objectivity and can be used by the teller to persuade others of the credibility of their cause (Robben 1995).

The personal and political reasons why victims decided to contribute to this book were, therefore, wide ranging. At the same time, numerous others did not want to give their story. The reasons for this may reflect some of the silencing tensions detailed above, but it also reflected the fundamental aspirations of storytelling. One particular aspect (that also affected those collating testimonies for the CAVR, see Chapter 7) was that victims did not want to continually repeat their experiences. Thus, Ana remarked:

> Following the violence of 1999, the International Red Cross came to take testimonies. I gave my story to them. The CAVR wanted to hear it. I told them that they must contact the Red Cross, they have my story. It is too much to keep giving it. And, nothing has happened from it. Why should I do it again?

The ways in which multiple organizations and individuals came to collect stories, without thereafter taking what was perceived as the appropriate action, meant that some victims had decided not to speak to any other people. For these individuals, the stories were just reappropriated by groups for their own ends, stories were used for the advancement of others, and there was no personal benefit to be gained from relating a painful past once more. This particular response provoked a clear evaluation of the motives for this research and the potential neocolonizing impact that it could reinforce. The ability of Western researchers to 'give voice' to people's suffering and to rewrite stories for their own ends illustrates privilege – stories can easily be reappropriated into a commodity and tellers can regularly lose ownership over their stories, a point intensified by unequal resources and access to global information flows (Ross 2003b). As Skeggs (2002: 362) outlines:

> Centuries of colonialism designate some people as knowers and some as strangers ... We are positioned by these relations and techniques and therefore acknowledgement of the unequal forms of exchange they reproduce is not about telling the self but being aware of positioning and the limits on the mobility of some groups.

The reproduction of stories in this book therefore reflects the researcher's own status; this scholarly work is imbued with power. That one can 'study, rather than endure' abuse is a reminder of the benefits that follow for some from the 'nature and distribution of assaults on dignity' (Farmer 2003: 224). The individual stories given for this book are 'saturated with meaning' (Lawler 2002: 252) and reflect wider social, national, and international realities. No story was given or taken lightly. In their reception and telling, it is hoped that the stories will work against terror, naming violations for what they are, and assist in ending the isolation of injustice (Suárez-Orozco 1992).

The research process

The primary research was conducted, over three fieldwork visits to Timor-Leste, from February 2004 to December 2005. Undertaking interviews with 74 individuals, the author also engaged in observations of the serious crimes process and truth commission activities, and had a broad range of informal meetings with victims, transitional justice workers, and other individuals.

Interviews were conducted with 21 victims of detention and torture (involving nine women and twelve men). All were adults – mostly aged between 30 to 50 years of age – and all had experienced life before Indonesian occupation. These victims mainly came from Dili, Aileu, Ermera, Baucau, and Viqueque. These central regions perhaps do not always identify the 'worst' of the repression that is often associated with the far east or far west of the country and, consequently, there were limits to these interviews. However, these gaps have been somewhat plugged by another project that the author established with the Judicial System Monitoring Programme (JSMP) during 2005–06. The author directed this project and subsequently wrote a report (Stanley 2007b), while JSMP outreach staff conducted in-depth interviews with 15 torture victims (three women, twelve men) in the districts of Oecusse, Liquica, Bobonaro, and Los Palos. These interviews are occasionally referred to in this book. Where this is done, the link to JSMP is shown in the footnote. In all other cases, interviews were undertaken directly by the author.

Interviews were also undertaken with those involved in transitional justice processes. The impetus of this approach was to gain a better understanding of the internal workings and pressures of the organizations established to provide truth and justice to the people of Timor-Leste. To this end, 18 interviews (five women, thirteen men) were conducted with those who worked within the serious crimes process; 14 (eight women, six men) interviews were undertaken with workers of the Commission for Reception, Truth and Reconciliation; and two Truth and Friendship Commissioners (both men) were interviewed. Finally, a further 19 (seven women, twelve men) workers from non-governmental organizations (NGO) and other UN organizations were interviewed.[11]

The chapters

The following three chapters provide a conceptual framework to the study on Timor-Leste. Chapter 2 illustrates the economic, political, and social conditions in which torture is used. It details the reasons why torture has remained a key, albeit devastating, tool for states and it explores the connections between this violation and structural relations of disadvantage. In particular, this chapter argues that torture is deeply linked to processes of marginalization and criminalization that determine who is tortured and how they are victimized. The aftermath of this violation is explored; while torture destroys human security and gives rise to a range of sequelae, this chapter argues that it is also a self-defeating activity for states.

Chapter 3 examines the broader issues of globalization, state power, and human rights. It contends that states remain central actors in the provision of justice for torture victims and, reflecting the work of political philosopher Nancy Fraser (1997, 2003, 2005), it establishes a tripartite framework to deal with injustice. This framework encompasses: (i) recognition – to address how torture victims are ignored or subject to cultural, legal, or political denigration; (ii) participation – to tackle how torture victims are frequently excluded from democratic processes due to their devaluation, limited capability, or as a result of institutional practices; (iii) redistribution – to deal with the structural and social injustices that hinder torture victims from participating on a par with others. This analysis – which highlights that human rights violations, and their claims, are bundled or intertwined together – encourages a justice response to victims that 'digs deeper' into the structures, institutions, and social relations that underpin torture.

These three factors of justice are applied, within Chapter 4, to an analysis of transitional justice. Transitional justice bodies, particularly truth commissions and trials, have enjoyed an expansive global rise over the last two decades and this chapter shows that they offer significant potential to provide justice for torture victims. Yet the practice of transitional justice has also restrained justice and, on many occasions, created further injustice. This chapter addresses the claims that transitional justice institutions may operate in ways that hinder recognition for victims – by impeding their participation – and that they undermine opportunities to pursue social justice.

The case study begins in Chapter 5 with detail on how torture was undertaken and experienced by different groups in Timor-Leste. It is shown that, while torture was used during the internal civil war, it was a systematic, pervasive tool for Indonesian officials and their auxiliaries. Torture was applied for various ends; however, ultimately, it was employed as a means to maintain or coerce state power. This value was, however, short-lived as torture also became a significant factor in building the ultimately successful resistance to occupation.

Chapter 6 evaluates the two criminal justice institutions established to deal with human rights violations in Timor-Leste: the Jakarta based Ad Hoc Human Rights Courts and the Dili-based serious crimes process. It argues that these mechanisms have provided political cover – they have given the appearance that justice has been done – but they have entrenched impunity for Indonesian officials. This chapter, and its related appendix, shows that the serious crimes process has provided a partial recognition of torture; however, this 'success' has been devalued as a result of numerous problems. The repercussions for torture victims have been extensive: they have continued to be subject to denigration, inequality, fear, intimidation, and violence under the new dynamics of transitional justice.

Chapter 7 assesses whether justice for torture victims has been secured through truth-telling mechanisms, particularly the Commission for Reception, Truth and Reconciliation (CAVR) and the ongoing Commission on Truth and Friendship (CTF). It details that the CAVR has presented a significant contribution to recognition and participatory justice in Timor-Leste. Applying culturally relevant practices, this Commission ensured acknowledgement for many torture victims and encouraged re-engagement between previous opponents. Nonetheless, these advances have been undermined by other institutional and personal factors, including the fact that Indonesian officials continue to evade censure while the vast majority of victims have not enjoyed reparations. These issues are shown to have intensified with the arrival of the CTF; a Commission that has proposed an amnesty for perpetrators and has foregrounded 'friendship' rather than redistributive demands.

In line with the aim to provide ongoing context to the lives of torture victims, and to look towards the future, Chapter 8 examines the wider programmes of social change in Timor-Leste. It demonstrates that, in the move to independence, international actors have continued to play a significant state-building role in this country. This chapter progresses two main arguments. First, through their disregard of local histories and capacities, and by their inadequate provision of resources and training, international actors have imposed Western state models over local conditions. Second, international actors have, through state-building measures, reconfigured local political, economic, and strategic priorities in their own interests. These activities have already begun to have a significant impact on torture victims. They have brought problems of deepening inequalities, dependency, and violence; they have also further undermined transitional justice mechanisms.

The conclusion, in Chapter 9, argues that the provisions of transitional justice in Timor-Leste have reflected and reproduced many of the same injustices that underpin torture. Albeit not directly violent, transitional justice institutions have continued to entrench the structural and power relations that sustained torture in the first instance. For the majority of victims, most of these activities have not provided any sense of justice. The potential and limits of transitional justice, as experienced 'from below' in Timor-Leste, raise significant questions about the whole project of transitional justice as a panacea for state-led violence. In response, this book concludes with some ideas on how future initiatives to 'deal with the past' might be undertaken in order to provide better outcomes for the victims they are established to serve.

2   Contextualizing Torture

According to the 1984 UN Convention Against Torture and Other Cruel, Inhuman or Degrading Treatment or Punishment (Art. 1.1), torture is severe pain or suffering (mental or physical) that is inflicted by or with the acquiescence of a public (state) official.[1] Also, it is conducted for a particular purpose such as to punish or obtain information from a victim. To pursue a legal case thay may reach the threshold of torture, the victim has to have experienced an intense degree of suffering. In reality, as campaigners like Amnesty International (2000) argue, these different harms often overlap; and, none are permissible.

Torture is condemned throughout an array of international human rights instruments and bodies, including the UN Convention, the Universal Declaration of Human Rights, the International Covenant of Civil and Political Rights, three regional mechanisms,[2] a Special Rapporteur, and a focused UN Committee (Rehman 2003). It is one of the few international human rights that is universally applied and cannot be derogated from. As the UN Convention against Torture (Art. 2.1) states, 'no exceptional circumstances whatsoever, whether a state of war or a threat of war, internal political instability or any other public emergency, may be invoked as a justification of torture'. More broadly, torture is seen as one of the most serious violations that an individual can endure.

For victims, torture represents shocking forms of violence, including: beatings; kickings; stretchings; whippings; burnings; electroshocks; genital mutilation, rape, and other forms of sexual assault; cuttings; suspensions, including hangings and crucifixions; breaking bones; amputations; teeth or fingernail extractions; *falanga*, the blunt trauma to the soles of the feet; attacks by animals; *submarino*, forced submersion into water, urine, vomit, blood, faeces, or other matter; injections or the use of chemicals to cause, for example, blindness; *teléfono*, boxed ears; asphyxiation; and the deprivation of food, water, sleep or sanitary conditions (Allodi *et al.* 1985; Arcel 2002; Rasmussen *et al.* 2005; Rejali 2003). It can also encompass psychological pressures such as: humiliation (for example, forced nakedness); brainwashing; infested surroundings (for example, by lice or rats); sensory overload; confined isolation; mock executions; death threats or the forced witnessing of

others being tortured (Arcel 2002). Torture can include regimes of detention – such as solitary confinement – and does not just refer to the infliction
of bodily pain. Still, many victims do die from torture and those who survive
often endure chronic long-term physical pain and psychological dis-
turbances.

Nonetheless, in the late twentieth century there was a marked resurgence
in torture's use (Evans and Morgan 1998). Between 1997 and 2000, torture
was inflicted in 70 countries by three-quarters of the world's governments
(Amnesty International 2000). More recently, this resurgence has been
clearly illustrated in the treatment of prisoners held within US-governed
detention centres in Iraq, Afghanistan, Cuba, and elsewhere. The initial
graphic depictions of detainees being subject to violations brought international attention and a military tribunal – unusual results for most torture
events. In return, a vigorous legitimizing discourse in support of torture has
emerged within political, academic, legal, and social spheres.

In the light of this conflict between codified norms and practice, and in an
attempt to make sense of torture's persistence, this chapter examines the
instrumental nature of torture. That is, it evaluates the use value of torture to
state operations. A historical analysis of the development of torture is not
presented as this task has already been undertaken by scholars such as
DuBois (1991), Langbein (1976), Lea (1878), Peters (1985) and Ruthven
(1978). Instead, the chapter develops an historical overview that critically
examines the ways in which structural forces, institutional, ideological, and
social practices, and personal relations combine to underpin torture practices
across the world (more specific analyses on how torture emerged and consolidated in Timor-Leste can be found in Chapter 5).

The chapter shows how torture operates along dichotomies: while certain
techniques of torture may emphasize 'stealth', other forms are overt in their
brutality; while torture may be denied, it can also be given legitimacy by
state practices; while the use of torture may face sustained resistance, it can
also garner widespread public support. In addition, the chapter illustrates
that the decisions as to which individuals will be tortured, and how, are
linked to issues of status, particularly with regards to class, 'race', and
gender relations. These relations are also fundamental in terms of victims'
abilities and resources to cope with their situation. Thus, this chapter shows
how torture can reflect and underpin global disparities within structural
relations, an issue further intensified by the ways in which torturers build
status through their work.

Finally, in exposing the personal, social, and structural consequences of
torture, this chapter details how torture links to numerous sequelae that
effectively destroy human security, create conflict, and give rise to further
status disparities. With particular attention placed on how torture survivors
are personally affected, yet often ignored, this chapter sets the ground for a
human rights ethos that is based on a full recognition and condemnation of
violations.

The historical use of state torture

Torture is frequently rationalized by states as an unpleasant but necessary means to an end – a tool to obtain information about alleged threats. However, torture has other recognized uses, most of which relate to aspects of state control and power over populations. This section provides a short historical overview of torture; it explores how torture has been given 'value' within state operations despite sustained resistance.

Torture is commonly linked back to the rise of Western civilizations – particularly to the ancient societies of Egypt, Greece, and Rome (Evans & Morgan 1998). In these societies, torture took a central role in the legal system (DuBois 1991). In ancient Greece, for instance, torture was undertaken as a 'test or trial to determine whether someone or something [was] real or genuine' (ibid.: 7). Torture was directly linked to official truth-finding; it was believed that any required proof for offences could be marked out or derived from the body.[3] The infliction of pain was seen by the judiciary to be the quickest way to gather proof and its use became so established within Greece and then Rome that torture was systematically developed with clear rules and safeguards for its application (Lea 1878).[4]

These early legal codes were reflected in torture's 'reemergence' across most European states from the twelfth century. From this time, torture became an integral part of policing and legal procedure as accused individuals were presumed guilty from the outset and the role of the judge was to prove this by obtaining a confession (Evans and Morgan 1998). Such persecution also emphasized secrecy: the prisoner would not know the charges against them and could not be represented by others in his or her defence. The safeguards held within the ancient societies were disregarded and torture was often recklessly applied (Peters 1985).

The early modern period of torture was, therefore, linked to pre-emptive actions against threatening 'others'; however, it is also associated with overt spectacles of state power. The torture so graphically illustrated in Rejali's (1994) work on Iran or in the first sections of Foucault's (1977) 'Discipline and Punish' presents an exhibition of violent excess; 'the fact that the guilty man should moan and cry out under the blows is not a shameful side-effect, it is the very ceremonial of justice being expressed in all its force' (ibid.: 34). This kind of torture served to produce meaning and secure the consent of the wider population through the victim's pain. Consequently, torture took place in the public streets or squares and the punishment of the criminal act, on the body, was symbolically and quantitatively applied (ibid.; Rejali 1994). The public was encouraged to meditate on the crime, the punishment, and the judicial system by witnessing the event. Thus, '[t]he victim was an integral part of the ritual performance of [state] power through their confession, bodily destruction and public agony' (Humphrey 2002: 30).

These forms of torture gradually faced opposition – notably as the spectators who were positioned to learn their lessons from the ceremonies also found a place to express their revolt (Foucault 1977). Towards the end of the eighteenth century, public displays often became regarded as the pinnacle of unjust violent state power; their usefulness as a tool to collectivize sentiment against individual offenders and to reiterate the social norms was regularly lost. The growing disdain felt towards torture in this period can be linked to a shift to civilizing and humanitarian practices, bolstered by the writings of Beccaria, Voltaire and others (Evans and Morgan 1998). Alongside this, there were legal and political changes that provided pragmatic reasons for the decline in torture: in particular, the formation of a professional judiciary, changes in the law of evidence (to a system where circumstantial evidence was accepted), the introduction of new criminal sanctions, and the development of state institutions (ibid.).

Modern states began to find new ways to control their populations and other forms of power and subjugation developed – the administration of bodies could now be undertaken through education, health, and work systems that might more securely guarantee domination in line with the growth of capitalism (Foucault 1977). And, for those who did not conform as they should, punishment was redirected in the 'birth of the prison'. The contemporary systems of punishment represented a move away from the public spectacle of brutality – accordingly, the nineteenth and early twentieth centuries are often regarded as a period in which torture significantly declined.[5]

However, the moral claims put forward during this 'humanitarian period' may be viewed with scepticism (Evans and Morgan 1998). Punishments continued to be harsh for those brought before the courts (who were, invariably, those most economically disadvantaged) and while some states took the moral high-ground regarding the use of torture at home, '[o]utside Europe, the white man's burden was almost everywhere eased with a rather free resort of force and brutality of every kind' (ibid.: 12). Sir James Fitzjames Stephens could, then, flippantly explain the use of torture in Madras by British officials: 'It is far pleasanter to sit comfortably in the shade rubbing red pepper into a poor devil's eyes than to go about in the sun hunting up evidence' (ibid.: 7).

The processes of colonization – a theory and practice that was grafted onto the needs of emerging capitalism and the quest for lands, goods, and markets – were regularly entwined with torture, genocide, and other forms of violation. The violence sustained in colonies across Africa, South East Asia, the South Pacific, India, Latin America, and elsewhere had the purpose of killing populations, but it also sought to retain a compliant, albeit dehumanized, population to provide labour and act as a potential market of goods (Fanon 1963; Taussig 2002). In colonial settings, torture was used to 'encourage' productive bodies for labour; it presented a means by which economic and ideological control could be established through the colonies.

Of course, this forceful control was not necessarily sustained. Torture, like other violations, solidified resistance from those who opposed colonial advances. From Algeria to Northern Ireland to South Africa, torture attracted more individuals to the cause of the opposition (MacMaster 2004). In these instances, torture contributed to a loss of legitimacy for the colonizing regime and eventually led to its demise. Given these long-term consequences of harm to state power, torture once again became self-defeating.

But what of the situation in the so-called 'post-colonial world'? The global dispersal of modern forms of control that entrench state power (such as those related to the advanced global economy, migration, surveillance, or policing) might lead us to presume that torture would have little value in the contemporary world; and the wide-scale legal, social, and political resistance to torture would similarly seem to indicate that states have also come to this conclusion on pragmatic as well as moral grounds (Evans and Morgan 1998). However, as Peters (1985: 7) opines, '... in an age of vast state strength, ability to mobilize resources, and possession of virtually infinite means of coercion', official policy has paradoxically focused on the idea that Western governments remains insecure and vulnerable to attack.

In recent times, the use of torture has been 'regarded by many practitioners to be a practical necessity' to ensure state control of 'crime', 'terrorism', and 'disorder' (Morgan 2000: 182). In this context, torture has never been abandoned, but has progressed in new and varied ways. Torture continues to be made officially acceptable for use against those who threaten state control, and the ethos of security has underpinned situations in which torture is readily viewed as acceptable when directed at those deemed to pose risks to the nation. At the same time, torture continues to invoke resistance. The US-led torture in the 'war on terror', for instance, has simultaneously consolidated opposition to the US government, its ideologies, and actions (Brody 2005).

Thus, when state power is in question, torture presents a 'wholly convincing spectacle' (Scarry 1985: 27); it can terrify and disband perceived opponents, and demonstrate to the general populace the risks of acting against powerful interests (Stanley 2004). Torture remains, therefore, a product of measured decision-making to facilitate state domination (Crelinsten 2003). Nonetheless, given the historical opposition to torture as a means of control, this state power is relatively short-lived and self-defeating. These ideas provide a useful background to the following section which explores how torture is simultaneously hidden and exposed.

Managing and legitimizing torture

This section explores how torture is managed. It shows how torture is sometimes hidden or denied while, in other circumstances, it is carefully exposed by violators. This dichotomous nature operates to make it more difficult for victims to gather proof; it isolates them and embeds anger, confusion, and fear among the wider population. Overall, it can incapacitate the ability of victims and their communities to challenge torturers. These limits on resistance are intensified by the academic discursive support for torture as well as the ways in which torture gathers legitimacy through global, institutional frameworks.

It is clear that states engage in techniques of denial to minimize their involvement in torture (S. Cohen 2001), but torturers also employ 'stealth' techniques – such as forced standing; electric shocks; torture by water, ice, heat or cold; and psychological pressures – to hide evidence and to 'isolate, and cripple the prisoner's "soul"' (Rejali 1994: 14). Stealth techniques are not necessarily innovative, for example the use of sleep deprivation was viewed as one of the most refined and effective forms of judicial torture in seventeenth century Europe (Peters 1985).[6] However, the popularity of stealth techiques rests on the fact that they 'leave no obvious physical marks other than the looks of vacant exhaustion' (Evans and Morgan 1998: 19). The methods are useful to states that wish to counter monitoring, or want to appear compliant to human rights norms and laws (Rejali 2007).

Yet the invisibility of torture is not meant to be total as regimes often seek to control what is said and not said and they want to ensure that individuals and groups remember fear (Stanley 2004). At a societal level, the fact of torture will emerge through local gossip, by strange sounds behind walls, in unusual arrests on the street, and through the blank faces that emerge from detention centres (Humphrey 2002). In some situations, knowledge about torture will also surface through photographs and film – pictorial evidence that is crafted by the torturers and distributed between officers, local communities, and occasionally the global media. These representations tend to be carefully managed; their powerful, symbolic evidence of a victim's denigration sends a deterrent message to the wider population (Kappeler 1986). However, it also encourages isolationism by distancing the viewer from the debased tortured subject – the humanity of victims and the richness of their ordinary lives (for example, as workers, brothers, artists, or parents) is erased (A. Davis 2005).

The control of messages is apparent, too, within modern torture methods that reflect the historical spectacles of state power that involved whole communities (Green and Ward 2004). For example, during the recent 36-year-long conflict in Guatemala that killed over 200,000 people, villagers would be forced to watch the torture, rape, and execution of their neighbours or family members by military officials and their militias; they would also be continually reminded of violations by the victims' mutilated bodies which would be displayed in prominent sites – along roads or at the entrances to schools, churches, or other public institutions (Rothenberg 2003). This overt presentation of power was 'designed to inspire generalised fear, mistrust and uncertainty'. The torture had a performative role to magnify militaristic threats and create an atmosphere of constant terror (ibid.: 476). Torture can, therefore, operate openly to control or incapacitate individuals and whole communities.

As a result of fear, confusion, isolation, shame, or lack of evidence, victims find it very difficult to be recognized *as* victims. Consequently, they struggle to access assistance, seek redress, or take their case through criminal justice systems. Their plight is further hampered by the legitimization of torture within official and academic discourse. For example, in the current 'war on terror', torture has been cast as an 'appropriate' and 'civilized' response given the circumstances. Dershowitz (2002), for instance, calls for the introduction of torture warrants so that torture can be subject to judicial review and accountability. Ignatieff (2004) argues that there is a distinction between torture and, to him, the more acceptable 'torture lite' involving psychological or stress induced violence. And, Bagaric and Clarke (2005) propose that torture is morally justifiable as an act to collect information, even if it results in the victim's annihilation. Such writings reiterate others, such as the political philosopher Cicero of 45 BC and the seventeenth-century jurisprudist Sebastian Guazzini, who attempted to instil support and enforce regulations for torture when the ruling powers were threatened or experiencing crisis (Peters 1985). These neutralizing texts legitimize torture, constructing the violation as a possibility within certain 'civilized' limits.

Some academics have, then, recently attempted to legitimize torture. However, legitimacy is also invoked through torture's use in sustaining employment and trade for individuals, groups, and states. Torturers tend to operate within policing or military bodies that promote a hierarchical culture marked by male domination and the persistent use of force (Green and Ward 2004; Huggins *et al.* 2002). These institutions benefit from an insular culture that depicts who belongs on the basis of 'bonds of solidarity, the sense of common purpose and mutual understanding' (Chan *et al.* 2003: 256). This culture may assist officers to shield themselves from feelings of alienation or criticism from the public, but it can also encourage officers to perceive that 'outsiders' have a degraded status (ibid.). The institutional context can therefore create situations in which violence is more likely to be operationalized and accepted – it can mobilize 'ordinary' people, men and women, to torture (A. Davis 2005: 64–65). It also creates situations in which individual torturers are regarded as legitimate and rational professionals who are deserving of national awards, good pay, career enhancements, and standing privileges (Conroy 2001: Haritos-Fatouros 2002; Huggins *et al.* 2002).

Added to this, torture can incorporate numerous state officials. Institutionalized torture requires a network of officials working towards a common aim. Thus, in reality, 'there is no such thing as "THE torturer"' as all torturers operate within the 'complex institutional and social relationship [s]' of the state (Rejali 1999:9). Military personnel, police officers, prison officers, doctors, nurses, judges and magistrates, and psychologists, amongst others, contribute to the implementation and maintenance of torture (S. Cohen 2001). For instance, Weschler (1998) notes how, in 1985, at the height of repression in Uruguay, more than one-fifth of all medical personnel were involved in torture activities. This sustained involvement was based on 'professional ambition and financial reward' (ibid.: 127). Commitment to torture brought its own benefits; however, the risks of non-participation were also strongly felt and, as Scarry (1985: 42) highlights, those doctors who refused to cooperate with the Uruguayan regime 'disappeared at such a rate that ... medical and health care programs entered a state of crisis'. Medical personnel had to give themselves over as 'servants of the state' or suffer the consequences.

Finally, the legitimization of torture is also apparent in the way that some states and corporations pursue brisk trades in torture technologies such as stun guns, leg shackles, trauma inducing drugs, electroshock weapons, and chemical gases (Wright 1996). Such torture equipment is often directed along established trade routes, and is designed and made in European or North American states (notably from companies in France, Germany, the UK, and the US) and shipped to other perpetrating states around the globe (Amnesty International 2001a). The research for and training of personnel can be undertaken along similar tracks, as shown by the way that Latin American torturers learnt and adapted their techniques through training manuals, courses, and practical instruction acquired from US professionals (Weschler 1998).[7] Consequently, while conflicts and gross human rights violations may be discussed as being localized, in reality they can also be connected to international structures of dominance (Galtung 1994). For these reasons, torture has to be viewed within a global economic context, 'not merely as a problem of infraction of human rights in the country where torture shows up, but as one of the strategies of capitalist and social imperialism' (ibid.: 133). Such relations of power will be assessed in the following section which explores the ways in which torture is connected to status disparities.

Torture victims and status

It is evident that some individuals are more likely than others to be devalued and tortured. This section examines how status disparities – linked to structural relations of class, 'race', and gender – impact on decisions to torture and the kinds of treatment that victims receive. For convenience these relations are examined separately here, although it is important to consider them together to understand how individuals and groups become vulnerable to victimization (Farmer 2003). In addition, these structural relations also connect with other status concerns – such as those relating to sexuality, ability, age, culture, and politics – that are briefly addressed here for reasons of space. Overall, torture tends to be experienced by those groups who are most marginalized within societies and a victim's status will often impact on whether and how they will face violation.

Class

From the writings established in ancient Greece and in the Roman Empire it is apparent that torture was governed directly by issues of status and identity. During these periods there was a strong ethos of 'torturability' that governed who could and who could not be subject to torture (DuBois 1991: 56). Slaves and non-citizens (foreigners) were deemed torturable as their low standing (compared to the citizens or 'freemen' of Greek and Roman societies) ensured that they could be marked out as different, non-logical, and, importantly, completely dependent on their bodies as a source of capital (ibid.; Lea 1878).

The idea of torturability rests on a fluctuating notion of appropriate treatment of individuals, dependant upon their social status, background, or class. As Rusche and Kirchheimer (1968 [1939]) expose in their work on punishment in the late Middle Ages, torture gains justification as the poorer individuals become, the more poisonous or threatening they are deemed to be. Their writing shows that the social and economic conditions in Europe that gave rise to the mass growth of economically dispossessed individuals also spurned increasingly authoritarian punishments that paid little attention to guilt or innocence. As they put it, the 'plague on the land' or those who were homeless or of low social status were to be dealt with at any cost (ibid.: 18). Conversely, merchants and those of standing could purchase their way out of trouble. Status, rather than individual actions, was the ultimate differential with regard to torturous punishment and justice. As Ruthven (1978) similarly argues, those individuals and groups that hold economically marginalized positions within society – having non-productive bodies – fall below the 'threshold of outrage'; their pain cannot be subject to the same level of indignation as that of an individual who is economically productive and valuable.

Torture has historically gained increased official support when inflicted on bodies that are perceived as lacking in their productivity. This does not mean that those with social standing cannot be tortured. Certainly, while torture victims are likely to bear the brunt of conditions of severe social inequality (Sottas 1998), it is not a hard and fast rule. In Chile, for example, torture was targeted at poor indigenous populations, such as the Mapuche people, but it was also directed at academics and other professional workers who held social and economic status within their society (Bacic and Stanley 2005). Similarly, Chandler (1999) shows that high-ranking individuals – those who had previously held positions in government ministries or political organizations – were tortured in Cambodia.[8]

Yet, it remains a brutal truth that those placed at the edge of markets – those who are at the bottom of the socio-economic hierarchies – are more likely to face a range of violations, including torture, than those who hold economic capital. In these instances, the essential feature of torture practices is that 'one class of society claims absolute power' over those with lesser class status (Vidal-Naquet 1963: 167).

'Race'

These perspectives on marginalization and economic disparity resonate with the manner in which torture gained popular support within colonizing conditions. As established above, the 'circumstances ... of colonial rule' were guided by desires of economic expansionism and this was ably assisted by settler beliefs that the colonized were racially inferior.

The management of the identity of colonized peoples has been a central element in torture's expansion and acceptability. Cast as 'other', the colonized person was an abject body, presumed incapable or guilty from the outset (Fanon 1963). Accordingly, MacMaster (2004: 5) details that the French use of torture in Algeria during the war of 1954–62 was justified through an 'unquestioning faith in the higher destiny' of French civilization 'founded paradoxically on the universal Rights of Man of 1789'. Algerian people were cast as evolutionarily 'backward' and 'racially inferior'. Because of their supposed intellectual weakness and poor cultural refinement, they also represented a 'dangerous class' that could not hold legal power (Peters 1985). Subsequently, Algerians stood outside the daily proceedings of due process and the rule of law – they could be arrested without trial, they enjoyed little legal representation, and they were not protected by habeas corpus (MacMaster 2004). Torture formed an 'integral part' in the arrest of Muslims who would be 'brought before the courts which were both biased and permeated with a spirit of racialism' and then imprisoned (Vidal-Naquet 1963: 31).

This ideological stance was further strengthened by beliefs that the colonizers and the colonized country could be more economically stable or affluent as a result of colonizing activities, and that violence was a worthy cost given the prize (MacMaster 2004). And, if the use of state torture was antithetical to public opinion, colonizing states have also been known to encourage torture victims to become torturers themselves. In Algeria, for instance, French officials hired and violently 'persuaded' Algerians to torture other Algerians. The advantages to this were that 'by keeping the task of torturing Algerians in the hands of other Algerians, the police could keep its hands clean' and maintain the prejudicial construct that Algerians were 'savage' people (Vidal-Naquet 1963: 115).

Such racist underpinnings have inevitably formed the setting for contemporary forms of torture. It is perhaps of no surprise that indigenous populations, travelling people, and ethnic minority groups are regularly targeted for torture. Such groups are easily identified as 'different' and their marginalization within societies means that there is little risk of anyone 'coming to their defense' (Birch 2003: 537). However, these racist ideologies have also dovetailed with other notions of identity that operate across geographical, political, and economic boundaries. That is, racist-based torture operates not just across black and white divides, 'but [against] the newer categories of ... displaced and dispossessed' or 'outsider' people (Sivanandan 2001: 2). This xeno-racism, as Sivanandan (ibid.) calls it, is more about status than skin colour. In this light, the new torture technologies – such as taser anti-personnel mines, high-powered microwaves or chemical incapacitants – that are being developed to respond to the mass movement of vulnerable people across borders due to political or environmental disasters makes sense (Wright 2007).

Gender

The issues of gender and patriarchy – the latter term representing a set of social relationships by which men, as a group, maintain power over women and children – have also impacted on the way torture is conducted. It can be argued that torture is a significant patriarchal practice as it is explicitly gendered, and serves to reinforce the structural inequalities between men and women.

The historical evidence for this argument is clearly expressed in the inquisitorial panic over witchcraft in the sixteenth and seventeenth centuries. The knowledge that women possessed was said to threaten Christendom and, in England, witchcraft was subject to such intense denigration 'no means were considered too severe to secure the conviction' of an accused woman (Lea 1878: 506). The tortures experienced by these victims were sometimes specific to the apparent threat of the female voice; for example, the witch-bridle (a band of iron that was fastened around the face with four metal points thrust into the mouth, and then secured to the wall) cruelly symbolized the common perception that women were unable to follow a 'chatterless' life (ibid.).

The gendered method of torture has also been recently exemplified with the photographs emanating from Abu Ghraib prison in Iraq. Some of these photographs detailed male prisoners stripped naked with electric wires attached to their genitalia, others depicted naked men held on a leash by a petite, smiling woman. At the centre of these techniques lay the idea that male Muslim prisoners would endure psychological harm through both the measured attack on their sexuality and by their enforced subjugation to a white, female officer. Officers took the view that using a woman during torture was the quickest way to induce prisoner degradation and powerlessness (Hersh 2004). The technique struck at the heart of patriarchal societal ordering.

While the majority of political prisoners in Iraq, and elsewhere, have been male, female victims do endure particular forms of torture that emphasize the continuum of male power. In particular, it is evident that women will often face sexual forms of torture. For example, the recent Chilean Commission on Torture report stated that almost all of the nearly 3,500 women known to have been tortured during the Pinochet dictatorship had suffered sexual torture (Bacic and Stanley 2005). This acknowledgement of sexual violence and rape as forms of torture does, however, still remain contentious for two reasons. First, in many instances rape continues to be dismissed as a private act undertaken by aberrational officers (Kois 1998; Seifert 1993). This has meant that, until relatively recently, rape has not featured as a worthy charge in prosecutions or literature.[9] Second, if these acts are acknowledged as torture, it is often done so in a way that equates female experiences with sexual violence alone (Ross 2003c). That is, sexual violence can become the dominating focus of the female experience of torture, so much so that other forms of violence that women endure (as well as sexual violence against men) are overlooked.

Further status disparities

Finally, albeit briefly, the use of torture is connected to other status disparities. For instance, torture has been related to the issues of: age, for example, children are subject to torture, including sexual torture (Amnesty International 2001b; Blaauw 2002) and may be violated in front of their parents to make the adults comply with officials (Suarez-Orozco 2004); ability, through enforced medical experimentation on individuals with mental or physical disabilities (Hornblum 1998); and, sexuality, in relation to the torture of gay men, lesbians, bisexuals, and transgendered people (Amnesty International 2001c). In their marginal and 'outsider' status, these groups are also seen as 'torturable'.

However, status disparity may also be linked to what people think and what they represent. Groups that are perceived as politically or culturally dangerous are more likely to face torture. During the European Inquisition, for instance, torture consolidated around heretics who were seen to be dangerous as a threat to ruling powers. During this period, anyone could be tortured, but those who demonstrated some kind of resistance to the dominant beliefs of Christianity were a particular focus – as the Pope Innocent IV argued, heretics 'were thieves and murderers of souls' and their capability to root themselves within families and neighbourhoods had to be destroyed (Peters 1985: 65). Such a position illustrates the early acceptance that torture could be applied to perceived 'enemies' of the ideological order; it also underpins the reason why torture is so often directed to 'ordinary' criminal prisoners too (Fellner 2005).

In these instances, torture is not just directed at an individual, but at the group that the individual represents. Further, threatening representations of 'enemies' are instilled in the common psyche through political talk, media reporting, and state institutional action, and these representations often strengthen support for violations. For example, in Chile those tortured during the Pinochet regime were often politically represented as 'terrorists' and, despite the knowledge about regime brutality, it is still not unusual in Chile to come across those who argue that 'they were tortured, but they *must* have done something!' (Stanley 2004). Victims, therefore, are regularly attributed with responsibility for the violence inflicted against them and this misrecognition of the implicitly guilty ensures that torture is widely thought to be acceptable and necessary.

Generally, torture does tend to be directed towards those groups who are most marginalized within societies and, from this, it is evident that structural relations do impact on how individuals become the targets for torture and, then, how they are violated. These status disparities are intensified by the fact that torturers are rewarded for their efforts by professional and social advancement and enjoy material and ideological benefits. Torturers rarely face sanction and, even when their roles have been exposed, they may still be promoted and sometimes cherished. These conditions stand in stark contrast to the consequential realities that victims endure. Such disparities are often significant in terms of how victims are able to move forward following torture.

Torture's aftermath

For survivors the aftermath of torture can be a period in which the status disparities between the torturer and the tortured are often sustained and even widened. The repercussions of torture for victims – which form the focus of this section – are wide ranging and encompass medical, psychological, social, economic, and political arenas. These issues are intensified by the way in which, as previously illustrated, torture victims are often silenced in the wake of their violation. Given this, it is perhaps not surprising that torture victims will readily express anger at their situation as they take the view that their torturers have enjoyed economic and social gains at their expense (Stanley 2004). For most victims, the opportunities for acknowledgement, compensation, pursuit of criminal prosecutions, or an ameliorated living situation remain distinctly limited.

As shown above, torture victims sustain numerous injuries as a result of their treatment and they can emerge from their experiences with an array of medical complaints that require treatment (from broken bones to burns to unwanted pregnancies or sexually transmitted diseases). Alongside this, while some survivors demonstrate no after-effects, many victims suffer numerous psychological sequelae. These bring significant challenges to the individual's very sense of identity and impact on how victims are able to function (Arcel 2002). Among other effects, victims may: report feelings of depression, anxiety, anger or irritability; have disturbed or violent behaviour; lack energy, cannot sleep or sleep all the time; suffer nightmares and flashbacks; become utterly dependent on others and fear being alone; avoid situations, locations, or things[10] that remind them of their violation; have feelings of shame, self-blame, dirtiness, humiliation or embarrassment; be unable to eat; feel suicidal or want to harm themselves; no longer desire sexual relations; constantly fear another attack; have a diminished ability to concentrate; and, fear that they are going crazy (ibid.; Allodi *et al.* 1985; Becker *et al.* 1990; CODEPU 1989; Feitlowitz 1998; Haenel 2003; Hardy 2002; Stanley 2004; Turner and Gorst-Unsworth 1990). These conditions impact severely on the abilities of individuals to move forward from the status of 'victim' to that of 'survivor'.

The psychological repercussions are, therefore, long lived. Victims can also experience such sequelae in ways that resonate with the debates on structural relations and status detailed above. For example, women who have experienced sexual assault may transfer their fears and begin to see their partners as potential 'attackers' (Arcel 2002: 13). They can also experience intense shame because of the humiliating sexual practices inflicted against them (Becker *et al.* 1990). Male victims of sexual torture, who can also experience crises of sexual identity, may also share these feelings. Following sexual violation, heterosexual men can perceive that they have lost their 'manhood', they may feel feminized and sense that their sexual orientation has been compromised or changed (Hardy 2002). These reactions are explicitly tied to dominant notions of masculinity, manhood, and sexuality that underpin mainstream gender relations. Thus, torture practices impact differently on different groups as a result of structural relations and social norms.

Family members of torture victims may also experience a range of trauma. This 'secondary traumatization' is common and it shows how trauma has 'systematic and ripple effects that go through space and time, beyond the initial impact' (Kira 2004: 39). As a result, 'children of tortured parents reveal more psychosomatic symptoms, headaches, depression, learning difficulties and aggressive behaviour' (ibid.: 40). In other circumstances, children born as a result of rape may suffer subsequent victimization from other family or community members (Blaauw 2002). More broadly, victim's families can endure a devalued social status. For instance, families can be deeply affected by the fact that the victim is no longer able to work, is incapacitated, or has had to move to another area or country. Victims and their families can endure a 'marked downward mobility' in their social status (CODEPU 1989: 738).

Given these experiences, it is important to recognize that torture victims are not a homogenous group and each (along with their family and community) will face unique medical and psychological consequences. These effects will link with other social, cultural, and political repercussions, including: family breakdown; the collapse of trust between community groups; dislocation and exile; continued criminalization; increased drug or alcohol use; a rise in self-destructive behaviour, self-harm, and suicides; the loss of schooling; or problems in accessing work or appropriate health care (Arcel 2002; Hardy 2002; Kira 2004; Stanley 2004). The lived realities of these issues cannot be underestimated. Torture rips apart social and personal relations, it creates short- and long-term problems not just for those directly affected, but for their families, friends, and communities. Moreover, these after-effects illustrate how torture, as a civil and political violation, connects with 'second generation' violations related to work, health, housing, education, and so on.

The official and societal responses to torture victims often underpin and reinforce these consequences. The demonization of those subject to torture permeates most aspects of political, social, and cultural life, and victims are often imagined to be complicit in their own violations (Crelinsten 2003). As a result, many audiences distance themselves, disbelieve, and do not engage with stories of torture (Rivera-Fuentes and Birke 2001; West 2003). Perhaps the denigrated and abject status of victims can be perceived as being contagious or transferable (Kristeva 1982). To demonstrate allegiance with a torture victim is to potentially present as a member of the maligned group. In these circumstances, torture invokes solitude as it envelops its victims in silence and disrupts 'normal' relations (Weschler 1998). This silencing is a perpetuation of violence as it 'becomes a second form of negation and rejection' for the victim (Scarry 1985: 56).

The silencing or lack of recognition of torture victims is no more apparent than within the criminal justice system and even within truth commission procedures. These are issues covered in greater depth in the following chapters; however, it is clear that victims rarely encounter an official acknowledgement of their predicament, legal or social sanctioning of their perpetrators, or reparational support to assist them (Stanley 2004). In this way, victims are 'twice silenced'; in the first instance, they are silenced by those who torture them and, in the aftermath, they are silenced by those who close down opportunities for dialogue (West 2003: 356).

Conclusion

While torture is prohibited under international law, it continues to be applied with some vigour across the world. Despite the fact that it is frequently resisted, and that it is often ultimately self-defeating, its persistence may be understood in terms of how it is used as a short-term tool to build or consolidate state power. The real value of torture is as a systematic and institutionalized technique of control, and it is subsequently applied to incapacitate opponents or terrorize communities that are perceived to be 'criminal' or 'threatening'.

In this context, torture tends to be experienced by those most marginalized or criminalized within society. The relations of class, 'race', gender, sexuality, age, culture, and politics are all pertinent factors with regard to which individuals become the targets for torture, how they are violated, and how the victim subsequently copes with their treatment. Yet torture is not an individualized violation as it produces a range of medical, psychological, and social consequences for victims, their families, communities, and countries. Torture wipes out 'normal' social relations and, in this way, it destroys human security, creates conflict, and provides a platform for further violations.

Finally, it is evident that those who suffer torture face cultural, participatory, and violent injustices. As shown in this chapter, victims are regularly demonized through official discourse in ways that make acceptable their violent victimization. While torture is often tempered by techniques of distancing and denial, it is also made palatable through legitimizing discourses and institutional practices that emphasize torture's acceptability within certain circumstances. Victims find that their perpetrators are rarely brought to account and they realize that the spaces for them to speak out or to air their grievances are limited. These latter points, revolving around the debates on justice, are the subject of the next chapter.

3   Introducing Justice

This book has, so far, established the ways in which torture has been historically used as an instrument of power by states and their allies. Those individuals and groups who become targets for torture also tend to be socially, politically, or culturally devalued; they are individuals that are deemed to have a lesser, or sometimes no, status in humanity. Torture also connects with wider injustices as the ways in which individuals are targeted for torture, and the possibilities for victims to deal with their violation, are deeply linked to their structural location as well as to their personal history and experience. Given these routes to, and repercussions of torture, this chapter focuses on how justice for victims of such violations might be approached.

What might justice mean for torture victims? The dominant sense of justice is one that is usually linked to the arrest, prosecution, and punishment of the offender. Certainly, the criminal justice processing of torturers remains one of the vital aims of campaigning by victims, their families, and representatives. Victims want their suffering to be formally recognized by the criminal justice system in the same way that other victims of 'domestic crime' (such as burglary, car theft, or assault) might be. However, many victims aspire to a more complex form of justice, one that also addresses their social needs and places them as participants in future actions.

Drawing from the work of Nancy Fraser (1997, 2003, 2005), this chapter argues that victims of torture can suffer three forms of long-term injustice: the first is cultural or symbolic (in the socially devalued representation, non-recognition, or misrecognition of victims); the second is structural[1] (in the economic, gendered, 'raced', or age-based exploitation, marginalization, or deprivation); and the third is participatory or representational (in the exclusion of victims from democratic decision-making processes and activities). These forms of injustice often combine and reinforce each other: they are linked to which individuals or groups become victims to torture; they underpin the opportunities available to victims to have their suffering or their perpetrators recognized; and, they contextualize prospects for criminal or social justice.

Fraser's (ibid.) arguments were focused on attaining justice in 'peaceful' states, yet her analysis resonates with debates on the provision of justice in 'transitional' states. Justice that acknowledges cultural recognition alongside structural equalities and democratic opportunities is, arguably, particularly important during a transition from widespread state criminality. The reasons for this are: (i) that cultural misrepresentations are central to how torture comes to be legitimized and how those involved (as perpetrators or victims) come to be viewed and responded to. Denigration or silencing is such that victims will often lack authority, status, or respectability in the wake of violation while perpetrators will rarely experience a status 'demotion'; (ii) that victims of torture and other violations are also likely to face structural disadvantages within their own societies and if these arrangements remain unaddressed, victims will be more likely to face continued injustice; and, (iii) that torture victims may also find that they are unable to take part in democratic decision-making processes either because of their incapacity to perform or because they have been excluded from participation following their violation. This means that the institutional structures that give rise to torture are rarely tracked, questioned, or overhauled.

Given these linked forms of injustice, victims of torture (like other subordinated groups) require social arrangements that can ensure their status parity and provide opportunities for their political participation (Fraser 2003, 2005). The solutions for injustice should, as Fraser (2000: 115) proposes, address 'what precisely the subordinated parties need in order to be able to participate as peers'. The remedies are diverse and depend on what individual victims require to gain parity with others. For some torture victims, having their distinct identity and experiences acknowledged may be enough. For others, there may be a need for changes that develop new values into institutional policies and practices (for example, to challenge the institutionalized discrimination through which violence propagates). Other victims may need reassurance that they have full access to political, legal, or social structures (such as enabling them to take cases through court proceedings or to become involved in institutional change). In other situations, a redistribution of resources may be required (for example, to deal with economic inequalities by focused financial assistance or by transforming economic systems in ways that do not reinforce inequitable conditions). The interventions to deal with injustice have to be made to fit victims' needs and their desire for non-violent and equitable conditions.

Before progressing these strands of inquiry, however, this chapter will first examine the role of states[2] in the globalizing world. The reason for this interlude is that an understanding of globalization, human rights, and state action is vital to an analysis of how justice might be secured for torture victims. As shown in the previous chapter, states have used and continue to use torture, along with other violence, to build and sustain their power. However, states also remain key actors in protecting individuals from torture and in providing avenues for justice. These issues of protection and redress regularly traverse national boundaries.

Globalization, human rights, and the state

While the term 'globalization' has been defined and discussed in multiple ways, it can simply be articulated as being about the 'social and political implications' of a 'growing world interconnectedness' (Hayden and el-Ojeili 2005: 2). With this in mind, the human rights movement is undoubtedly a product of globalization (Freeman 2002); its activities are regularly based on the international connections that have emerged in law, politics, cultures, and communications. Yet this is not a coherent movement and the successes of human rights have been unevenly felt across the world. The protection of rights has often reflected a range of factors and decisions, including the political imperatives of individual states, demands from transnational organizations, as well as structural conditions (Galtung 1994).

The ideas and practices of human rights have turned on the idea of a state-centric political space in which state protection of citizens is assumed in return for consent and order. Some commentators have recently regarded this contract as outdated as, under conditions of globalization, state activities are 'enmeshed' within complex transnational networks and states are certainly not the sole guardians of human rights. Moreover, states are not the only perpetrators of human rights abuses as violations are regularly undertaken by corporations, militias, or international financial institutions that are seemingly outside state control. Thus, states are often viewed as reacting to, rather than dictating, policies and events (Evans 1998). In this context, much debate has questioned how rights might be protected in such a non-state-centric world (McGrew 1998).

Yet how far can the argument that states are tending to irrelevance be sustained? Throughout history, states have been built along diverse boundaries and have been organized in relation to other powerful actors. Historically, state powers have regularly incorporated third-party actors, as well as diverse discourses, to bolster their activities and to attain control of trade and resource flows. During colonizations, for instance, state officials operated alongside 'powerful private economic organizations (the early multinational corporations) and cultural entrepreneurs (eg. missionaries)' to build their power (Freeman 2002: 154). It is evident, then, that states are *crafted* and continually in the process of being made (Coleman and Sim 2005: 104). The shifting political, social, and economic contexts in which states operate have not necessarily meant that states have crumbled;[3] rather, state institutions have transformed with the changing landscapes of power. For example, the retreat of some Western states from engaging in direct colonial violence might lead one to suspect that Western states withdrew their power from colonized nations. But this has not been the case as more anonymous Western-led systems of power have been introduced that could 'retain hegemonic positions over former colonial territories' through the 'invisible government' of transnational organizations, financial institutions, and business (Held *et al.* 1999: 43). While states are undoubtedly 'undergoing a profound transformation' due to economic globalization, it has not translated 'into a diminution of state power; rather, it is transforming the conditions under which state power is exercised' (ibid.: 440–41).

State sovereignty and control is in a constant process of realignment and, at any one time, states remain central actors 'in building collaborative power arrangements' to respond to economic, ideological and political challenges (Coleman 2003: 95). The difficulties in determining who is responsible for violations and the argument that states no longer have the capacity to effectively provide justice for violations must therefore be reflected upon with reference to such *statecraft* (Stanley 2007a).

Of course, these processes of globalization are unevenly applied and the characteristics and nature of power, through political and economic circuits, cannot be downplayed (ibid.). For instance, economically powerful states have not shied away from using their status and offers of financial support to gain compliance from economically weak states on a range of issues from the environment to the 'war on terror' to bilateral agreements on the International Criminal Court. And, transnational corporations that have trade levels which surpass the GDP of many states regularly base their investment decisions on nation-state adherence to their demanding conditions on environmental conditions, employment rules, and labour laws that violate rights (Evans and Hancock 1998). Moreover, these corporations rarely connect with those individuals who experience their decisions and policies (Hayden and el-Ojeili 2005) – a charge that can also be made against international financial organizations, such as the World Bank and the International Monetary Fund (IMF) (Evans 1998).[4] With such a disconnection between powerful interests and local needs, opportunities for states (or others) to protect rights may be distinctly limited.

Despite all this, and to reiterate, the integral role that states do play in sustaining and orchestrating these conditions of globalization cannot be ignored (Evans and Hancock 1998). Powerful governments will appoint their political allies to the boards of transnational organizations and corporations. Similarly, states will promote firms and ease trade conditions for corporations, they will engage in violent force to quell dissent or strikes, they will forcibly displace communities in the interests of industry, and they will regulate national economies. Further, as shown in Argentina, where the government refused to pay back IMF loans because of national economic instability, states may also have the ability to not act upon international financial demands. In short, ' … globalization is what *States* have made of it. States themselves have established the rules and institutions to maintain order amid the diversity of their cultures' (Dunne 1999: 28). While states have certainly had to 'carve out a new role for themselves', they retain a significant role in contemporary global affairs (Woods 2000: 213).

In addition, the central position that states continue to take in the actual committal of violations cannot be overlooked. As shown in this book, violations in Timor-Leste have involved a variety of actors yet the responsibility of states has rested on a continuum (Kauzlarich *et al.* 2003). State officials directly engaged in violations and they also funded or directly supported other states or bodies that undertook violations; they failed to regulate the activities of parties where they held a clear mandate to do so; and they displayed distinct indifference to violations, hampering attempts to bring perpetrators to account. A number of states gained political, economic, and strategic power from violence in the region.

It is clear that states cannot be easily decentred from the global frame; despite the emergence of new global actors, states sustain a central position in setting the rules and conditions of justice opportunities. With this in mind, this chapter now turns to the first aspect of justice for torture victims, that of cultural or symbolic recognition.

Recognition

Torture is often hidden from view. Perpetrators will regularly employ 'techniques of neutralization' to distance themselves from violations (Sykes and Matza 1957) and, as S. Cohen (1996a 2001) has demonstrated, human rights violations are frequently subject to denial as states euphemistically rename violent situations and act in ways that deny the reality of criminality or the ensuing pain and trauma, hence: torturers were only following orders; violations of torture are relabelled as 'intensive questioning' or 'challenging conditions'; 'harsh' treatment was appropriate given the circumstances; torture, if it occurs, is necessary to save civilization; and, any detractors are hypocrites! These techniques, undertaken in conjunction with isolationist explanations that emphasize the activities of individual 'bad apple' officers, serve to reappropriate criminal behaviour as the consequences of either benign state control or non-institutionalized practices. Consequently, as Mathiesen (2004: 33) establishes, most violations do not generally appear as a problem and if they do, they are taken to only require short-term fixes that may give '*the impression* of fundamental change'.

The political management of torture will regularly find popular support and legitimacy, particularly in situations where state actions are presented as politically unavoidable or 'for the greater good' (S. Cohen 1996a). However, when there are conflicts of interest, the law also provides a framework in which violent state activities can be cast as justifiable. Green and Ward (2000), for instance, illustrate how the Turkish state gained legitimacy for torture through decisions of the European Court of Human Rights that normalized a state of emergency. Similarly, Morgan (2000) has highlighted how the Landau Commission, reporting on the activities of the Israeli General Security Services (GSS), presented and legally consolidated the case for the GSS to use methods that involved 'moderate physical pressure'. The common presentation of law as being orderly, rational, and peaceful covers the reality that violence is an inherent feature of its operation (Hudson 2003) and, as a result, when state acts of killing or serious harm garner legitimacy through law, there may be little opposition.[5]

In such a mediated context, those involved in human rights violations are likely to be masked or misrepresented. Bauman (1995: 203) proposes that state violence against individuals is not undertaken 'for what they have done, but for what they are'. Thus, in their representation of 'political signs' (Humphrey 2002: 27), torture victims do not tend to be seen as 'victims'; instead, as S. Cohen (1996a) and Crelinsten (2003) detail, they are either depicted in danger-linked ways (e.g. as 'terrorists' or 'criminals') or as being outside the human experience altogether (e.g. as 'animals' or 'vermin'). Whether representations are political or pathological, the end result is an essentialist 'othering' in which groups, perceived by powerful definers to be threatening, are depicted in a falsely homogenous manner. Indeed, whole societies may be deemed to be culturally dangerous; their 'otherness' is used to rationalize the perpetration of violence – 'they use torture to deal with offenders there, it is their way' – and power is disregarded; culture becomes 'an alibi' for suffering (Farmer 2003).

Jock Young (1999: 117) argues that such essentialism 'furnishes the target, it provides the stereotypes, it allows the marshalling of aggression' and facilitates social exclusion. Individuals and groups portrayed in ways that conflict with 'what we represent' are more likely to be denied full legal rights and protection (Hudson 2003) as 'they are put out of sight or below the threshold of moral vision' (Humphrey 2002: 32; I. Young 1990). Those who are tortured are also seen as implicitly to blame for their treatment – their perceived dangerousness and difference makes them 'deserving' of their violation (Huggins *et al.* 2002; Kauzlarich *et al.* 2001). Accordingly, torture becomes acceptable in a culture of denigration in which individuals, groups, and even societies are 'othered' or 'excluded' from the rest of the world. In this situation, the suffering of disparaged victims is not recognized 'because they fall outside any moral relationship of care or responsibility' – this 'political exclusion' makes 'suffering invisible' (Humphrey 2002: 32–33).

From these arguments it is clear that torture victims tend to go misrecognized or unrecognized altogether. This can often have long-term consequences. As C. Taylor (1992: 26) argues, this is not just about a lack of due respect as denigration 'can inflict a grievous wound, saddling its victims with a crippling self-hatred' and low self-esteem. A lack of recognition can imprison torture victims in a false state of being or not recognize their 'being' at all (Bauman 2001). Moreover, cultural devaluations can mean that torture victims will rarely receive the care that they need to deal with their violation and they will struggle to experience equal treatment before the law (Honneth 2004).

For such reasons, the dominant liberal, human rights agenda has foregrounded legal and cultural recognition as a principal means of struggle against violations. For some, recognition is deemed 'a vital human need' (C. Taylor 1992: 26); it is viewed as a 'balm'; and to recognize what happened to victims in cultural and legal fora 'can provide at least a symbolic redress which can allow some healing to take place, and individual societies to move on' (Hoffman 2003: 280). For victims, such 'speaking out' has a therapeutic potential (Herbst 1992); as highlighted in Chapter 1, intervening in the representational management of torture is a method of taking control, of denouncing and challenging the state.

In this context, justice for torture victims has to incorporate strategies of recognition that will expose violations and upwardly revalue the identities of victims.[6] Such acknowledgement can set the ground for wider effects: it can highlight how state violence comes to be legitimized and accepted; it may provide a start to symbolic healing for victims; and, it can invoke the provision of social, legal, or institutional assistance for them.

One means through which this can be achieved, as agencies like *Amnesty International* and *Human Rights Watch* have long realized, is through the dissemination of evidence that counters the official discourse on torture. The use of testimony to expose the myths of state violence and to provide recognition for those who suffered can be observed in many arenas, including the documentation of non-governmental organizations, investigative media reporting, UN materials, court proceedings, and truth commissions. Hence, while contemporary patterns of globalization may provide limited opportunities for the majority of the global population to experience human rights standards (see the following section), the acceleration of communications and cultural technologies has simultaneously increased a global, cultural awareness of rights. Information on injustice cuts across state borders; political recognition can be globalized (Hayden and el-Ojeili 2005).

Redistribution

While the issue of recognition (the acknowledgement of identity) is undoubtedly important, it cannot stand alone in an analysis of justice. The reason for this is that a sole focus on identity politics could move an engagement to deal with the context of human rights violations off the agenda. Who people are would become more important than what those people need to live a 'good life'.[7] As Fraser (2000) argues, identity politics can displace or supplant struggles for structural equality.[8] For her, justice is entwined with questions of economic redistribution – any portrayal of redistribution and recognition as being mutually exclusive is a 'false antithesis' (Fraser 2003: 16). Consequently, a critical theory of justice must not decouple recognition from issues of social justice (Schwendinger and Schwendinger 1975).

This combined approach appears particularly useful in relation to torture victims who, as noted previously, tend to suffer different forms of injustice. First, they suffer cultural/symbolic or recognition-based injustices (victims are likely to suffer distorted social representations) and, second, they often experience structural (economic, gendered, 'racialized', or age) disadvantage. Thus, to attend to their injustices, victims require both recognition and structural redress (Stanley 2005b). Any claims for recognition must, as Fraser (2003) argues, be connected to measures to overcome their subordination and to establish victims as full partners in social life. This 'status model' can allow victims to self-define what they need to socially participate on a par with others (ibid.).

These arguments are extended here in terms of highlighting the connections between economic justice and the structural concerns of gender, 'race', and age. In doing so, this section considers what structural inequalities are and how they impact on the lives of torture victims. It also exposes how mainstream human rights law, policies, and practices tend to downplay the structural context of human rights violations. It shows that there has been a silencing of economic, social, and cultural violations in dominant human rights thinking, and that this has, inevitably, decreased opportunities for justice for torture victims.

Structural injustice

Galtung (1994) used the term 'structural violence' to expand thinking on human rights violations. Taking the premise that an actor-oriented approach to human rights (which focused on individual 'evil' officers, bad institutions, or rogue states) was ineffective in the examination of the wider relations of repression, exploitation, or marginalization, he espoused an analysis that revolved around the 'patterned interactions' in violating systems (ibid.: 50). In doing so, the legitimate, everyday structures of global, national, and local relations – the 'social machinery of oppression' that is 'exerted systematically ... by everyone who belongs to a certain social order' (Farmer 2004: 307) – could be connected to seemingly individualized or *ad hoc* violence. Such analyses relate directly to a global economic order that has exploited and replicated inequalities through slavery, imperialism, and the workings of advanced global capitalism.

Certainly, from an economic perspective, inequalities continue to widen and vast numbers of the world's population live in extreme poverty so that millions do not even have their basic human needs met. Thus, Pogge (2005: 3–4) states:

> Out of a total of 6.2 billion human beings (2002), some 799 million are malnourished, more than 880 million lack access to basic health services, 1 billion are without adequate shelter, 1.1 billion without access to safe drinking water, 2 billion without electricity, and 2.4 billion without access to basic sanitation ... Some 50,000 human deaths per day, fully a third of all human deaths, are due to poverty-related causes and therefore avoidable insofar as poverty itself is avoidable.

For victims of torture, who are likely to face political and economic dis-advantage within their own societies, such structural violence can dominate their lives. As Farmer (2004: 315) clarifies: 'Structural violence is ... *stric-turing*. It constricts the agency of its victims. It tightens a physical noose around their necks, and this garroting determines the way in which resour-ces ... are allocated and experienced.' The social conditions of poverty, hunger, poor sanitation, illiteracy, or unemployment sustain a victim's long-term suffering.

Of course, many of these social conditions will impact on all devalued populations. That is, if a country is poor – as Timor-Leste certainly is – then most people will require redistributive change. The issue, here, is that social injustices can impact in deeper, or different, ways on those who are also struggling to deal with state violence. If, for instance, torture victims cannot access medical or psychological assistance, or they are unable (as a result of their injuries) to work or continue education, then they will face multiple injustices that reflect not just their economic standing, but also their victi-mization. Alongside desperate social conditions, they will have the added burden of not being able to deal with or redress their past violation.

Yet these historically driven processes and relations that entrench inequalities and suffering are not solely economic. As they are gendered, 'raced', and aged-based in that the injustices of economic maldistribution are more likely to be felt by women, minorities, children, and the elderly. The 'political economy of brutality' rests within multiple relations of power and status in which certain historically devalued groups face simultaneous dis-advantages (Farmer 2003: 43). Further, as shown in the previous chapter, violations evolve under specific relations of patriarchy, neocolonialism, abil-ity, and age. That is, individuals may well be victimized because they are female or black or homosexual or because they are young or for some other status reason. The mass rape and torture of women during conflict, for instance, does not occur because women are poor, but because they are female and because their violation can, under global patriarchal conditions, simultaneously harm men (Seifert 1993).[9] Similarly, the recruitment of chil-dren to engage in violent conflict exemplifies the lesser status that children have in many societies – they are often seen as easily expendable (Singer 2005). For these victims, redistributive justice has to encompass actions to deal with their denigration within personal, social, institutional, and political frames.

Of course, those who do have access to funds will have increased choices in terms of avoiding or resisting their violation. At a personal level, if an individual enjoys significant economic power, it stands that their 'identities' as being, say, female, or black, or gay, or having a disability, or being a new migrant will have lesser 'other' value. That is, 'It is one thing to be a black taxi-driver, quite another to be a black football idol; it is one thing to be a woman working as a domestic servant, quite another to be the first lady of the land' (Boff and Boff, cited in Farmer 2003: 49–50). Being wealthy, and having access to status circles, may offset the structural conditions that relate to other personal attributes.

Rights are then, as Blau and Moncada (2005) note, bundled – that is, victims will tend to have a range of rights claims that are linked to their unique structural location or their difference. For example, structural relations of class intersect with other relations (of age, 'race', or gender) to create a situation in which certain torture victims (such as indigenous populations or ethnic minorities or women) are more likely than others to experience difficulties in accessing judicial procedures or social support.[10]

It must be borne in mind, however, that such structures are not encompassing or deterministic; these structural conditions do not relate to all human rights victims by any means. It is clear, for example, that there are torture victims who have not previously experienced social inequality and there are also torture victims who progress to positions of power following their experience. For instance, as detailed previously, Chilean torture victims were often those who held high status positions in education, politics, local government, and entertainment. These individuals were victimized as a consequence of their official labelling as political subversives (Stanley 2004). And, as shown in the example of the Chilean torture victim turned President, Michele Bachelet, the experience of violation does not automatically equate to a future of poverty, unemployment, or inability to cope.

Victims of human rights violations tend, then, to be 'differentiated ... by virtue' of both their structural location and their cultural value within society (Fraser 1997: 19). Consequently, to work towards justice for torture victims, one has to be mindful of difference and the ways in which personal experiences are embedded within particular historic, cultural, social, and structural contexts. To fail to do this can mean that 'we are likely to endorse traditional social forms that sustain those differences' and lead to further subordination and oppression (O'Neill 1993: 307).

Obscuring the structural landscape

Notwithstanding these sharp connections between inequalities and violations, the dominant human rights tradition has continually obscured the understanding that human rights are contextualized by structural forces (Galtung 1994). While the UN has developed conventions that relate directly to structural issues – such as the Convention on the Elimination of Discrimination Against Women and the Convention on the Elimination of Racial Discrimination – states, and other regulatory bodies, continually appear reticent to challenge such inequalities. To illustrate this problem, this section will examine the mainstream distancing from economic, social, or cultural violations and show how this approach maintains the status quo of inequalities.

Economic, social, and cultural rights bear the same legal status as civil and political rights, each gives rise to binding obligations to preserve the

inherent dignity of individuals,[11] and it can be argued that economic violations cause far more deaths and suffering than political violations. Despite
this, the dominant version of human rights that is presented at an international level gives a distorted emphasis to civil and political rights (Evans
2001; Green and Ward 2004; Thomas 1998). Indeed, for most politicians in
the 'global north', the legal documentation regarding economic, social, and
cultural rights are just unfeasible demands (Chomsky 1998). Or, as Herman
(2002: viii) argues, human rights are not seen to be violated at all 'if immi-
seration follows from the normal workings of the market system'.

The concentration on civil and political violations is perhaps derived from
a belief that some events are so atrocious they should never be repeated –
that is, there is a hierarchy of suffering and those who suffer direct, physical
violence should receive most attention. Yet this concern for particular kinds
of victims 'is ... highly superficial' (Chandler 2002: 227) as it undermines the
reality that civil and political rights are intertwined with economic, social,
and cultural rights.

Civil and political rights, for example, give people the opportunity 'to
draw attention forcefully to general needs and to demand appropriate political action ... the exercise of political rights (such as voting, criticizing,
protesting, and so on) can make a real difference' to people's economic,
social and cultural opportunities (Sen 1999: 92). Likewise, the ability to
legitimately distribute information or protest has been crucial in struggles for
those seeking national independence or equality. Conversely, the strength of
'equality' rights has wide implications for how individuals and societies
experience civil and political rights. For example, illiterate people, who have
not had access to education, will be disadvantaged in their ability to 'exercise
political speech on a basis of equality with others' (Nussbaum 2006: 289)
and less likely to know about their legal protection. Similarly, if individuals
are in poverty they will have less ability to pay for legal representation, to
protect themselves against violations, or to seek redress (Smart 1989).

To concentrate on one aspect of rights while disregarding others can
mean that levels of oppression or violence remain unchallenged. For
instance, a statement that a population will enjoy freedom from torture or
inhuman treatment will have lesser meaning if the population 'experience ...
growing impoverishment' that 'wears down the fabric of sociality in other
ways and consigns an increasing proportion of the population to prisons'
that are governed by untrained, underpaid staff (Gledhill 2003: 217).
Therefore, in order to effectively protect the right not to be tortured there
has to be simultaneous improvements in wider economic and/or institutional
structures.

The attempt to unpick one set of violations from another does not, therefore, reflect the ways in which human rights are violated, protected, and
fought for. Part of the problem, here, is that violations of 'equality' rights are
not often understood by those who have most power to make changes. As
Pogge (2002) and Farmer (2003) argue, those who do not live in poverty

tend to be extremely isolated from the experiences and realities that such circumstances entail: they often have no understanding of what this suffering might feel like; they perceive that the sheer scale of suffering makes it impossible to deal with; and, they do not understand how this suffering is distributed (who is affected and how their position fits with historical events, political economy, culture, or global politics). Debates about justice, therefore, have to work against this lack of awareness, and to illustrate how even minimal economic changes could make a significant difference.[12]

However, it can also be argued that this disconnection may be pursued as a means to consolidate power and provide legitimacy for certain states and systems. With a focused attention on civil and political rights, human rights talk tends to reflect Western interests and constitutes a 'dominant discourse of legitimate statehood' (Reus-Smit 2001: 522; McGrew 1998). Under this management, the major violators will be shown to reside in less powerful countries and so the 'burdens of compliance' for rights ralliers will be minimized and attention will shift to those who hold less cultural, economic, or social capital (Pogge 2002: 5). That is, those states that have most responsibility and ability to change the structural conditions in which violations occur are shielded and they claim that they have relatively little to do (Ewing 2001). The response to violations, then, 'is to focus on actions or inactions of relatively powerless individuals' or states rather than to trace back to institutional, societal, and structural conditions (Slapper and Tombs 1999: 145).

This hierarchy of rights norms also connects with the standards of global economies and free trade (Evans 2001). For instance, it fits more easily with international financial institutions, such as the IMF and the World Bank, that regularly use the 'stick' of civil and political rights to exert control over countries that require monetary assistance. Paradoxically, such bodies also impose 'austerity packages', in which states with weak economies have to 'tighten their belts' to repay debts (Stanley 2007a). Such policy decisions, often leading to cuts in health, housing, education, and food, facilitate dramatic negative 'financial and human consequences for large numbers of especially vulnerable people' (Friedrichs 2004: 147). However, they also inevitably lead to 'increasingly repressive policing measures' and the encouragement of 'deviant alliances between states and corporations, and states and organised crime' (Green and Ward 2004: 188).

The economic globalization structured by international financial institutions and corporations along laissez-faire lines has therefore helped to manage, 'reinforce and legitimize' forms of economic exploitation, social inequality, and political repression, all of which worsen and shorten the lives of affected populations (Thomas 1998: 171). These international bodies have been further criticized for embedding a 'one-size fits all' attitude to development that prioritizes market forces, individualism, and private ownership (Chossudovsky 1997). This situation ensures that developing states – that have become material reserves for western states – have even less ability to foster conditions that are conducive to human rights.[13] In this way, the violations that occur in many countries may be regarded as the end result of power differentials, or as Farmer (2003) puts it, they are 'pathologies of power' that impact heaviest on devalued populations.

The picture painted thus far is that, notwithstanding the mainstream management of human rights as being disconnected from structural conditions, violations cannot be viewed as separate from the entrenched inequalities that contextualize lived realities under contemporary conditions of globalization. Injustices are bundled together and victims of torture will regularly have a variety of rights-based claims that link not just to their direct suffering of violence, but also to their denigration and oppression within their daily lives. These latter injustices may be connected to localized interpersonal and social relations, but they are also often reflective of wider institutional and structural conditions that cut across national borders, serving the interests of individuals and groups that reside in other countries.

Consequently, a critical perspective on justice for torture victims is centred on a recognition that involves the acknowledgement of identities (who people are and what they have experienced) alongside actions that assist victims to redress the balance, enabling them to engage as a peer in social life (responding to what people need to have a 'good life' free from inequality and oppression). Without these dual elements, victims are likely to suffer continuing violations. For torture victims, then, justice will entail diverse affirmative and transformative strategies – for instance: to get victims out of poverty; to open up educational opportunities for them; to ensure their access to adequate health care, stable housing, safe drinking water, and food; to facilitate opportunities to acknowledge their violations through educational curricula or social monuments; or to encourage cultures that are free from discrimination. The possibilities, here, are diverse and, while they often require a global engagement, they have to fit local conditions and needs. With this in mind, this chapter now turns to the prospects of democratic participation in formal institutional processes.

Participation

The argument presented so far contends that torture victims can aspire to provisions of justice that relate to recognition as well as to structural change. These claims are global as well as local in nature, which raises significant concerns – notably, how might torture victims (and others) ensure their participation within institutions and structures that, while being intensely significant to their lives, operate in different towns, countries, or continents? How might a victim garner representation for their claims?

In response to such issues, Fraser (2005: 73) proposes that justice perspectives should also take note of the 'political dimension of *representation*'. That is, thinking on justice has to encompass issues of 'who is included in, and who excluded from, the circle of those entitled' to recognition or structural redress; similarly, it has to consider 'who can makes claims' and 'how such claims are to be mooted and adjudicated' (ibid.: 75). In other words, justice responses need to address the problems that victims often face in taking their claims to a higher authority, such as: How can a victim seek redress if there is no institutional space to take a claim forward? How might a female victim progress her case if institutions operate to give ascendancy to male claims? How might a victim, living in poverty, access services? What happens when a torturer is hidden by institutional structures or resides in another state? What happens when a victim is so culturally devalued that they fall outside the boundaries of justice?

Torture victims may well find that they are unable to procure justice for a myriad of reasons. Three reasons why this might occur are: (i) victims are 'framed out' of the claims-making community and perpetrators are often hidden from view; (ii) victims do not always have the capability to progress a claim; and, (iii) relevant institutions are structured in such a way that opportunities to seek justice are closed down.

Misframing

Fraser (2005) argues that many individuals and groups are excluded from being able to make justice claims on the basis of misframing. Misframing occurs when groups are excluded from political participation or protection on the basis of a devalued recognition, such that their identity lacks authority, status, or respectability (Young 1990). For instance, as shown above, perceived 'enemies', who are so distant from 'what we represent', have often found that in the face of repressive measures they stand outside full legal representation and protection (Hudson 2003).

Such perspectives can be readily seen in the post 9/11 world as 'globalized fear' has generated a situation in which states have readily engaged in clampdowns, surveillance strategies, and other authoritarian measures on the basis that 'enemies' must be fought by any means (M. Davis 2001; Giroux 2004). Those criminalized within political discourse – such as those represented as Arab, Muslim, or an 'other' minority – have been subject to increasing levels of violence at the hands of other civilians, who are rarely sanctioned or prosecuted (M. Davis 2001; Poynting *et al.* 2004). Further, some states have invoked strategies to place victims of torture outside of legal protection altogether – as seen in Guantánamo Bay, victims can be placed in inaccessible 'legal black holes' where legal oversight is significantly hindered; victims can be 'outsourced' to states that have fewer constraints regarding violence; and, victims can be vilified to such an extent that the 'human' does not exist and legal rules do not apply (Jamieson and McEvoy 2005: 515–17). Placed at the 'criminalized margins' (Bauman 1995: 216), those individuals who 'suffer' misframing '… become non-persons with respect to justice' (Fraser 2005: 77).

A further element of Fraser's (2005: 78) concept of misframing relates to the ways in which political space and global systems tend to 'insulate' powerful actors from 'critique and control'. While the conditions of globalization, detailed above, are inevitably central to these discussions, it is evident that states will also invoke strategies to obscure the relationship between human rights violations and state activities. As Jamieson and McEvoy (2005) illustrate, state officials may resort to perfidy (hiding their affiliations), engage in collusion with paramilitary groups, hire private mercenaries, militias, or military firms, and give special favour to specialist units that operate outside established rules and laws. Each of these strategies makes it harder for bystanders to connect violence with state activity.

In summary, states play an active role in the ways that torture victims are sometimes 'framed out' of the claims making community and, simultaneously, how their perpetrators can be 'framed out' of debates on responsibility or accountability. Under such conditions, victims can find that they are so culturally devalued that they fall outside the domains in which human rights claims are heard and dealt with. For justice to occur, therefore, states and other global actors need to acknowledge the testimonies of those who have suffered violations and open up effective, 'democratic arenas' where all social actors can participate 'as peers' and where victims' 'claims can be vetted and redressed' (Fraser 2005: 85).

Capabilities

The second point on representational justice relates to the idea that participation within democratic arenas cannot be readily secured by those who do not have the full capability to advance their claims. Individuals and groups are more likely to be excluded from positive recognition or from processes of structural improvement if they occupy a position in which they cannot make a claim. Thus, poor or uneducated people are far less likely to insist on their rights, or to enjoy provided services, on the basis that they might not know what their rights are, or that they do not have the knowledge, economic backing, position, or support that is necessary to take their case forward (Pogge 2002; Young 1990). Accessing services and participating in institutional decision-making is far more difficult for those who occupy positions of structural disadvantage, as torture victims do.

Nussbaum (1999) has been a key proponent of a capabilities perspective on human rights. Her basic thesis, reflecting that of Sen (1985), has been that we need to question 'what people are actually able to do and to be' (Nussbaum 1999: 228).[14] The capabilities approach, therefore, requires that attention be paid to how individuals and groups are able to function and what opportunities they have to achieve a dignified and good quality life. While human rights may exist on paper, a capability perspective requires that claimants have the choice and ability to pursue their rights; their rights must be potential realities. 'In short, thinking in terms of capability gives us a benchmark as we think about what it is really to secure a right to someone' (ibid.: 240).

A capabilities analysis usefully emphasizes the structural, social, and cultural conditions in which people live. It clarifies, for example, that individuals who experience poverty may well require more than material resources to ensure that they are capable of functioning. In such instances, a rationale can emerge that those who are disadvantaged will need extra money, but that they may also need resources (such as employment training, education, health care, or housing) 'to assist their transition to full capability' (ibid.: 241). Further, this analysis is specific – that is, it takes an approach that accounts for the ways in which resources and opportunities are differentially distributed and it notes that individuals will 'vary in their ability to convert resources into functionings' (ibid.: 232). So, as detailed above, groups cannot be approached as homogenous entities; rather, the differences between, and within, groups in terms of their access to resources and services must be specified.

To progress this approach for torture victims, there needs to be a clear understanding of the ways in which certain victims are differentially affected by historical, structural, social, or cultural factors when they face multiple injustices. For example, female victims who are located within patriarchal structures of subordination are more likely to be economically dependent on male family members or partners; in many states they are also less likely to have access to education, paid employment, or to have ownership of land or property (Freeman 2002). In line with these injustices, women are far more likely than their male counterparts to be underrepresented in decision-making bodies at local, national, and global levels (ibid.). As a result, female torture victims will often be ignored within schemes to recognize or provide redress for victims. And, many female victims will lack the knowledge or economic independence necessary to pursue rights claims (Smart 1989). Furthermore, if a woman has suffered the loss of her husband or male partner, she will face other injustices – for instance, she may suffer sexual harassment from community members, and she can often face the loss of land and property that is tied in to male ownership. Female victims will, then, face specific participatory injustices that inhibit their realization of human rights. A capabilities approach is one that attempts to recognize such different needs and status to ensure that inequalities or disadvantages are not reinforced through further decision-making (Nussbaum 1999).

In summary, participatory justice is directly linked to people's capabilities to actually change the world around them (O'Neill 1993) and to live under conditions that enable them to do things (Young 1990). Capabilities are therefore connected to the social structures that guide daily realities in states, institutions, and societal networks (ibid.). In many circumstances, however, individuals and groups are not in a secure position to choose, criticize, or to change such relations. In these instances of incapacity, justice becomes directly linked to the institutional arrangements that frame lives.

Institutional frameworks

The capacity for individuals to work towards justice must also be directly linked to the ways in which institutions operate. The reason for this is that 'major economic, political, and cultural institutions' systematically reproduce structural injustices, and their deficiencies regularly lead to violence and suffering (Young 1990: 41).

Undoubtedly, some institutions may well be 'criminogenic' or 'socially dangerous' because they operate in ways that directly violate rights, or in a manner that causes the conditions for the violation of rights (Slapper and Tombs 1999: 135–38). For instance, it may be argued that the inherent and legitimate workings of state institutions may actually sustain violations like torture – this might be seen, for example, in penal establishments that offer supermax or death row 'services' or in policing units that revolve around paramilitary techniques. Further, while many state institutions may 'readily secure an appearance of consent', they do not always allow 'those whose capacities and opportunities are limited' to renegotiate their position or to refuse to comply with the institution (O'Neill 1993: 320–21); institutions can be structured in a way that shuts down opportunities to seek justice.

In a response to such debates, Pogge (2002) proposes that human rights thinking should be refocused directly onto institutional practices. In these terms, human rights are, primarily, moral claims to be made against 'coercive social institutions' and, secondly, they are claims against the individuals or groups that are 'involved in' such institutions (ibid.: 46). In taking this approach, he (ibid.) moves away from a human rights frame that is dominated by individualized responses (for example, in the mainstream responses that may condemn individual torturers through legal processes without a simultaneous examination of the global, institutional frameworks that facilitate torture) to one that fosters the redesign of international or state bodies to ensure that rights can be securely accessed. Hence, Pogge (2002) argues that there is a collective responsibility to ensure that 'coercive social institutions' should be designed or reformed so that all human beings have access to their rights. Similarly, Nussbaum (2006) notes that decent institutional structures have to be created to ensure that individual capabilities are secured.

The reform of institutions may be a difficult task at a national level, yet it is made even harder under a rubric of globalization – many individuals and groups can find that they do not have ready access to the institutions that govern them and attempts to bring violating institutions to account can be extremely difficult (Fraser 2005). As previously shown, many institutions in less powerful states will 'depend on the structure of the international order and also on that of the national institutions of more powerful states' (Pogge 2002: 33). In such circumstances, the responsibility for institutional change in developing countries encompasses those in a position to influence and guide the activities of powerful, western bodies. This participatory justice requires 'overlapping spheres of engagement and decision-making' (Blau and Moncada 2005: 160).

So, how might institutions be evaluated in terms of justice for torture victims? Young's (1997: 153) suggestions may be helpful here. She proposes that evaluations be based on the institution's 'patterns of distribution of goods and resources', 'their division of labour', 'the way they organize decision-making power', and 'whether their cultural meanings enhance the self-respect and self-expression of all society's members'. Institutions should therefore be measured according to how they operate with regard to structural differentials, representation, and recognition; any evaluation should focus on whether the institution functions in a way that constrains victims in their attempts to 'develop and exercise their capacities' or whether the institution is free from domination, providing emancipatory conditions that enable them to 'express their needs' and to realize a 'good life' (Young 1990: 22–37).

An institutional approach to justice allows the role of state and international institutions in the violation of torture to be clarified and questioned. It encourages further contextualization of the lives of those who suffer violations and of the structures that may compel or legitimize violations (Young 1990). In addition, in questioning the ways in which individuals and groups can be excluded from institutional decision-making, it advances a framework that implicitly encourages the exercise of political rights and participation (Sen 1999). In pursuing institutional changes that might shape capabilities, more victims might enjoy democratic decision-making and procedures.

Conclusion: Working towards status parity

This chapter has presented a tripartite framework to evaluate the 'just' treatment of torture victims. The interlinked injustices that relate to the concerns of recognition, structural differentials, and participation/representation are central to the ways in which certain individuals and groups are targeted for torture, and how victims continue to face injustice following their violation. As shown above, victims are regularly demonized through official discourse in ways that legitimize or make acceptable their violent victimization. In the wake of violations, victims find that their perpetrators are rarely brought to account; they realize that the spaces for them to speak out or to air their grievances within state bodies are limited; and they find that their capacities to function, to work, to have positive relationships, or to access much-needed social or legal services are also diminished (Stanley 2004). In addition, victims may be made aware that their victimization is not just deeply tied to local relations of power, but that it is also linked to national and global concerns of maldistribution, marginalization, limited political participation, as well as institutional exclusion. The suffering of torture victims extends far beyond the direct violence that is inflicted on their bodies and minds.

Given these realities, any analysis of justice for torture victims has to incorporate a recognition of their victimhood alongside actions to ensure that they can participate, as equals, in society. As the transitional justice literature shows (Boraine *et al.* 1994; Hayner 2001), there are no simple solutions to deal with state repression and violence. However, as indicated here, torture victims cannot easily disconnect the injustice of misrecognition from their social status. Moreover, as Fraser (1997, 2003) argues, the prevention of harm will not be attained if structural or institutional corrections are directed solely to piecemeal change. Therefore, she calls for transformative strategies, which address the root causes of injustice, to be placed alongside affirmative action that focuses attention on short-term need. Ideally, the emphasis is on an integrated approach that pursues recognition, representation, and structural concerns together.

It seems clear that justice responses to torture victims have to tie processes of recognition to practical changes that can ameliorate the social status of the victim as well as end further violation and produce more democratic structural and institutional frames (Bauman 2001; Fraser 2000). This position may well present a stark challenge to the dominant response to human rights problems that has strengthened '*the legitimacy of the state and of a society*' which has been productive of violations in the first instance (Mathiesen 2004: 68). The official debates and responses have been 'frequently 'orthodox', keeping 'inside the circle of officially accepted and acceptable disagreements' rather than digging deeper into the underpinning structures (ibid.: 104). With this in mind, the next chapter examines the dominant transitional justice responses to violations in states that are emerging from periods of conflict and repression.

4 Transitional Justice

The previous chapter built a framework of justice that revolved around three central tenets: (i) recognition – how individuals are identified or recognized in terms of their experiences, histories, or status; (ii) representation – the ability of individuals or groups to participate in democratic processes and institutions; and (iii) redistribution – the ways in which status disparities are addressed to ensure that each human being can operate on a par with others, as a peer, in social life. This chapter builds on these ideas by evaluating how justice is secured for torture victims in transitional states.

Roht-Arriaza (2006) notes that anything that is devised to deal with past violations, from a renewed school curricula to the making of memorial quilts to museum exhibits that focus on a painful past, can be viewed as part of a transitional justice framework. These activities demonstrate how widely transitional justice thinking permeates into cultural, social, and political life. This book takes a more confined view by focusing on just two aspects of transitional justice – criminal trials and truth commissions – that frequently illustrate 'top down' processes to deal with violations like torture. This narrowed approach means that the broader fabric of transitional justice initiatives, including the plethora of 'bottom up' measures that emerge in transitional states, will inevitably be omitted.

Nonetheless, the official mechanisms of truth commissions and trials have begun to dominate the transitional justice landscape. These bodies are often deemed to offer significant potential in terms of securing a more peaceful future for victims and their societies (Boraine et al. 1994; Hayner 2001; Kritz 1995). They are commonly the first step to open discussions and facilitate further responses to gross human rights violations.

This chapter highlights that trials and truth commissions can facilitate justice for torture victims; however, this success is mostly connected to how they provide a partial recognition of violence, victims, and perpetrators. The recognition built through these transitional justice bodies tends to be simply and differentially applied, and does not often reflect the socio-economic, or other structured, injustices that regularly bolster human rights violations in the first instance (Stanley 2005b). This, it is argued, can prove problematic as the promotion of recognition as an issue of identity, and not status, ensures that those who have suffered torture are dissociated from their social and structural location (Fraser 2003).

Moreover, the chapter details that transitional justice mechanisms can also shut down representational justice.[1] As a result of institutional deficiencies or rules, certain victims come to be excluded from processes of justice, and institutions do not often provide 'safety nets' for those victims who do not have the capability to participate. Such problems dovetail with more personal decisions – by victims, perpetrators, or bystanders – on whether to engage with transitional justice.

Further, it is apparent that transitional justice bodies can also inhibit the occurrence of redistributive justice; that is, they do not necessarily facilitate social, economic, or political change. Victims often find that they are subject to further denigration or control and that their needs are ultimately downplayed during or following these mechanisms. For victims, these limitations may well undermine transitional justice attempts altogether. They also mean that victims' limited abilities to participate in institutional life or to lead a 'good life' are hampered.

A final point on the structure of material: given the deep interconnections between representational justice and issues of recognition and redistribution, this chapter weaves the analyses of the former into discussions of the latter. This is undertaken to show how the concerns of participation are central to how, or whether, people come to be identified as torture victims, and how they are assisted to participate as a peer among others. It is also done to confirm that these tenets of justice are not mutually exclusive (Fraser 2003).

The rise of transitional justice

Lawrence Weschler (Harvard Law School 1997: 26–27) highlights a dynamic of torture in which the torturer tells the victim: 'Go ahead and scream. Nobody will hear you; nobody will ever know what's going on in this room.' The imposed secrecy, the not knowing or forgetting of torture, is a means to 'demoralize the victim' and to make them feel utterly alone; however, it also gives the torturer 'confidence' that they will never be caught, shamed, or punished (ibid.). Exposing such violence and providing some redress in times of transition, from a repressive regime to a more democratic situation, is the basis of transitional justice (Fletcher and Weinstein 2002). Transitional justice invokes legal and social responses; it ' ... includes that set of practices, mechanisms and concerns that arise following a period of conflict, civil strife or repression, and that are aimed directly at confronting and dealing with past violations of human rights and humanitarian law' (Roht-Arriaza 2006: 2). It is an attempt to get rid of the 'arrogant strut' of the torturers (Weschler, in Harvard Law School 1997: 27); it threatens the silence and impunity of perpetrators.

The birth of transitional justice is often attributed to the Nuremburg Trials and the Tokyo Trials that followed World War II. These trials, directing their attention not just to the prosecution of individual perpetrators but to saving civilization itself, set the ground for internationalized responses to human rights violations. They propelled the idea that law could deal with the most extensive, gross crimes, and they were swiftly followed by a range of international Conventions and Covenants (Neier 1998). However, these trials also highlighted the dangers of dealing with the past – principally, in how international law could be applied as a form of 'victor's justice' in which the 'losers' faced denigration and punishment while the 'victors' (that were also undoubtedly responsible for egregious violations) sustained their power and supposed innocence (ibid.).

The decades following the Nuremburg and Tokyo trials were marked by limited responses to gross human rights violations. This situation, attributable to the Cold War, rather than the problems of taking action, began to change during the 1980s and 1990s, a period in which the fall of Latin American dictatorships demonstrated the need for official acts of 'social repair' (Fletcher and Weinstein 2002: 578; Teitel 2000). As a result, by the end of the twentieth century, calls for transitional justice measures – such as criminal trials, truth commissions, reparations, memorials, apologies, or lustration (the removal or exclusion of perpetrators from public office) – had become a regular feature in transitional states, sometimes years after violations had taken place (Teitel 2000, 2003).

The subsequent 'global justice cascade' has been such that, over the last three decades, there have been almost 40 international courts and tribunals and over 35 truth commissions established to deal with the past (see Sikkink and Walling 2006). These global responses to violations regularly traverse national boundaries, as exemplified by the emergence of the Ad Hoc Tribunals for Rwanda and the Former Yugoslavia, the International Criminal Court, as well as the Pinochet case that crossed British, Spanish, and Chilean jurisdictions. Overall, the expansive rise of transitional justice practices has been dramatic. Doing nothing, it seems, is no longer an option and this upward trajectory of truth and justice measures does not look set to reverse (Sikkink and Walling 2007).

The escalation and international 'success' of these measures is reflected in the way that transitional justice has been widely promoted by influential institutions and politically powerful states. The UN (2004) has firmly supported transitional justice measures and has recently condemned the use of blanket amnesties for perpetrators (Bell *et al.* 2007) and a number of states, including the US, have begun to claim truth-telling and accountability measures as vital ingredients for conflict resolution (Leebaw 2008). Alongside such support, new institutions offering training courses and academic journals,[2] established to promote transitional justice ideas, norms, and practices, have emerged. The global transfer of transitional justice knowledge and 'best practice' has become increasingly common and potential practitioners can prepare themselves with short 'toolkit' courses in New York and Paris, among other cities.

Trials and truth commissions

Despite the idea that the rule of law should prevail for democracy to flourish (Neier 1990), and notwithstanding the fact that human rights law has become the 'dominant language of successor justice' (Teitel 2000: 38), the issue of criminal accountability has been difficult to attain in practice. Historically, criminal justice responses have been *ad hoc* in their implementation (for an overview, see Sikkink and Walling 2006) and their emergence has reflected the changing nature of political will and the resources of local and international actors. To operate effectively, legal processes also require support from the official regime, the local population, and often the 'international community'. Consequently, many courts or tribunals have been charged with being political because of their very formation (Minow 1998).

Nonetheless, there remains a 'feel good' factor about the potential of criminal trials to produce a variety of positive outcomes: to name crimes and record what happened; to bring key perpetrators to account; to quell calls for revenge; to deter individuals and groups from future repression; to redefine societal norms; to underpin the democratic rule of law and demonstrate that no one is above the law; to inspire reforms in and respect for democratic institutions; and to make a distinction between the old and new regime (Malamud-Goti 1990; Méndez 1997; Mertus 2000; Orentlicher 1995; Teitel 2000). In addition, the duty to prosecute is consolidated by the presumption that failing to do so would enhance the power of the perpetrators and undermine the legitimacy of the new government and their institutions (Orentlicher 1995). Trials have, therefore, been connected to wide-ranging, useful ends.

Historically, truth commissions have been implemented by new regimes when their balance of power is such that there is no political will to indict, arrest, or prosecute key human rights violators. So, while commissions seek to deal with past violence, by investigating patterns of abuse, they do not necessarily directly challenge officials from the previous regime (Stanley 2002). Notwithstanding this fact, truth commissions have become a popular feature of transitional conflict resolution over the last two decades and it appears that their use will continue to grow (Hayner 2001).

Commissions are considered to have a number of positive benefits, including: promoting healing for individual victims and their families; shaming perpetrators; building national reconciliation; encouraging nation-building; and, supporting initiatives to prevent future abuses (Hayner 2001: 15–16). As is illustrated below, truth commissions have the further potential to satisfy some demands for justice as, in their hearing of multiple stories, they can detail the complexity of violations and the contexts in which they occur. From this, truth-telling processes may present a unique opportunity to recognize victims, give them 'equal respect', and provide an authoritative acknowledgement of previous harms (ibid.; Stanley 2002). The power of truth does not necessarily end with the closure of truth commissions either as the 'opening up' of debate can facilitate a range of reactions over decades (Osiel 2000). The 'increasingly porous legal fabric' means that 'promises of amnesty or immunity made at the national level cannot be airtight' (Roht-Arriaza 2006: 11).

On the whole, trials and truth commissions are argued to offer great possibilities. While many outcomes tend to be assumed (Nagy 2008) – for example, there is no real evidence that truth commissions or trials might deter further violations – transitional justice mechanisms are represented as being desirable and undoubtedly beneficial on some level. As a result, these processes often present a starting point for dealing with past violations (Phelps 2004). The issue, now, is not whether transitional justice should be done, but how (Nagy 2008).

Providing recognition

While some torture victims just want to forget and to move on (Stanley 2004), others do want formal acknowledgement of their suffering. Given the 'othering' of torture victims – that dehumanizes victims or puts them out of common sight or support – many victims want to have their identities socially reassigned through a process of mutual recognition (Fraser 2000), they want to renegotiate the 'language of political violence' (Teitel 2000: 85).

Recognition-based justice can be a central component in dealing with a violation like torture. As highlighted in the last chapter, justice is linked to victims' opportunities to have their experiences heard and for there to be an official denigration of the perpetrators and the institutional framework that facilitated violence. A central aspect of the 'justice' in transitional justice mechanisms, therefore, lies with their ability to provide recognition of who has been victimized and who has perpetrated human rights violations. These processes offer an opportunity to 'undo power' (Breytenbach 1994) by highlighting the scale of terror, specifying that violence was legally or morally wrong, recognizing who suffered under repression, rehumanizing victims, challenging the denials of repressive regimes, and exposing the myths on which violations come to be distorted and ignored.

The ensuing acknowledgement of victims' experiences is a means by which to contest cultural injustice; it is an opportunity for the state to upwardly revalue the disrespected identities of maligned groups (Fraser 1997). Truth commissions, as well as trials, can make be serious challenge to the negative representations of victims espoused by previous regimes; they allow a purge of 'depreciating self images' (C. Taylor 1992: 65). In doing so, they present opportunities to turn the identity tables around in a way that dismantles past 'common sense' narratives.

Some commentators argue that trials are the best means to build a new record of previous repression (Malamud-Goti 1990). Criminal justice proceedings and findings are more likely to be viewed as credible by onlookers, as legal investigations and decision-making have an air of legitimacy and objectivity (Méndez 1997). As Teitel (2000: 73) notes, while we might not always remember who was condemned in a particular case or what their punishment was, we tend to remember trials for producing 'a lasting record of state tyranny'. In addition, the drama of court proceedings – shown so clearly in the recordings of the Nuremburg Trials, the Ad Hoc Tribunal for the Former Yugoslavia, and the trial against Saddam Hussein – can encourage viewers, and thereby build a national narrative (Osiel 2000).

However, truth commissions are quite unique in their ability to hear multiple testimonies. Often travelling around states, commissions can encourage thousands of people to participate and engage in processes of recognition. Indeed, truth commissions depend on the participation of large groups of people to be successful in building a narrative of truth. Here, victims are the 'centre-piece of truth production' and the participatory process of truth commissions may well be just as, if not more, important as the end product of a report (Humphrey 2003: 172; Méndez 1997). For participants, the simple act of publicly telling a story in their own language, in their own town, can provide a sense of symbolic liberation (Hamber and Wilson 2002). In the official belief in and acceptance of each individual 'truth', commissions may assist healing for participants and communities (Orford 2006).

Commissions also have the potential to provide a wider recognition of events by illustrating how human rights violations are linked to decision-making at international, national, institutional, and personal levels (Crelinsten 2003). In El Salvador, for instance, the truth commission recognized that direct perpetrators as well as colluding bystanders (such as the judiciary) and international supporters (particularly the US government) each contributed to systematic violations in that country (Kaye 1997). This commission mapped the relationships that sustained and maintained violations, and emphasized that violence was institutionalized at governmental and international levels.

It seems, therefore, that both trials and truth commissions have potential to 'do justice' through recognition. While criminal justice processes can offer a focused response to violations, truth commissions can provide a more extensive access to justice for victims. Yet, sometimes it is clear that both courts and commissions are established and operated in ways that exclude certain participants and shut down opportunities for justice for different groups. Transitional justice mechanisms can inhibit representation and recognition for certain individuals and groups.

Inhibiting recognition

This section illustrates how transitional justice measures can obstruct recognition on the basis of two principal concerns: first, the institutional frame of transitional justice; and, second, the structural, social, and personal factors that impede participation and testimony.

Problems of the institutional frame

The global transfer of knowledge has, as detailed above, become a prominent aspect of the transitional justice realm. This transmission of norms and experiences has brought some benefits. For instance, local practitioners can learn from the successes and mistakes of other transitional justice workers across the world. However, in the wake of this transfer, 'transitional justice goals and methods' have also become standardized (Lutz 2006: 333) and normalized (Bell *et al.* 2007). The dominant frame of transitional justice is now commonly cast in terms of 'top-down' initiatives – reflecting the notion that responses to violations require formalized, centralized programmes (such as criminal trials and truth commissions) which comply with international legal norms (Nagy 2008). At the same time, traditional local customs and laws to deal with conflict – the 'bottom-up' initiatives – are more likely to be obscured or delegitimized (Cunneen 2008). Instead, dominant transitional justice practices are manipulated to fit diverse conditions, sometimes (as shown in the following study of Timor-Leste) with 'ambivalent consequences' (Bell *et al.* 2007:151).

The acceptable, Western frame of transitional justice has narrowed the options in terms of how conflict can be resolved (Cunneen 2008). Invariably, this means that local populations do not always have the opportunity to play a part in recognizing violations. For example, consider the nature of prosecution processes: while criminal justice outcomes are directed towards the general populace at large, the actual process revolves around relatively few individuals, specifically court personnel, victims, defendants, and witnesses. Few individuals actually participate in legal proceedings and victims become just 'one source of evidence, amongst others' (Humphrey 2003: 172). This fundamental basis of legal proceedings means that victims, together with other local actors,[3] can feel distanced from court activities.

Furthermore, the operation of law can mean that many individuals do not see their case recognized at all. For instance, while harms against victims may be 'horrible' or 'morally reprehensible', they can stand outside international legal definitions of crime (Mertus 2000: 150). Legal institutions and actors are positioned to set the vocabulary and to name harms, and their omissions mean that certain perpetrators or victims can go completely unrecognized in court proceedings (Rosenblum 2002). It is only recently, for instance, that crimes such as sexual slavery or rape have been admitted to the categories of international crime. Similarly, whole categories of violations (in the form of economic, social, and cultural harms) continue to be ignored within most international legal processes. As previously discussed, the legal hierarchy that prioritizes civil and political violations has stifled recognition of the diverse forms of violence suffered by vulnerable groups.

Even in cases where an event is classed as 'crime', victims can also be frustrated in their quest for recognition because there are too many crimes to try (Mertus 2000) or because their violation is hidden under prosecutorial attempts to build a 'winning case'. Victims are 'so thoroughly represented' by professionals that they are 'pushed completely out of the arena' and they are denied the right to freely participate (Christie 1977: 3). For instance, prosecutors can reconfigure 'facts' to produce a particular legal story, discarding certain aspects of violation to build a picture that is more legally convincing (Osiel 2000). Testimonies of harm may be 'considered inadmissible' or 'discounted as subjective and unreliable' (Rosenblum 2002: 80). Legal language works against narrative that depicts painful experiences or emotions (Mertus 2000). The recognition of the minutiae of repression and violence gets lost in administrative responses that seek to classify, categorize, and explicitly name violations. As a result, individual traumas are 'truncated and skewed' into neat legal categories (Rosenblum 2002: 82; Mertus 2000). Victims become part of this mediated process as they have to make their testimony legally 'digestible' to fit the precise boundaries of the case (Humphrey 2000: 11). The despair, the smells, the sounds, and the smaller details and feelings that are experienced during horror are sidelined (Strejilevich 2006).

The strength of commissions has been that they provide a victim-centred space to recount pain and trauma; they allow some opportunity to see the 'human costs', that is the 'small stories' (Minow 1998: 76). Yet, commissions are also limited by a narrow mandate. Truth commissions tend to be established for short periods of time (sometimes for less than a year) and, as a result, they can never hope to fully acknowledge all human rights violations. This means that certain groups are excluded from truth-telling, resulting in them being less able to 'participate in a newly emerging culture of respect for human rights' (Rolston 2006: 657). Alternatively, it creates further antagonism. In Chile, for instance, the 1991 Rettig Commission limited its investigations to 'death' cases. This decision, reflecting both a lack of time for investigations and money for reparations (Hayner 1998), meant that the Commission did not recognize survivors. Embittered about this, torture victims staged a prolonged campaign for recognition that culminated in the 2004 establishment of the Valech Commission that officially acknowledged 27,255 victims of torture (Bacic and Stanley 2005).

In addition, commissions still collate their data on specific categories of violations and identities. Those giving testimonies on suffering have to ensure that their experiences fit into an authentic identity of being a 'torture victim' or a 'rape victim' or a 'victim of arbitrary detention', and so on. Commissions are increasingly positivistic and technological in their focus – the issue of how many people were killed or injured during conflict has become a central part of official programmes. Subsequently many commissions spend significant amounts of money and time trying to get the classifications, measurements, and numbers right.

While highlighting the extent of suffering and trauma is an important aspect of truth-telling, the reliance on classifications and figures can be sanitizing, distracting, and sometimes harmful. The issue of who is classified, and how, and who decides which kinds of harms are noted while others are omitted can be particularly contentious. After all, the ability to classify, and to make decisions on how categories are formed, is a significant indicator of power (S. Cohen 1985). The capacity to place individuals into particular categories of experience can provide relief for victims, but it can also silence them or force them into remedial action to gain some recognition.[4] While some victims will be omitted from the count completely, others may design their testimonies in an effort to fall into a particular category (Wilson 2001).

The sustained approach to get the 'numbers right' may operate, therefore, to create artificial understandings about the nature of violence and suffering; for example, by highlighting the 'difference' rather than the 'continuities' 'between past and present violence' (Hamber 2006: 219). The imposition of simplified identities can deny the complexity of lives (Wilson 2001); it may sanitize suffering and cut out difficult to hear experiences. It can also mean that people are solely recognized for who they are identified to be, rather than for what they might individually need (Fraser 2003). Moreover, the pragmatic solution of collating hard data also presumes a certain, linear outcome that providing irrefutable data *will* provoke change. Yet, the underpinnings of violence are frequently historical, social, and political, and while the exposure of violation statistics may represent an 'end product' for truth commissions, it will not necessarily lead to reconciliation, peace or even truth (Nagy 2008).

Further, commissions – with an eye on political stability and nation-building – may also streamline testimonies and suppress diversity, imposing simplified or homogenized group identities for reconciliatory purposes (Wilson 2001). Individually complex stories can be selectively channelled in ways that undermine difference in favour of building political consensus (Humphrey 2003). In the South African Truth and Reconciliation Commission, for example, Archbishop Tutu would make frequent pronouncements that everyone had been wounded through apartheid; he proposed that there should be no boundaries between groups and their treatment. This proposal ran against dominant victim perceptions that there is a moral distinction between actions that supported and resisted apartheid, and that individual suffering was unequal in its distribution and intensity (Humphrey 2002). For victims, whose distinctive experiences were subsumed for political nation-building ends, this focus meant that their psycho-social needs went unmet (Hamber and Wilson 2002).

Finally, here, the individualism that is so often espoused by both criminal justice and truth commission mechanisms hinders a complex recognition of responsibility and victimhood. These transitional justice processes tend to focus on the bipolar structure of 'individual victims' and 'individual perpetrators' (Humphrey 2003). While this approach is useful in terms of stating that particular people were directly responsible for violations or that specific people were victimized, this individualism has a number of repercussions. First, the exclusive definitions of 'victim' or 'violator' hide the reality that some individuals will occupy both categories. This is particularly so during periods of armed resistance to repressive regimes (Stanley 2001). Second, even if a case is successful, the outcomes will only benefit individual claimants despite the fact that numerous other individuals may have suffered similar violation (Smart 1989). Third, it propagates a flawed discourse that emphasizes 'evil' individuals or aberrant policies as being at the heart of violations (Galtung 1994). Individualism hides the social, political, and economic structures in which violations take place and the causes of violations are regarded as exceptional deviations from 'normal' state or institutional behaviour or from 'normal' international relations (Orford 2006). Thus, individualism tends to disregard economic, social, or cultural violations that pervade lives across post-conflict societies and shifts attention away from the networks that sustain inequalities and violence (Humphrey 2003; Osiel 2000). It is a convenient focus for 'those who most benefit' from existing structures (Evans 1998: 16–17) and who may be relieved of responsibility (Fletcher and Weinstein 2002; Phelps 2004).[5]

In summary, trials or court processes may present a solid opportunity to attribute responsibility for violations; however, they are limited by the fundamental requirements of law to focus on acts classified as 'crimes' and to limit narrative to legally convincing 'facts'. While truth commissions may permit subjective stories and further detail, they also operate with an eye on political consensus, and according to a specific mandate and related classifications. The standardized nature of these transitional justice initiatives inevitably means that local attempts to understand or deal with violence and trauma are overlooked or delegitimized, and the complex experiences of victimization and perpetration are sidelined in favour of an individualistic, smooth, and fast process that is dominated by 'professionals'. However, the recognition of violations is also hampered by a range of participatory difficulties to which this chapter now turns.

Problems of participation

In terms of opportunities for criminal justice, one well-trodden concern is that there is little equality to the law (Ewing 2001). Critical legal scholars have repeatedly detailed how law is not a 'neutral arbiter' or 'protector of the weak' (Smart 1989: 140). Human rights law – like law in general – continues to be identified as supporting those who are white, able-bodied, heterosexual, affluent, and male (ibid.; Otto 1999; Peterson and Parisi 1998). And, in its construction of official identities and definitions, law tends to disqualify alternative knowledges and experiences, including those it purports to advance (Otto 1999).

Certainly, the ability to access criminal proceedings is not fairly experienced and many groups are excluded from legal processes. For example, uneducated or poor people – often women, minorities, children, elderly individuals, or those with disabilities – may not know what their entitlements are and they can lack the legal understanding or economic independence needed to pursue claims (Pogge 2002). The wider political context in which human rights operate has meant that economic support to progress cases (including the availability of legal aid) is invariably limited (Tushnet 1984). For most individuals without significant funds, making justice claims is not an option. Rights are established, yet subjects do not enjoy equal, secure chances of participation, even in civil and political cases (McColgan 2000; Pogge 2002).

Social exclusion from transitional justice can also be reinforced, in different ways, by the very institutions that have been established to provide pathways for justice. Some authors (such as Byrnes 1988–89 and Galtung 1994) argue that mainstream human rights institutions – for example, the UN, governmental bodies, and courts – operate in ways that are not neutral and which entrench inequalities further. Mainstream institutions often fail to address economic, gendered, or other structured 'difference' that 'inhibit' the 'accomplishment' of formal rights (Chinkin 1998: 120). For instance, despite some progress in recent years, gender inequalities and difference can still be ignored by mainstream institutions as a result of: the dominance of males in institutions that implement and interpret rights;[6] the exclusion of women or 'women's issues' from institutional discussions or focus; the limited attention to economic, social, or cultural violations, or to violations that occur in private spaces; the failure to recognize that gender has a differential impact on violations; and, the reticence to engage in investigations or court procedures in ways that are 'woman-wise'[7] (Byrnes 1988–89; Franke 2006; Rowland 1995). The consequences of such frames, policies and practices are that female victims 'remain unrecognised by broader political processes, and outside the sphere of full political and legal inclusion' (Ní Aoláin 2006: 844).

These critiques can also be directed towards truth commissions. Recognition is hampered by the frequent inability of commissions to collate testimonies from and on groups that are relatively powerless among victims. Certain groups, such as indigenous populations, working-class populations, children, and women, can find that they are less likely than others to be recognized and provided with a space for dialogue in the aftermath of violations (Pérez-Sales *et al.* 1998; J. Taylor 1994). For instance, in South Africa, women frequently did not highlight their own suffering in truth commission testimony. In an attempt to address the emerging gendered imbalance of 'truths', the commission began to draw explicit attention to the sexual violence of women. The end result, as Ross (2003c) argues, was that the categorical linking of women to sexual violence ensured that their other forms of suffering, and women's status within societal power structures, went unnoticed. Such 'mis-recognition or over-recognition' (Franke 2006: 823) distorts the acknowledgement of victimization during conflict; however, it also impacts on how women are subsequently treated by relevant institutions, communities, or others.

As a result of structural and social conditions, then, many groups find that they have limited ability to participate. Transitional justice institutions often disregard these vulnerabilities in their operations and fail to build in safety nets to address these concerns (Ross 2003c). Status and power differentials are central to whether justice will be secured, the possibilities that victims have to pursue their claims, and the response they receive from domestic and international actors. The mainstream response to victims who hold a devalued status is not a positive one and those in most need often have little power to 'define which rights should be guaranteed by law' or capacity 'to secure redress against violations of rights' (Hudson 1993: 197). That said, it is also clear that even with the best intentions, transitional justice mechanisms can fail to recognize victims or perpetrators as a result of social resistance to the project. The success of transitional justice processes in providing recognition of violations is heavily reliant on their participants and bystanders.

Even the most far-reaching transitional justice bodies have struggled to access victims. Notwithstanding the promise of reparations for officially designated victims in South Africa, for example, thousands of individuals still chose not to share their experiences with the truth commission (Stanley 2001). Alternatively, victims who do participate in transitional justice processes often remain silent about, or they discursively manage, their own experiences. Perhaps this is to be expected; after all, the idea that after months or years during which victims silenced themselves, to protect themselves and others, they should be able almost magically to speak freely is illusionary (Stanley 2004). Moreover, giving testimonies or telling stories 'like other social phenomena, have unanticipated consequences' and bring their own risks (Das and Kleinman 2001: 21). Participation or inclusion in transitional justice bodies can retraumatize victims as well as 'heal' them. Silence or the careful management of stories can therefore 'emerge' for numerous reasons. They can, for example: allow people to cope with their situation; sustain a facade of normality; ensure that an individual is not identified as a victim; be a form of resistance to a process that is not politically supported; be a way to protect oneself from shame, humiliation, or future repression; or be about keeping a secret. Silences within transitional justice mechanisms can be just as important as what is said (Motsemme 2004; Ross 2003c; Stanley 2004).

The official recognition of human rights violations is played out within a managed context in which individual victims make decisions about whether or how far to participate. Of course, these decisions are also made by perpetrators and it is apparent that most perpetrators do not share their testimonies with transitional justice bodies. Perpetrators regularly sustain power during transitions; they often hold too much status and require significant exclusionary practices to dislodge their position within societal structures.

While criminal trials proceed with some perpetrators in attendance, commissions generally operate without any input from this group and regularly choose not to name perpetrators at all (Hayner 2001).[8] In instances where perpetrators have participated, as in South Africa, a certain amount of tactical storytelling has also been operationalized. Perpetrators, interested in obtaining an amnesty for their crimes, often made political choices on what to tell and, of course, what to leave out (Stanley 2001). Powerful people (such as Winnie Mandela, Chief Buthelezi, and F. W. de Klerk) used their influence, legal representation, and money to sideline their own involvement in atrocities and negotiate a lesser form of truth (ibid.).

Thus, powerful individuals or groups are not averse to using transitional justice bodies for their own ends (Smart 1989). While lending authority to claims that rights defend the weak, official responses to violations can be manipulated by those who have the most and who seek to advance their particular interests (Chinkin 1998; Connell 1995). This issue has been clearly highlighted in the recent establishment of the Iraqi Special Tribunal by the US Administration. This tribunal, focused on the crimes of the Hussein regime, held no jurisdiction to consider crimes committed by the US and their allies since the invasion (Bell *et al.* 2007). Consequently, there was no recognition of the violations emanating from US-led actions in Iraq, from the illegality of the intervention itself to killings, torture, or 'disappearances', to the corruption of the 'oil for food' programme (Boraine 2006; Nagy 2008). Transitional problems were purely cast as Iraqi problems rather than issues of 'occupation, insurgency, and the war on terror' (Nagy 2008: 280).

This tribunal illustrated the capture of transitional justice for powerful interests.[9] However, it also shows that court processes can also be used by defendants to espouse and reinforce their own assumptions and values, and subvert the intentions of prosecutors and their supportive regime (Osiel 2000). Arguments that this tribunal did not fulfil standards of due process (ICTJ 2006) bolstered defendants' claims that they were being ill-treated by a retributive, aggressive force. In short, transitional criminal justice processes can sometimes enhance the standing or 'victimhood' of perpetrators and institutions can 'function to construct political myths, whether deliberately or inadvertently' (Leebaw 2008: 111).

Finally, for the recognition of violation or status to occur, there 'must be at least some comprehension of the other's point of view' (Hudson 2003: 212) and there has to be a certain degree of active discourse – telling and listening. Yet when those with power do not want to sustain discourse, they either show open disdain or they begin to look elsewhere; that is, they become disengaged (Fletcher and Weinstein 2002; Giddens 1994). In the transitional justice context, the disengagement of powerful perpetrators and bystanders can be clearly identified: the Afrikaan population in South Africa chose not to watch the truth commission media coverage (Paris 2000) and the Chilean security services have consistently demeaned the legal findings related to 'disappearances' and torture (Stanley 2002). In effect, those with power can just choose not to listen or can claim that any 'truth' or 'justice' is the result of an attack against them. These activities, in which perpetrator or bystander groups do not concede 'at least partial legitimacy to the narratives of others' means that victims' truths continue to go unrecognized (Rolston 2006: 656).

To conclude, although criminal justice processes and truth commissions may present a vital means to recognize those involved in human rights violations, and to start discussions on 'the past', they can also inhibit recognition in diverse ways. It is clear that neither mechanism is particularly useful for recognizing perpetrators – in legal terms, most perpetrators avoid examination while truth bodies are unable to compel their participation; and powerful groups can capture transitional justice mechanisms to propel their own interests. However, as a result of limited time, mandates, and powers, and skewed practices, these bodies do not recognize certain victims either. In this way, it seems that transitional justice bodies 'perpetuate silences' and myths as much as they build recognition (ibid.). The recognition they provide is always incomplete, partial, and constructed (Osiel 2000). These limits on justice may well 'frustrate' victims 'and inflame their sense of having been wronged' (Rosenblum 2002: 83). Yet, ultimately, their situation depends on those who are engaged in listening – when bystanders disengage completely from transitional justice initiatives, recognition is deemed not to socially matter and opportunities for redistributive justice become much less likely.

Promoting redistribution

As highlighted in the last chapter, Fraser (2005) argues that claims for justice must be viewed not just in terms of participation and identity, but also social status. In other words, any individual's claims for representation or recognition must be connected to measures to overcome subordination and to establish that person as a full partner in social life (ibid.). The need for recognition is regularly entwined with calls for changes in the disadvantaged social status of victims. While establishing the truth of events is important, 'truth, for truths sake is a pretty pointless exercise … unless it is coupled with some form of social transformation' (Hamber 1998: 98); to prevent further repression and discrimination there has to be political, social, and personal change for victims. Alongside recognition of 'victimhood', there has to be distributive corrections to ensure that the social esteem of victims is combined with material changes that permit all members of society to interact with one another as peers (Fraser 2003).

Redistributive possibilities are wide in their scope. In torture's wake, some people will require direct medical assistance, while others may require psychological counselling or educational scholarships or economic support for loss of earnings caused by them being unable to work following trauma (Stanley 2004). Evidently, given the issue that 'torture victims' are not a homogenous group, it is likely that different people will face different impediments to overcome the injustices that they have suffered. So, for example, children might have particular needs, as might women or indigenous populations. Provisions to ensure that such individuals have an ability to fully participate in their social world have to be flexible and meet individualized demands.

Torture victims may also support initiatives that redistribute power within transitional states. For example, reparations and compensation are likely to enhance the lives of individual victims or affected communities; while schemes like rewriting educational curricula or building official memorials or insitituting days of remembrance can each enhance the status of victims by showing that their experiences are culturally important. Alternatively, the redistribution of power can be pursued by strategies that are also aimed at perpetrators. Thus, the shaming of perpetrators, their punishment, or their lustration can each support a 'balancing out' or a restoration of equal power relations (Phelps 2004: 123).

Torture victims can also request significant institutional changes to ensure that torture is less likely to occur in the future. To this end, there may be a need to entrench new values into the institutions that have allowed violations to occur unhindered (Hayner 2001). Linked to this, victims may be keen to reorganize institutions so that they operate along political democratic lines. In many instances this institutional change cannot stand alone, but must be interlinked with provision to ensure that individuals and groups are capable of participating 'on a par' with others. This may well require large-scale and prolonged social change and capacity-building in order to ensure that all individuals are able to make effective claims.

Additionally, victims are often all too aware that the obstacles to parity that they face are connected to wider structural inequalities. While directed compensation or reparations may offer some relief, these focused payments do not transform the conditions that give rise to economic and social inequalities. In certain situations, the solution needed to address injustice may require a focus to, say, re-establish community lands or resources (and provide the opportunities for devalued groups, like women or indigenous people, to enjoy equal ownership), or to make a significant challenge to globalization practices that privilege markets over people (McCorquodale and Fairbrother 1999). From this standpoint, as Farmer (2003) proposes, justice entails standing firm on fundamental human rights and about learning to change the world in ways that transform structural inequalities, institutional shortcomings, and interpersonal relations.

Given these obstacles to parity, trials and truth commissions have to be dovetailed with redistributive initiatives that work to change the factors that inhibit victims from operating 'on a par' with others. To be effective in the long term, these measures have to be seen as more than a one-off 'quick fix' that shields states from taking further, more politically difficult, action. For victims, the need to be identified as having been wronged is combined with the need for disruptions to their disadvantaged status; they recognize that 'the profound implication of the revelation of knowledge is that it introduces the possibility of future change' (Teitel 2000: 111). Consequently, without a tangible response to the official recognition of violations, the work of transitional justice mechanisms is 'undermined' and their impact considerably 'weakened' (Fletcher and Weinstein 2002: 630).

Yet the possibilities of redistribution, emerging directly from court processes or truth commissions, are narrow. As shown earlier, each of these mechanisms has the ability to offer recognition of victimization, as well as the condemnation of violators – in this way they can provide justice by restoring the reputation of individual victims and shaming those responsible (Mertus 2000). Trials can invoke punitive responses to perpetrators – individuals can face fines, community sentences, lengthy jail terms, and even the death penalty. Truth commissions may have the ability to allow a re-engagement between victims and perpetrators; they can offer reparations to those designated as 'victims'; and they can put forward extensive recommendations to direct relevant powers to make positive changes to structural, institutional, and personal realities. These transitional justice processes can, therefore, facilitate redistribution in diverse ways; however, as detailed in the next section, they may also inhibit this form of justice from developing.

Impeding redistribution

Undoubtedly, trials or truth commissions cannot be expected to solve the many issues of redistribution. Yet, these processes might be expected to promote or prepare the ground for relevant changes. At the least, it might be anticipated that transitional justice provisions are imbued with the 'spirit' of redistributive justice. In many instances, however, this is not the case. As shown here, transitional justice measures can cut off redistributive opportunities as a result of their failure to recognize the diverse needs of victims or to pre-empt political resistance. Further, redistributive opportunities are also hindered by institutional systems that increase possibilities for future victim inequality. Overall, the opportunities for trials and truth commissions to encourage redistribution are limited – this is significant as, currently, these institutions dominate the transitional landscape. The ascendancy of such transitional justice initiatives may well distract thinking from issues of structural, social, and institutional injustice.

Victims often hope that transitional justice measures will rebalance unequal power relations between themselves and those who perpetrated violence upon them. For some victims the issue of parity is defined in terms of the status of their perpetrators – for example, torturers do tend to be mis-recognized as good professionals who hold prestige within their institution (Huggins *et al.* 2002). The issue regarding parity, then, is that such individuals require some devaluation in their standing; a balancing out is required. Yet, as already shown, transitional justice mechanisms often proceed on the basis that most perpetrators will not be touched. The use of *ad hoc*, individualized criminal justice, for example, means that most perpetrators are not brought to account. Similarly, as detailed above, truth commissions often fail to expose those responsible for violations. Besides, in many states, amnesties are used to smooth the transition to a more democratic situation.[10] Amnesties, often employed to retain political cohesion (Humphrey 2003; Stanley 2001), challenge the notion of redistribution. In their illustration of 'where political power lies' (Teitel 2000: 56), they show how perpetrator resistance to 'rebalancing' can determine political policy (Méndez 1997). These institutional features mean that perpetrators do not have to give anything up – they will not be identified as perpetrators or prosecuted; they do not have to illustrate remorse or responsibility; and most will continue to work in their positions of power.

This resistance to 'rebalancing' can also emerge from transitional justice bodies that simplify or fail to expose the redistributive needs of victims in favour of making statements on reconciliation or forgiveness. This issue was particularly illustrative in the South African truth commission. Here, commissioners made regular statements that victims were willing to forgive and be reconciled with perpetrators, and that they only sought symbolic reparation (Simpson 2002). Victims who did not request any redistributive response, or who spoke without anger, were praised; those who made statement claims (for example, for the return of bodies, for reparations, or for criminal prosecutions) were depicted as being 'needy' or as undermining the national project of reconciliation (Wilson 2001). In effect, the Commission managed victims' feelings and misrepresented their needs to make them more acceptable to transitional powers (Simpson 2002). In quelling claims for justice, the Commission weakened its ability to move victims' needs forward, to push for radical change and, to inform South African society about the complexity of victimization (Hamber *et al.* 2000).

Transitional justice mechanisms can be employed, therefore, to meet wider political ends. Thus, perhaps the most crucial element that informs the redistributive possibilities of transitional justice bodies is the way in which they are responded to by transitional states and other relevant powers. More often than not the redistributive options that are advanced by transitional justice bodies are ignored (Hayner 2001). And, even though most victims have 'relatively realistic expectations', such as to 'get medical attention, a tombstone, exhumations, further investigations' and so on (Hamber *et al.* 2000: 34), transitional states rarely attend to basic concerns. This inability of transitional states to respond to what victims need ensures that the injustices of the past remain open; it leads to feelings that transitional justice procedures are incomplete or weak (ibid.).

Victims may also discover that their opportunities to make legal claims are hindered by a backlash from those who feel threatened by what are regarded as self-interested advances (Smart 1989). It is not unusual for human rights victims to face intimidation, threats, or assault from those who face censure or punishment. However, victims may also find that they are denigrated or distanced by a wider population that perceives that they are demanding too much. For instance, the Argentinian 'Madres de Plaza de Mayo', who have marched every Thursday to acknowledge and campaign about 'disappearances', have been ostracized and ignored. For some, their persistence is an unwanted reminder of a violent past and their perseverance has, over time, generated hostility (Feitlowitz 1998).

The backlash that victims suffer can also be sustained in less overt ways – for example, in how victims can find that their claims for justice are positioned against others who advance competing claims (Smart 1989). In such situations, decisions on the balancing of rights 'are likely to favour those already advantaged through allocations of power and influence' (Chinkin 1998: 120). Inevitably, this can stop human rights claimants from further action. For instance, in 2005, a group of Chilean torture victims commenced a legal process to claim reparations (as is their right under international law). They were informed by the government that, if successful, their reparations would be paid from the milk budget for schools and their claim would disadvantage the welfare claims of schoolchildren (Bacic and Stanley 2005). What could the victims do – stand against already disadvantaged children to claim their rights? Imagine the criticisms from the general population if they did – 'what a clamouring group of needy individuals!' This issue of counterclaims poses a real problem for any human rights strategies (Smart 1989).

Alternatively, victims can find that their claims are accepted at the price of their integration into a disadvantageous system. In particular, those making justice claims can be subject to heightened surveillance, regulation, and enforcement (S. Cohen 1985; Smart 1989). Thus, claimants tend to have their histories, lives, and relations mapped and recorded, and their daily activities become subject to new rules. Galtung (1994) goes further by arguing that the dominant human rights tradition increases the power and legitimacy of transnational bodies and state governments as it makes individual claimants dependent on these institutions to make amends or to provide redress. In such instances, victims may resist becoming incorporated within mainstream, discriminatory systems – at the expense of justice.

In conclusion, the perceived results of trials and truth commissions, among others – to bring closure, promote peace, build nations, or strengthen democratic institutions – are overstated. Transitional justice bodies, by themselves, cannot do these things. While these bodies, operating under very difficult circumstances and often struggling with limited support, are powerful in their promotion of previously silenced voices, questions do need to be raised about their usefulness to prime transitional states for change.

Of particular concern, here, is that these bodies regularly represent the only 'eggs in the basket' (Rolston 2000: 324) and their implementation can detract from other useful initiatives. With regard to opportunities for justice during transition there is often nothing else and, in this position, trials and commissions reiterate the liberal approach that human rights claims can only be made in terms of 'special identity and suffering' – the simplified version of what victims *are* supplants what individuals *need* (S. Cohen 1996b: 15). In effect, these mechanisms make no challenge to the subordination linked to the institutionalized relations of exploitation, marginalization, and deprivation that give rise to human rights victimization. They direct attention to identities rather than inequalities (Fraser 2003).

This remit displaces structural differentials as a central injustice (Fraser 1997) and the end result, as Bauman (2001: 147) points out, is that social justice is abandoned and recognition becomes 'toothless, ineffective' and 'easy'. This issue undermines the potential of trials or truth commission because if people continue to live in desperate poverty, or they see that their violators retain a high status, transitional justice processes hold less legitimacy (Fletcher and Weinstein 2002: 602).

Conclusion

In an era in which trials and truth commissions are being rapidly disseminated around the world, this chapter has shown that they provide an uncertain response for victims seeking truth and justice. While these institutions are heralded as providing significant solutions to violence, harm, or conflict, they are regularly problematic in practice.

Truth and justice are undermined by a range of factors, including: the formalization of Western approaches that delegitimize local endeavours to resolve conflict; institutional restrictions or failings that mean most perpetrators are not recognized or brought to account; individualistic approaches that simplify, and create hierarchies out of, violence; the political management of stories to sanitize accounts or to 'force' reconciliation; the limits on participation as a result of institutional rules, limited capacities, or resistance; the institutionalization of inequalities within presiding bodies; and, the limited capacity of institutions to build or enforce redistributive options, as well as the political distancing from redistribution. These issues can often mean that torture victims are not able to participate in transitional justice proceedings, that they remain unrecognized, and that they do not enjoy redistributive benefits.

A related aspect is that legal or truth-finding bodies may well divert attention from political issues (Teitel 2003). These 'limited' justice initiatives do 'not substitute for political action' and, vitally, they 'can lull those who would otherwise engage in political action into taking their "eye off the ball"' (McColgan 2000: 304–05). In the constant focus on 'mainstream' instruments and procedures, groups may well lose the forethought, imagination, or energy to propel the kind of long-term social movements required to transform the structural inequalities that accompany problems of rights (Byrnes 1988–89; Miller 1999). Mainstream rights talk may well close down other means of effective struggle and undermine the idea that there is life beyond trials and truth commissions.

Given this situation, it is important to remember that transitional justice initiatives are interdependent; that is, each mechanism is dependent on and contextualized by other institutions and programmes for their own success

(Orentlicher 2007). As a result, trials and truth commissions need to be implemented alongside other interventions and responses – such as: exhumations; psychosocial interventions; restoration of political, legal, economic, or social institutions that are capable of managing conflict and providing security; reparations; memorials; economic development; restitution of property; conflict resolution; or mourning rituals (Fletcher and Weinstein 2002). In order for justice to emerge, there has to be 'multiple', culturally-relevant 'pathways to justice' for victims (Roht-Arriaza 2006: 8). This position requires the creation of varied institutions and groups (at local, national, and international levels) to build the issues of representation, recognition, and redistribution in diverse ways.

Notwithstanding these criticisms, it seems appropriate to state here that these transitional justice bodies should not be 'thrown out'. The ideas expressed in this chapter are not meant to undermine the whole being of transitional justice bodies; rather, they are presented to begin an honest discussion of the possibilities and failings of transitional bodies. Transitional justice initiatives do continue to represent a number of possibilities: to raise consciousness and show the entitlement to human rights that all people possess; to provide some opportunity for victims to participate and be recognized in an otherwise 'silencing' world; to oblige states to consider the minimum international standards of human rights; to put rights claims onto the agenda of a visible institution; to energize social movements; to destabilize establishment values (such as institutionalized patriarchy or racism); to unmask the sources of power in transitional states; and to invigorate transformative challenges (Connell 1995; Miller 1999; Otto 1999; Smart 1989). They can, therefore, be strategic tools. Finally, it is clear that these institutions are wanted by victims themselves. As the forthcoming study on torture and transitional justice in Timor-Leste shows, those who have not enjoyed secure human rights argue that such transitional justice bodies – and the human rights thinking that underpins them – are deeply needed.

5 Torture in Timor-Leste

This chapter builds on the previous overview of repression (established in Chapter 1) to provide further detail of torture and ill-treatment in Timor-Leste. The chapter, which draws substantially on research interviews with victims, highlights that torture was undertaken and supported by various groups within Timor-Leste including local political party members, as well as militia members and intelligence agents. However, the majority of torture in the region was directly conducted and directed by Indonesian army and police force officials. These perpetrators used torture for different ends – to obtain intelligence, to gather confessions, to coerce compliance and defer-ence to the regime, to silence dissenters, to punish and eradicate resistance groups, to terrify the population, to 'turn' individuals into regime supporters or informants, and to satisfy the personal wants of individual torturers.

Many groups have been affected by torture in Timor-Leste; however, this chapter indicates that torture was differentially applied – according to the victim's social status and location. Alongside this, torture is shown to have been just one part of widespread gross human rights violations and abuses that affected vast swathes of the population – that is, torture was just one violation among many others and victims often faced a spiral of victimiza-tion in which the harms against them extended over many years.

This chapter also illustrates how victims have coped with or resisted their treatment. Victims' testimonies make clear that they engaged in strategies to avoid being 'caught' in the first instance; that they attempted to subvert the repressive techniques against them during detention; and that they sought to secure their freedom through various means. In detailing these aspects of victimization and resistance, this work highlights that the Indonesian-led torture and repression in Timor-Leste invigorated and gave spirit to the whole resistance movement, both within Timor-Leste and abroad.

General overview

Within the context of extensive repression, arbitrary detention and torture became an integral and commonplace feature of the occupation (Human Rights Watch 1994). The Commission for Reception, Truth and

Reconciliation (CAVR) identified 17,169 victims of arbitrary detention, 8,508 victims of torture, and 6,872 victims of ill-treatment (CAVR 2005: Ch. 7.4.28). Given the issues around data collation (discussed further in Chapter 7), it seems reasonable to suggest that these figures minimize the true extent of such violence.

In 2000, the International Rehabilitation Council for Torture Victims undertook a national psycho-social needs assessment in Timor-Leste (Modvig *et al.* 2000). Following interviews with members of 1,033 households, they concluded that, despite under-reporting, 587 respondents had been exposed to torture. As they (ibid.: 1763) further set out:

> Psychological torture (411 [40%]), physical beating or mauling (336 [33%]), and beating the head with or without a helmet (267 [26%]) were the most common forms reported, and other forms of torture included submersion in water (126 [12%]), electric shock (124 [12%]), crushing of hands (102 [10%]), and rape or sexual abuse (54 [5%]) .... 207 (20%) respondents believed that they would never recover from their experiences, and a further 424 (41%) believed they would only recover with some help.

Torture has been widely experienced in Timor-Leste. However, like other violations, it was used more frequently in particular time periods and spaces. In terms of time periods, the CAVR illustrates three peaks of torture – in 1975, during the internal armed conflict and the Indonesian occupation; between 1976 and 1984, when large-scale Indonesian military operations were used to crush the resistance; and, in 1999, at the time of the referendum and the subsequent departure of the Indonesian military and supportive militias (CAVR 2005: Ch. 7.4.23–27). Between 1985 and 1998, torture was low-level and mainly used for specific, targeted individuals. In terms of space, all regions were affected by torture yet, given the network of prisons and interrogation centres, torture occurred regularly in Dili. During the initial and final periods of occupation, torture was used more extensively in the western districts that bordered Indonesian West Timor while, between 1980–85, torture occurred more often in the eastern districts where resistance activity was seen to be strong (ibid.). Generally, the CAVR report (2005: Ch. 7.4.570) details that torture was coordinated as 'there was clearly no limit on what police and military officers could do to obtain information'.

Torturers and their motives

This section establishes who was directly responsible for torture during 1975–99. It is shown that the Indonesian military and police officials committed most of the torture; however, the direct involvement and support of East Timorese in torture is also clear. This local participation in human rights violations has created a legacy of mistrust and anger between the Timorese population – an issue that has required significant transitional justice attention in the move to a more democratic situation.

The role of UDT and **Fretilin** *in torture*

The internal civil war in Timor-Leste was rooted in the actions of the Timorese Democratic Union (UDT) who, on 11 August 1975, launched an armed movement to purge '*Fretilin* communists'. This movement lasted until 20 August 1975, when *Fretilin* commenced an armed insurrection. However, during this short period, UDT members attacked and burnt villages where there was strong *Fretilin* support. Many people were detained in improvised, overcrowded prisons and torture was common albeit not systematically applied (CAVR 2005: Ch. 7.4.798–99).[1]

In response, *Fretilin*'s armed action targeted hundreds of UDT leaders and supporters, as well as *Apodeti* members, Portuguese administrators, civilians, and even its own members. Over the following four years, *Fretilin* engaged in killings and wide-scale detentions of suspected enemies, collaborators, and those who criticized *Fretilin* leadership. Those detained were held in an array of improvised spaces – prisons, military barracks, warehouses, and 'rehabilitation' centres;[2] they faced overcrowded, unsanitary conditions and suffered severe food shortages. Detentions were also brutal as torture (including heavy beatings, whippings, burnings, strippings, stabbings, and humiliation techniques) was widely undertaken during interrogation and as punishment (CAVR 2005: Ch. 7.4.800–801).[3] In addition, *Fretilin* actively engaged the civilian population to violate suspected enemies – during political rallies, leaders would encourage locals to commit violence against each other. Although aware of these activities, *Fretilin* leaders failed to intervene (ibid.) and this issue, of Timorese turning against Timorese, intensified old community divisions and created new ones – a reality that was undoubtedly manipulated by the Indonesian military (CAVR 2005: Ch. 4.75).

Indonesian torture

The techniques employed by the Suharto-led Indonesian government in Timor-Leste mirror earlier attempts to control and destroy the Communist Party of Indonesia (PKI) in 1965–66 (Cribb 2002; Nairn 1997). During this period, the same government implemented policies in which those identified as PKI members or supporters were persecuted and murdered – while Amnesty International (1977) estimated that more than one million people were killed in less than two years, even the head of the Indonesia's state security system assessed the toll at half a million people (Jardine 1997). It is also thought that over one and a half million were jailed or sent to prison camps over the following decade on the basis of their supposed communist connections (Cribb 2001). During detention, many individuals were subject to extreme torture and maltreatment (Amnesty International 1968;

B. Anderson 2000; Budiardjo 1974; Nusa 1987). These activities were undertaken to obtain evidence and confessions, and they formed part of the 'retraining' to turn people away from their perceived communist ideals (Nusa 1987).[4]

Torture pervaded the criminal justice system of Indonesia and, thus, the torture in Timor-Leste was a continuation of similar treatment (Lawyers Committee for Human Rights 1993). Further, as the UN Special Rapporteur on Torture (1992: 73) noted, Indonesian torture occurred in cases that were 'considered to endanger the security of the state'. In areas like Timor-Leste, which were thought to be unstable, torture was routine and extensive – indeed, the CAVR (2005: Ch. 7.4.33) found that the Indonesian military and police, together with their Timorese auxiliaries, were responsible for 82.4 per cent of all reported torture and ill-treatment cases.

Part of the reason for this extensive use of torture was that the military and police operated everywhere in the region. Soon after the start of occupation, special commands were established to ensure that all aspects of life in Timor-Leste were militarized, policed, or controlled. There was the East Timor Regional Defence and Security Command (Kodahankam Timor Timur), Sub-Regional Command (Korem), District Military Commands (Kodim), Sub-district Military Commands (Koramil), Combat Team Regiments, Intelligence Task Forces (Intel), Elite Counter-Insurgency Forces (Kopassus), Military police, riot control Mobile Brigade (Brimob) as well as provincial, district, and sub-district police units (CAVR 2005: Ch. 4.39).

Violent interrogation was institutional practice to obtain confessions or information about *Fretilin* members, the location of weapons, or political strategies (CAVR 2005: Ch. 7.4.807). Torture was also used to coerce compliance and deference to the Indonesian regime – individuals were tortured for being unwilling to take part in military operations such as the 'Fence of Legs' Operation; because they refused to join militia groups; for falling asleep during night patrols; or for failing to attend welcome demonstrations when international delegations or dignitaries visited. Alternatively, torture was used as a preventive means to 'silence' perceived dissenters when such internationals visited (Amnesty International 1985: 74–75, 1991). Contacting international organizations or journalists to provide human rights information was viewed as a suspect activity, as was listening to foreign shortwave radio (Nairn 1997: xv; HRW 1994). As a result, both East Timorese (particularly students) and foreigners were carefully monitored, investigated, and hindered in their movements during visits (Amnesty International 1989, 1991).

On many occasions, deference to the Indonesian regime was enforced through torture in which victims had to perform symbolic or cultural actions to demonstrate their loyalty – often this included swearing allegiance to the Indonesian flag or publicly rejecting Portugal or *Fretilin* and their related insignia and songs (CAVR 2005: Ch. 7.4.339). In addition, torture was applied to stop perceived associations with *Fretilin*. Long-term prisoners would be tortured every six months and classified according to their supposed attachment to the party (CAVR 2005: Ch. 7.4). Similarly, detentions and torture were used to undermine political opposition and communication between *Fretilin* members. As Lino detailed:

> In 1994, the freedom fighters came and organized us to take letters and food to and from the jungle. When the military found this out, we were arrested and detained for a month. They tortured us with electricity, hit us and put chairs on our toes. They used a razor to cut my forehead and I collapsed. They cut me with a knife, across my face, ears and arms, and cut my hair off. They also threatened to kill my family. After that, I escaped to the bush and hid for six months.

Families deemed to be 'political' were also subject to regular intimidation techniques and family members could face 'proxy punishments' in which they were violated on account of their association with another individual (CAVR 2005: Ch. 7.4.803–4). Family members, particularly women who took a central cultural and community role in the independence movement, were often the initial targets of such punishments (Franks 1996). They 'became a substitute for punishment' when male relatives 'could not be captured' (CAVR 2005: Ch. 7.4.377). For example, Ana, who was detained during 1980–81 after being suspected of taking guns and food to *Falintil* relatives, commented:

> I was held without clothes for three weeks. For two weeks, my hands were tied up and my hand has been broken as a result. They asked questions about my husband and about *Fretilin*. I was raped again and again over 10 days, and I was threatened with snakes. There were about 20 men – both Indonesian military and Timorese army. I was lucky not to get pregnant.

While Isabel stated:

> They arrested me because they discovered that my husband was in the forest. They tried to get me to tell them where he was hiding. At the time, I didn't even know.

Such punishments had a number of different objectives – to intimidate specific families, to stop any assistance (such as food, medical help, or information) going from families to *Fretilin*, to weaken the resolve of *Fretilin* fighters, and to warn others of the consequences of resistance (Pinto 1997; Stanley 2004). For many resistance fighters, this treatment of family members was one of the worst aspects of the struggle – to know that loved ones would be arrested, raped, tortured, or killed on the basis of their relationship was a deep burden to bear.

This wider application of violence was also apparent in the collective tortures undertaken by Indonesian officials. These techniques sought to spread terror and thereby compliance. As Jacinto Alves, CAVR Commissioner, detailed:

> I know of cases in which individuals had their throats cut and then were made to walk through the village where their family and friends lived. The wives of the victim would not be able to contain [cope with] the scene, they couldn't watch and would collapse. But then the military would force her, the wife of the victim, to stand.

Such events constituted torture of the forced observers – a technique that (as shown below) was widely applied by militias during 1998–99.

At an individual level, torture sought to undermine a victim's psychological and political integrity. From the outset, captors often regarded torture victims as 'less than human'. Alberto stated:

> They thought that we were less than pigs. They treated us worse than animals. They didn't see us as human at all.

This misrecognition was combined with popular techniques (such as stripping, sexually abusing, and photographing detainees) that were employed to shame and humiliate victims. Thus, Maria, who had engaged in clandestine activity, was detained on several occasions. She suffered a variety of tortures including being beaten and burnt and she experienced the miscarriage of her child. Over the course of three months she was placed (along with two other women) in a toilet-less 'iron cell', which was a small, completely dark space surrounded with iron. The three women were stripped naked and continually photographed. These photographs were to be passed and swopped around the Indonesian military; and much like 'cigarette cards', they became tokens of service within perpetrating units.

Other activities to disempower victims included using fellow detainees to 'confess' and testify against each other or making detainees torture each other. Thus, Mariano described his own experience as follows:

> I was surrounded by lots of people, other detainees. I was passed from one person to another, and they were made to beat me. Some people as they hit me were crying, others couldn't look at me.

This strategy, to implicate victims in the torture of others, worked to disturb collective cohesion within resistance groups, which was an issue that was also related to the creation of informers or the attempts to 'turn' individuals into regime 'supporters' in order to get 'clandestine members and former Falintil guerrillas to work for the Intelligence Task Force' (CAVR 2005: Ch. 4.110).

Finally, alongside these strategic reasons, torture was also undertaken for the personal gains or wants of individual torturers. Torture was sometimes applied to extort money from the prisoner or their family or because the torturer had particular sadistic motives (Amnesty International 1985). In Ana's telling of her detention and torture, she remarked:

> There was one man who attacked me often. I think that he enjoyed being able to dishonour women whenever he pleased. I know that he always raped the women that were held.

Such testimony illustrates that some perpetrators used, and were allowed to use, their bureaucratic position for personal ends and sadistic pleasure.

Torture formed a central plank of Indonesian control (Amnesty International 1985). While the victims tended to be male, of between 20–40 years of age, with a real or suspected association with *Fretilin* or *Falintil*, they came from a wide range of backgrounds. Victims also included women, children, elderly people, students, teachers, local government officials, educated Timorese, whole families, those suspected of witchcraft, or anyone deemed to be 'political' (Amnesty International 1991). The reported victims – picked out for what they politically represented – 'have come from virtually the whole spectrum of East Timorese society' (Amnesty International 1985: 11).

Of course, the Indonesian authorities attempted to minimize and distort their involvement in such torture. In an attempt to deflect criticisms, those detained were often depicted as ordinary criminals, rather than political actors (Amnesty International 1991). Minimization of criticism can also be identified by the training manuals, constructed 'in-house' for serving military officers, that instructed soldiers how to avoid public antipathy by not photographing prisoners stripped naked or being tortured by electroshock,[5] not circulating photographs, and by ensuring that witnesses from the local population were not present during interrogations (Amnesty International 1983).[6] Further, in response to allegations of brutality from international organizations, Indonesian representatives would argue that torture was contrary to the state philosophy;[7] that torture undermined the basic values of the Indonesian people; that any alleged torture had now stopped; that it was always subject to disciplinary action; that preventative action was being taken; or that human rights organizations had collated unreliable evidence (Amnesty International 1985; Laywers Committee for Human Rights 1993). Torture was vigorously denied and neutralized by Indonesian authorities (S. Cohen 2001).

The militias

Contrary to much of the international human rights literature during the occupation, it is clear that Indonesian officials were assisted by Timorese auxiliaries. Locals would be involved in the arrest, interrogation, and torture of suspects and they took an active part in intelligence-gathering and searching for independence supporters. Over a third (37.1 per cent) of torture and ill-treatment cases recorded by the CAVR detail the participation of East Timorese auxiliaries (CAVR 2005: Ch. 7.4.33). Aside from the fact that East Timorese worked within the Indonesian Army itself,[8] they also partici-pated in 'ninja' gangs, militias, intelligence units, and civil defence forces. In these roles they provided a means by which Indonesian officials could dis-tance themselves from violence and avoid international scrutiny while pre-senting the idea that they were a neutral force in a volatile, conflictual country (Human Rights Watch 1995; Robinson 2001).

Paramilitary groups have a long history in Timor-Leste and their use can be tracked back to Portuguese administrators, the Australian forces during World War II, as well as the Indonesian occupation (Robinson 2001). In the early 1990s, for instance, the Indonesian military established local ninja gangs that engaged in 'death squad operations'. Dressed in black, and working at night, hooded ninjas would undertake raids on suspected inde-pendence supporters – their victims would be 'disappeared' or their executed bodies would be left in public view as a means to terrify the local population (ibid.). Given this history, the rise of militias in 1998–99 did not emerge out of the blue, but their role became increasingly significant as groups devel-oped throughout Timor-Leste.

The Indonesian military was central to the formation, training, and instruction of militia groups (CAVR 2005: Ch. 4.126). Militia commanders, who were given recruitment targets for each village, were paid a salary for the mobilization, coordination and retention of local members (Dunn 2003). The CAVR (2005: Ch. 4.134) estimates that 'US$5.2m was channeled to the militias through the Indonesian civilian administration' to implement the military plan. Robinson (2001: 277) notes that a considerable number of individuals joined militias 'under duress'. Those that refused to join would often have their homes or their families attacked. Some 'refusers' were detained for up to four months, tortured, and threatened with being burnt or raped (CAVR 2005: Ch. 7.4.563; Cribb 2001). However, a fair number of East Timorese chose to join the militias – to enact revenge for *Fretilin*-led violence in the 1970s, to gain power through the carrying of arms, or to show support to the regime in which their family had done well. Some mili-tia members had been previously part of criminal gangs, or were also enlis-ted as Army soldiers, and were just continuing their work under different auspices (ibid.; CAVR 2005: Ch. 4.129).

During 1998 and 1999, militia members asserted their power through random, often opportunistic, acts of violence. Torture was used to intimidate the population, to assert the authority of pro-autonomy forces over com-munities, and to punish those who supported the move to independence (CAVR 2005: Ch. 7.4.664–75). Yet, during this period, militias were see-mingly less likely to wish to keep people alive. As Emilia details, during

1998–99, the intention of militias was to kill rather than torture victims. Furthermore, torture was more likely to be used as a public spectacle – to humiliate the victims and terrorize others – than to be hidden away (CAVR 2005: Ch. 7.4.808). This strategy was highlighted in the killing and public display of bodies in villages.

The intelligence networks underpinning torture

While militia members engaged in widespread violent acts, like torture, the Indonesian military was also assisted by a developed network of intelligence gatherers and informers. For instance, many East Timorese joined civil defence forces[9] that aided the police and armed forces. Civil Defence members, engaging in combat, surveillance, and intelligence roles, could be found in every area of Timor-Leste. The CAVR (2005: Ch. 4.95) estimates that 'by 1982 nearly 12,500 East Timorese were involved in the various civil defence organizations ... this figure is roughly 2.25% of the population'. Alongside this contribution, East Timorese were employed as 'village guidance officers' (*Babinsas*), providing vital information to the local military, and some worked as spies or informants (known as Intel), monitoring and informing on fellow villagers. Of course, some informants were settling grudges, as well as undertaking political action, when reporting 'enemies' to the local military. Once named, individuals were far more likely to be detained and tortured (CAVR 2005: Ch. 7.4.400). Many interviewed victims remarked that their initial arrest was a result of being reported by another Timorese.

Despite the significant contribution such intelligence gatherers made to Indonesian military strategies – for example, this web of local workers meant that by the early 1980s arrests appeared to be targeted against perceived opponents to the Indonesian regime – they were not wholly supportive. Village guidance officers were not completely loyal and the Indonesian Armed Forces had trouble controlling civil defence groups. Individuals would defect to *Falintil* or *Fretilin* (CAVR 2005: Ch. 4.94) and, consequently, members of these groups were also targeted, arrested, tortured and killed by Indonesian forces (Amnesty International 1985).

East Timorese communities were therefore militarized and tightly controlled through expansive intelligence networks (CAVR 2005: Ch. 4.95). This situation destroyed trust within communities and underpinned an atmosphere of suspicion and fear as villagers would not always know who could or could not be trusted (Sherlock 1996) – 'Timorese were turned against Timorese' (CAVR 2005: Ch. 4.1–2), creating a legacy of mistrust in the region.

Experiencing torture

The specific forms of violence inflicted during torture were wide-ranging. During interviews, victims described numerous humiliating and painful experiences, including: beatings (with fists, wood, iron bars, lengths of cable, and bamboo); burnings with lit cigarettes (all over the body and on sensitive areas such as genitalia, eyelids, and mouth); cuttings (with knives and razor blades); being hit on the head (particularly when victims wore a steel helmet); kickings; whippings; electroshock (again, all over the body, but used particularly on the head, thumbs, genitalia, and breasts); submersion in fetid water and urine; being placed in small spaces and having animals (such as lizards or snakes) attack; sexual abuse (including being stripped naked and paraded); rape; having teeth or nails forcibly extracted; having feet crushed under table legs (the table being sat on by interrogators); having salt or lemon juice rubbed into open wounds; standing for long periods in the sun; being made to drink urine or blood, or made to eat their own or another victim's body parts; food deprivation; and, death threats to the victim and their family members. Thus, the following comments were not unusual:

> I was arrested in 1998 and detained for a few weeks ... I was held in a room with lots of other people. During the night, they would take us out, one at a time, to question us and hurt us. They did different things to me. I didn't know them, they were Indonesian Commanders. They put me in a barrel with water and added little lizards. The lizards bite. They are small but it hurts, especially when they bite down there [genitalia]. Then they beat me.
>
> Martinho

> They stripped me of my clothes and when I was naked they started to beat my body. The beating lasted a number of hours and, by the end, I had lost teeth and was bleeding heavily from my mouth and different parts of my body. I was then held for a few weeks. I couldn't eat much, my face was very swollen, and I got very skinny. They cut my hair.
>
> Fransisco

> They would put a metal military helmet on my head and beat the top of the head. On the helmet, they would write harsh things ... so they would insult you, or your family. They started beating on the top of my head with the stick.
>
> Adelino

> I was beaten until I fainted. When I woke up, my face was covered in blood. I had four teeth smashed out ... I was held in a cramped, dark cell in the prison. You couldn't tell whether it was night or day. Sometimes, we heard a cock crow but that was all that might tell us the time. I was held there for a few weeks. We were placed in just our underwear. It was so hot. There was no toilet, so we had to go on the floor.
>
> Mateus

The plain, unadorned description of torture belies the reality of the pain, suffering, and fear experienced in those particular moments and in the aftermath of attacks.

The majority of torture victims recorded by the CAVR were male – a point that fits with the fact that men were at the forefront of fighting and resistance networks. Of the cases of ill-treatment against female victims recorded by the CAVR, 12.3 per cent were cases of torture, 13.9 per cent detention, and 7.7 per cent ill-treatment. Given the problems in collating this gendered data (see Chapter 7), these percentages will not illustrate the true extent of torture against women.[10] Regardless of the recorded statistics, the CAVR details that while some men were sexually assaulted and raped during torture, the sexual violation of women was a 'widely accepted practice' that was 'covered by almost total impunity' (CAVR 2005: Ch. 7.7.11).[11] This issue was reflected in each of the interviews with female victims. While women suffered similar physical violence as men, they would also experience specific sexual tortures.

During sexual torture, women would face rape, genital mutilation, the insertion of objects (bottles, wood, or snakes) into vaginas, burning with cigarettes or electroshock on genitalia, and they would be forced to conduct sexual acts. Pregnant women were often beaten until they miscarried. In many instances women also suffered gang rape and prolonged periods of individual rapes. Emilia stated:

> I was arrested with my friend. We were investigated. During this, they stood on my feet. There were about 60 military members. There was no electricity. They took off my clothes so that I was naked. The Indonesian military raped us during the night. There were about five people who raped us. As women, we could not fight back. They had weapons. We did not get pregnant. We were made to stand during the rape because the floor was wet. … When their boss was there, they didn't do anything to me, they only insulted me … they destroyed us like animals.

Such violations were also directed towards children and young girls were also victims of rape. Generally, children (those 17 and under) account for 5.2 per cent of torture cases (CAVR 2005: Ch. 7.8.198). While civilian children were often targeted as a means to punish or inflict harm on their older family members, children were also attacked in their own right. Children aged 14 or 15 years were regular contributors to the clandestine networks and, as a result, they were 'sometimes tortured as a consequence of their own activities, rather than their family ties' (CAVR 2005: Ch. 7.8.220). During the 1990s, students were also fiercely targeted – some young people were repeatedly detained, particularly during the visits of foreigners, and torture was used as a regular form of recruitment, to 'encourage' them to become informants or militia members (CAVR 2005: Ch. 7.8.224).

Torture as one violation among many

Notwithstanding these brutalities, victims were also keen to identify that torture was just one violation among many. The very nature of detention itself was particularly horrifying for many interviewees. For example, prisoners were regularly passed from one site to another. This technique disoriented victims, isolated them, and placed them far from their family, friends, and support networks, while allowing different units to continue the torture (CAVR 2005: Ch. 7.4.569–70). The torture of individuals took place at multiple locations including: military sites;[12] large civilian buildings, such as warehouses, shops, and hotels; requisitioned private homes; police buildings; local government buildings, such as village offices and meeting halls; local prisons, particularly Comarca and Becora prisons in Dili, and Buruma prison in Baucau; prisons in Indonesia; victim's homes; transit camps that were used for mass surrenders and arrests; improvised structures, such as holes in ground; as well as public spaces (Amnesty International 1985; CAVR 2005: Ch. 7.4). Prisoners would also suffer various degradations during detention. They were given inedible food (that was mixed with glass or faeces), they were made to strip, placed in solitary confinement for extensive periods, put in dark cells (small cells with no light and limited ventilation), held in poor sanitary conditions (with prisoners toileting on the floor), or were subject to severe overcrowding (CAVR 2005: Ch. 7.4.806). These conditions made detention particularly traumatic regardless of whether or not prisoners were also tortured.

Alongside this, it is also clear that victims could also be subject to multiple violations, by different perpetrators, over different time periods. For example, two victims in this study highlighted that they had been detained on two occasions – the first time by *Fretilin* and the second by the Indonesian military. Alberto, for instance, was held in a *Fretilin* camp during 1976–77 (in which he was not directly harmed, but suffered food shortages and general poor conditions) and imprisoned by the Indonesian military in the mid-1980s. During this time, he was tortured badly, his toenails were pulled out, his feet were crushed by a chair, and he was electrocuted. Similarly, Maria Fatima was held in a *Fretilin* 'rehabilitation' centre for three months in 1976, a period during which she was placed in a pit and suffered severe food shortages, and from 1978 she was detained for eight years by the Indonesian government, during which time she suffered multiple tortures.

However, beyond these specific detentions, victims faced many other victimizations. For example, victims witnessed or suffered the killing of their family members and friends,[13] they had their houses destroyed, they had all their possessions and money stolen, they were displaced, they experienced malnutrition and starvation, they lost all communication with their families, and, for numerous women, they were forced into sexual slavery at military installations. In addition, victims often experienced a 'spiral of victimization' – one violation would invariably lead to another and certain individuals became particularly vulnerable to further attack. For instance, women who had been released from sexual torture and slavery often had nowhere to access medical care; they faced continued victimization by the local community and the church (which would often blame the women for their fate or consider them to be sexually loose); they had problems getting married and their husbands, if married, would often leave; and their children would also face victimization (CAVR 2005: Ch. 7.7.337). The initial basis of a specific violation could, then, provoke a range of harms that extended across a number of years.

Dealing with torture

So far, this chapter has shown how individuals either perpetrated or were victimized by torture. Yet it is also apparent that many people engaged in strategies to cope with and resist torture. This section illustrates that East Timorese took a variety of approaches to avoid torture in the first instance and to cope with their treatment during and after the violence.

Perhaps one of the clearest points to emerge out of this research is that torture did not stop political activity. Indeed, for those who were the principal targets of torture (the individuals who supported independence), the use of torture by Indonesian officials intensified their commitment to continue resistance. As Maria Fatima makes clear:

> I was dealt with in the same way as everyone else. I was given electric shocks, was burnt with cigarettes and stripped naked during interrogations. I accepted this treatment, I had to focus on the political fight for Timor-Leste. I understood the consequences of being active ... Torture did not stop political activity. People were fighting for independence and freedom. They had a focus, and torture did not stop them.

Similarly, Flisberto[14] details that, without such violations, the resistance movement would not have gained the momentum it needed to attain independence.

> They continued killing and hurting us but we continued fighting for our independence. The most important thing is, and I don't deny it, what else could we do? I can enjoy the independence of Timor-Leste and give thanks to those who did bad things to us, because if they hadn't created turmoil, we wouldn't have gained our independence.

From the late 1980s, political activism against occupation grew in the towns and cities. This activism focused on Indonesian-led violence and was directed to the human rights cause – the violence committed by Indonesian officials gave a focus to the resistance movement.

This fight was not, however, foolhardy and East Timorese would engage in different strategies to avoid being suspected or arrested. They would be careful in their movements, to ensure that they did not raise suspicions that they were connected to clandestine networks; they took on the insignia of the Indonesian officials; they would wave Indonesian flags at demonstrations and give the impression that they supported the occupation; they would pledge allegiance to UDT or *Apodeti* on identity registration cards; women would look unkempt or dirty so that Indonesian officers would not approach them and sexually violate them; and, as shown below, the East Timorese would work directly for Indonesian officials, as interpreters or informants, despite their commitment to work against their employers.

Notwithstanding these attempts, many people were imprisoned. East Timorese people experienced little redress, and they had limited ability to resist their detention through the criminal justice system. Trials, that convicted East Timorese who were suspected of supporting *Fretilin*, were often closed and relied on 'evidence' from suspect sources (Lawyers Committee for Human Rights 1993). Presiding judges would commence trials by speaking – at length – about their support for Indonesian progress in the region (ibid.). Timorese defendants would not have adequate access to defence counsel and they rarely understood the legal procedures (Amnesty International 1987: 1). Those who came before the courts were, then, highly likely to be convicted and imprisoned. While victims were detained, any complaints against torture were met with similar processes – there was no clear complaints procedure, no judicial independence, and any investigations were undertaken by the Indonesian police (Lawyers Committee for Human Rights 1993).

During the subsequent periods of imprisonment, which could last days or years, East Timorese took action to secure their release or to assist themselves and others. For example, clandestine members used tactics to control what was said or not said during torture. Mateus emphasized that:

> I only told them what they already knew. I tried to be very careful with what was said and not said.

Similarly, those who were detained together tried to build a group effort to control information. Flisberto[15] described his own torture as follows:

> The room was as big as a coffee table. We were all just standing, there was no room to sit. One man took his pants off because it was so hot inside. I took off my shirt. We just stood there for the night. In the morning I thought we had better die than live in this condition. At least we would have done something. One man was crying and I told him not to mention the names of anyone. I knew that we could not reveal anything to them.

Certain victims had also, following torture, been transformed into interpreters and played a part in the interrogation sessions of others. In this role, some individuals would attempt to subvert the process – if the torture victim gave away too much by stating who had killed soldiers or where weapons were held, they would attempt to change the words and to cover up the information. This position could be tenuous and the CAVR (2005: Ch. 7.4.389) notes the case of the interpreter Antonio Peloy who would present an alternative story to the interrogators while simultaneously hitting the victim to ensure that his allegiance went unquestioned.

During detentions, victims would also take solace from the news and support that they obtained from outside. It is evident, through a number of testimonies, that bishops and priests played a vital role in supporting and encouraging prisoners to resist and be courageous in their situation.[16] Manuel[17] detailed one such visit:

> I wasn't frightened. Although, we were visited by Bishop Martinho from Dili and, when he arrived, we all cried. He asked if we had eaten, and we all said 'yes'. If we had said 'no', we would have been beaten when he left. He said, 'Endure with pride, Timor is yours'. He encouraged us. So, from then on, we were not afraid to die even though they beat us.

Similarly, the news that the Timorese cause had gained international recognition was also of significant help to people's ability to deal with their situation. As Alberto explains:

> I had heard that Bishop Belo and Ramos Horta had been given the Nobel Prize. After that, I knew we would win. It didn't matter if they tortured me, I was open to the possibility that I would die.

The possibility of dying was not, however, a preferred option and prisoners would try to secure their early release from imprisonment by different means. Prisoners could sometimes buy their way out of imprisonment, and related torture, with money, antique coins, or other valuable items. Alternatively, if a trusted individual would vouch responsibility for the prisoner, then a release might also occur. Release could therefore be contingent on a person's ability to pay or their social standing.

Prisoners would also 'give themselves over' to become workers for Indonesian authorities. If victims agreed to this, they would be placed on report (during which they would have to report to local military installations a number of times a week) and would undertake maintenance work, cleaning, or cooking for Indonesian staff. Failing that, prisoners could also agree to become intelligence workers or informants, a point explained by Antonio:

> The technique to survive depended on the individual. For example, the military would arrest people for visiting Xanana [Gusmão] in the bush. If they wanted to survive, they had to become a member of the intelligence. If you refused, you would be killed as the Indonesian military just

relied on intelligence workers. And, on release, you would have to report every day. I was reporting until independence.

Of course, as Antonio also noted, as an intelligence worker you could give Indonesian officials the wrong information and simultaneously pass on relevant details to *Fretilin*. As far as he was concerned, 'they never questioned whether the person was right or not'.

In summary, East Timorese victims engaged in various strategies to deal with or resist their detention, torture, and ill-treatment. In this sense, victims were never 'complete victims'. While free, many of these individuals engaged in subversive actions or supported the independence movement. During detention, these active struggles continued, often in the most dire of circumstances. The smallest of actions, even those that bore a 'hidden transcript' in which the perpetrators did not recognize the resistance for what it was (Scott, 1990), are illustrative of an ongoing vigorous dissent.

Conclusion

Torture in Timor-Leste was developed and used by a complex network of actors. Violations were most likely to be led by Indonesian officials, yet they also included local perpetrators. Of course, local populations suffered terribly. In detailing the horror of experiencing torture, this chapter has shown how certain groups experienced differential treatment on account of their status within society. Moreover, it makes clear that torture had been just one aspect of victimization for Timorese people – that is, some people had been subject to multiple victimizations (sometimes by different and opposing groups) and others faced a wide range of victimizations both during their detention and on release.

While victims have sought to cope with and resist these realities, it is fair to assume that these experiences will bring long-term repercussions for victims. For example, as highlighted above, torture victims face diverse psychological and physical difficulties; they may find themselves unable to work, or less able to cope with family life; they may also find it difficult to publicly acknowledge what has happened to them, especially when the violence inflicted is regarded as particularly shameful. Such repercussions are faced on a daily basis by many surviving torture victims in Timor-Leste. Alongside these issues, however, one aspect that victims have continued to stress is the need for truth and justice responses to their specific violations and to the wider repression in Timor-Leste. It is to these issues of transitional justice for Timor-Leste to which this work now turns.

6   Entrenching Criminal Injustice

In September 1999 the UN convened a special session to monitor the situation in Timor-Leste. Condemning the violence, the UN stated that all those responsible for human rights violations would be brought to account (UN 1999a). Three special rapporteurs subsequently sent to the region argued that there was 'little doubt as to the direct and indirect involvement' of the Indonesian army and police in violence and that, unless the Indonesian government made firm, quick arrangements to prosecute state officials, the UN should 'consider the establishment of an international criminal tribunal' (UN 1999b: para 59–74.6). As far as they were concerned, 'The East Timorese judicial system, which still needs to be created and tested, could not hope to cope with a project of this scale' (ibid.: para 73). A month later, in January 2000, a UN report from the International Commission of Inquiry argued that Timorese victims 'must not be forgotten in the rush of events to redefine relations in the region, and [that] their basic human rights to justice, compensation and the truth must be fully respected' (UN 2000a: para 146). Given the seriousness of the crimes, as well as the 'trusteeship' relationship the UN had developed with Timor, the Commission reasoned that the responsibility for addressing international justice fell on the UN (ibid.).

These early calls for criminal justice have been reflected, time and again, by torture victims in Timor-Leste. Victims argued that international prosecutions, particularly of senior Indonesian officials (the so-called 'big fish'), were vital to the emergence of the rule of law, a culture of human rights, and positive social development. For many, trials represented an opportunity to challenge the 'arrogant strut' of high status officials. However, the trials also connected to the idea that Timorese should have status parity with others in their access to international human rights law.

> Those who were involved should be brought to justice because only justice can ensure that this country will be well. In a country which has law and order, there must be justice
>
> Maria

Justice has to happen. Otherwise, what will this mean? Why should people follow the law if does not work for them? If we don't have justice, why should people follow international human rights?

Martinho

Independence was costly, it wasn't a gift. We can't just leave things behind because many Timorese people died. We need to have justice if we are going to work together to develop this country

José[1]

Kofi Annan, the then UN Secretary-General, downplayed the idea of an international tribunal. Arguing that he was 'encouraged by the commitment shown by President Abdurrahman Wahid to uphold the law' (UN 2000b), he recommended that the Indonesian government should pursue their own prosecutions. These efforts would be 'closely monitor[ed]' to ensure that they were credible and reflected human rights standards (ibid.; Burgess 2004: 135; Hirst and Varney 2005). Thus, instead of an international tribunal, two criminal justice institutions have been established to deal with gross human rights violations in Timor-Leste. These are the Jakarta-based Ad Hoc Human Rights Courts established by the Indonesian government in 2000, and the Dili-based 'hybrid' serious crimes process created in 2000 by the UN.

This chapter evaluates these institutions in relation to the tenets of justice that have permeated this book thus far. While detailing the approach of these institutions to the violation of torture, the chapter provides an indication of the generic problems that have affected all victims. It shows that these court mechanisms have provided 'political cover', and they have given the illusion that justice has been done while entrenching impunity for Indonesian officials. This situation – in which serious perpetrators have escaped recognition – has emerged through: a complete lack of Indonesian political or judicial will to bring perpetrators to account; the inadequate resources, poor planning and management afforded to trials by the UN; and, the Timorese government's decision to close down prosecutions in favour of friendly bilateral relations with its economically powerful neighbour (Stanley 2008a). Criminal justice practices have not, then, undone power.

Beyond these failings, these mechanisms have also led to the exclusion and 'othering' of Timorese people. Timorese individuals have been misrecognized or not regarded as victims, and some have been viewed as implicitly guilty for violations and subsequently ousted from legal protection. Further, few Timorese have known about and been able to directly participate in these bodies – for example, hardly any of the victims interviewed for this research knew about these processes and, consequently, had very little to say about the nature of criminal justice – a point demonstrated by the lack of their voices in this chapter.

In concluding, the chapter shows that these criminal justice institutions failed to make any challenge to status injustices at personal, regional, or international levels. The processes have embedded the power relations that underpinned violations in the first instance. In reproducing non-recognition, misrecognition, as well as participatory and redistributive injustices, these mechanisms have reflected a continuum of injustice that has placed state power ahead of those who are politically devalued. While sometimes well intentioned, human rights bodies have perpetuated and deepened the injustices experienced by torture victims.

Securing recognition for torture victims

Has recognition been secured for torture victims through legal processes? With regard to the Ad Hoc Courts in Jakarta, the short answer is 'no'. As shown in the next section, these courts did not deal with the issue of torture. However, the serious crimes process in Dili did provide some level of recognition for this violation.

The Special Panels for Serious Crimes (SPSC), a judicial tribunal that brought together international and national judges, was formed to try serious criminal offences. It took universal jurisdiction over charges of genocide, war crimes, and crimes against humanity, and could adjudicate over murder and sexual offence cases if they occurred between 1 January 1999 and 25 October 1999. Although the Panels, together with the Serious Crimes Unit (SCU, the prosecution unit) and the Defence Lawyers Unit (DLU), operated directly under the authority of the Prosecutor General, they were established and primarily resourced through the UN.

From first impressions, the serious crimes process appears to be quite successful. In May 2005, when proceedings closed, the SCU had brought 95 indictments against 391 individuals (and in 26 of those indictments, 121 individuals were connected with acts of torture). The Panels tried 87 defendants in 55 trials, and eventually convicted 84 people, 16 of whom were convicted on torture charges and one convicted on a charge of persecution that incorporated torture. This large number of convictions surpasses that reached by any other international or hybrid tribunal (D. Cohen 2006a; JSMP 2005a).

Key workers have credited the process with a number of accomplishments, including: establishing a historical record; bringing closure to cases; confirming respect for the rule of law; ensuring due process; deterring future offenders and building local capacity (DeFaria 2005; Koumjian 2004; Rapoza 2005). For reasons apparent below, these assertions are not entirely acceptable. However, it is evident that the process has facilitated the first two claims and, in doing so, has assisted in establishing a recognition-based justice.

For instance, prosecutors demonstrated the severity and the blatant openness of physical violence in 1999. As highlighted in the Appendix, indictments linked torture to events where victims were burnt with cigarettes or heated metal, cut with knifes, severely beaten, subject to multiple rapes,[2] suffocated, tied up and placed in unbearable positions, electrocuted, blinded with chemicals, stabbed, slashed with razor blades, attacked by dogs, starved, and forced to abuse other victims. In many instances, these tortures involved multiple assailants (both militia members and Indonesian officials) and they were often undertaken while the victim was detained in a militia house or restrained in a public space.

In addition, prosecutors were sometimes able to expose the depravity of the violence during this period. For example, in the *Lolotoe* (4c/2001) case, prosecutors laid two charges for the same event in an effort to make a particular point about severity. In this case, perpetrators had cut an ear off their victim, Mario Goncalves, and had then made him eat it. The prosecutors commented that they pursued two counts, of torture and inhumane acts, for this event as they wanted to draw public attention to its brutality. At trial, the judges agreed and it was held that the act of cutting off an ear was torture, while forcing a man to eat his own flesh was an inhumane act.

The psychological suffering that is endured through torture has also been highlighted. Indictments allege that victims and their families were threatened with death during torture and that some victims were placed in isolation, while others suffered humiliation techniques. The Special Panels also made a clear judgement on the psychological basis of torture. In the *Los Palos* (9/2000) trial, judges recognized that a non-physically violent act (in this case, the cutting of a detainee's hair) was a form of psychological torture. This act was viewed as a means to humiliate and threaten the victim and could, in such circumstances, be viewed as severe mental suffering.

These legal descriptions and decisions expose the historical truth of the torture that was inflicted during the chaotic period of 1999. They illustrate the personal realities of Timorese victimization and, in doing so, they may bring acknowledgement for select individuals. They also name alleged perpetrators who, as a continuation of the truth-telling process, are each listed in the appendix of this book. In this way, the serious crimes process did provide an element of recognition-based justice for some torture victims. However, less positive aspects of criminal justice processes have overshadowed this success.

Limiting recognition: The serious crimes process

The serious crimes process in Dili also undermined practices of recognition. This section shows that this occurred as a result of narrow institutional rules and decision-making, as well as institutional incapacity. These factors have impinged on the ability of victims to be legally recognized within legal processes; they have placed victims outside of legal protection. They have also ensured that powerful Indonesian perpetrators have been shielded from legal recognition and status devaluation.

Restrictive rules and decisions

Despite an initial remit to consider serious crimes from 1975 to 1999, the SCU narrowed its prosecutorial attention to those cases that occurred from January – October 1999. A former Deputy General Prosecutor, Nicholas Koumjian, argued vehemently that this 1999 focus was based on the lack of instruction to do otherwise from the UN Security Council, the General Prosecutor, or the Timorese government. Thus, while the UN established the process to deal with crimes from 1975–99, they subsequently retracted attention to less than a year (JSMP 2004a). In doing so, it placed most victims outside the legal frame.

This constricted time mandate may be explained by the issue of limited resources, the difficulties in collating evidence of historical crimes, as well as the desire of the UN to defend its own institutional status (by punishing those who had disrespectfully attacked the authority of the UN (UN 2000a). However, it invariably 'suppressed or ignored a broader truth' and wrote the context out of this legal history (Rae 2003: 173–75). For instance, it ensured that the vital international support and encouragement given to the Indonesian regime (detailed above) was omitted from any investigation or discussion. Moreover, it was also particularly confusing for victims. One SCU prosecutor pointed out that:

> In some areas, there may only have been a few murders in 1999 but many hundreds in 1998, just a couple of months before. And, in those situations, the families just do not understand why one case is taken forward, when the rest are left. It doesn't make sense!

Given this 1999 focus, the majority of torture victims were unlikely to experience the justice they demanded; institutional rules operated to exclude most victims (Stanley 2007a). This situation was made worse by a further streamlining of the SCU mandate in October 2003. Under new policies, as Nicholas Koumjian explained in an interview, indictments were restricted 'to those who organized violence and direct perpetrators of murder and sexual assaults' such as rape. This did not mean that torture was ignored completely but, from this time onwards, it took lesser prominence. Indeed, some SCU staff suggested that counts of torture were taken out of later indictments despite the existence of clear evidence and reliable witnesses.

Given the comparative severity of both torture and rape, it seems incongruous that torture was disqualified from investigations and indictments. SCU prosecutors proposed that rape was retained as a focus due to the vigorous campaigning of feminist groups on the issue, as well as a political commitment to prosecuting this violation by some SCU staff. Invariably, the omission of torture meant that its severity and extent was missed from official judicial recognition. These decisions have meant that none of the victims interviewed for this study, like thousands of others, have been able to make claims for justice. These individuals stand outside any legal protection. As Ana described, 'these courts have had no impact on my situation ... at all'.

Institutional incapacity

Recognition has also been undermined through institutional incapacities. As a consequence of limited funds,[3] staff, and resources, the serious crimes process failed to undertake investigative and judicial proceedings in a manner consistent with standards of due process (see also Stanley 2007a, 2008a).

For instance, in the SCU there was initially no prosecution strategy to investigate high-ranking Indonesian officials (UN 2005a) and investigators focused their attentions on those accused of 'domestic' crimes such as non-political or 'everyday' assault (D. Cohen 2002). Furthermore, in 2003, the SCU operated with between six to eight investigators who worked across 13 districts, sometimes without vehicles (D. Cohen 2006a). With each investigator having a responsibility for more than 300 murders, as well as other extensive violations (Stanley 2008a), one investigator noted:

> So, you'd be going and doing an investigation that might involve 20 or 30 murders and there might be between 50 and 100 witnesses ... and there's just you doing it. It was impossible. In other tribunals, there might be 50 investigating each crime.

Nor did the SCU have any criminal analysts, information sharing was poor, there was never any clear collation of information, and investigators were hampered by a database that was not responsive to multiple spellings of names (a significant problem in a region where individuals regularly have pseudonyms and multiple name spellings). None of this was helped by the high staff turnover that underpinned a lack of continuity and institutional memory in the Unit (D. Cohen 2006a; Reiger and Wierda 2006).

While the SCU struggled to operate, the DLU was even more poorly resourced. At the start, the DLU was staffed entirely by local defence lawyers who, given previous lack of experience, were 'trying *their first case ever* in Special panels' (D. Cohen 2006a: 17). Consequently, in the first 14 trials, no defence witnesses were called (D. Cohen 2002). Local staff were subsequently replaced by a very small international team, many of whom had no previous experience in human rights or international law, and who struggled without resources. A defence lawyer remarked:

> Look at this office. There's nothing in it! We have nothing to work with. This [here, he pointed to his body] is it! We don't have investigators, or law books, or internet access ... this is international justice in operation!

Generally, the Unit struggled to provide 'equality of arms' against the better resourced SCU.

Similar problems existed in the Special Panels. While a few international judges have garnered praise, others have not always acted in a professional manner – 'screaming matches' between international judges, judges laughing during testimony of sexual assault, judges arriving dramatically late, and judges sleeping through testimony have been observed during this research. In addition, international judges have not always had a firm grasp of the law. Judgements have sometimes lacked 'sufficient reasoning and analysis' (Open Society and CIJ 2004: 41–42), some have 'scarcely mentioned' international law (D. Cohen 2002: 5) and others have been based on law that is not actually applicable in Timor-Leste (JSMP 2005a). Further, defective decisions at trial have rarely been 'remedied on appeal because appeals judges [have also] lacked particular expertise in human rights and international law' (UN 2005a: s131).

On top of these problems, judges could not always access basic services – from telephones or computers to legal documentation – and, for a prolonged period they did not have assistants or stenographers – which means that defendants have been further disadvantaged in their opportunities for appeal by the lack of reliable court transcripts (Stanley 2007a, 2008a). Translation staff, an essential component in a court operating in four official languages (Tetum, Bahasa Indonesia, Portuguese, and English) and over 20 indigenous languages and dialects, were not always available and it was not so unusual for judges to translate themselves or for 'chain translations',[4] which greatly increase inaccuracies, to be undertaken (D. Cohen 2006a). Panel hearings have even been conducted when defence counsel and defendants could not understand most of the proceedings (Stanley 2007a).

Justice has therefore been dramatically subverted by institutional incapacities. Resources, staffing, managerial, and technological deficits undermined the ability of victims to take their cases forward or for those indicted to receive a fair trial. They have undone opportunities for Timorese people to attain justice.

Providing political cover

Ultimately, these institutional incapacities (backed by a lack of commitment from powerful 'bystander' states and organizations) have consolidated Indonesian impunity. The SCU could not compel the arrest of Indonesians and while final trial figures appear satisfactory, it is clear that those who have been prosecuted have been Timorese militia members who, as shown above, were often persuaded into participation – for example, all those prosecuted on torture charges have been Timorese (Stanley 2005a). While this may provide some sense of justice for those who have suffered, it cannot hide the issue that key perpetrators have not been recognized *as* perpetrators in the courtroom. Instead, those who bear most responsibility remain free with their high status intact. In all, 303 indictees, including all high-ranking perpetrators, remain out of reach in Indonesia, with many continuing in active service within political, military, and criminal justice institutions.

This situation has caused widespread consternation among torture victims who argue that the main role of the serious crimes process should have been to prosecute the 'big fish' – the Indonesians.

> When we say that we want criminal justice, we do not mean that we want the 'small fish' captured. We are talking about Indonesians, the 'big fish'!
>
> Mateus

> We can deal with Timorese militia members ourselves. But, we want the international community to prosecute the Indonesians as we can not do that ... not yet.
>
> Isabel

However, it has also led to disquiet among some UN workers who argue that their work was used as a smokescreen (highlighted in Stanley 2008a). One SCU worker, agitated at the skewed nature of prosecutions that did not touch Indonesian officials, argued that the UN should have halted the trials:

> Things should have been stopped ... instead, we continued and provided a cover – a sense that something was being done.

For this worker, the continuation of prosecutions took attention away from Indonesia. It made matters worse as it provided a space for perpetrating officials to strengthen their legitimacy and reconfigure their international identity as a 'good global citizen', which was an issue made all the more salient given that the 'international community ... seeks Indonesia's assistance in the so-called war on terror' (Kingston 2006a: 273).

Embedding impunity: The Ad Hoc Courts in Jakarta

In 2000, an Indonesian Commission of Inquiry reported on the strong links between Indonesian officials and militia activity (Komnas HAM 2000). Despite facing intimidation and uncooperative officials, Commissioners highlighted the involvement of more than 100 individuals in murder, torture, disappearances, sexual enslavement, rape, forcible deportation, and many other violations (D. Cohen 2003). Shortly thereafter, the Indonesian government established the Ad Hoc Courts.

Initially, the courts were to prosecute gross human rights violations that occurred from January to October 1999. A shift in Indonesian political commitment resulted in a Presidential Decree (96/2001 of August 2001) that restricted the jurisdiction. By the time the courts started work, in March

2002, the mandate excluded most violations; the courts would examine just three (Dili, Liquiça, and Suai) of the thirteen districts in Timor-Leste for events that occurred during two months, April and September 1999 (Stanley 2008a). Those who were finally indicted were charged with murder and persecution, meaning that numerous allegations of other violations, including torture, 'were not pursued' (UN 2005a: s224). Legal rules operated to exclude most claims and they placed most victims outside of legal protection. For torture victims, justice was not a potential reality in these courts.

Aside from problems of limited jurisdiction, the political and judicial subversion of justice was exemplified in numerous other failings, including: the failure of prosecution staff to undertake professional investigations or to produce relevant evidence regarding crimes against humanity, command responsibility, or the links between militia groups and Indonesian state officials; a lack of support from political leaders; the reticence of judges to punish individuals in ways that reflected the seriousness of the violations; and, the failure of courts to provide or offer compensation to victims (Amnesty International and JSMP 2004; D. Cohen 2003: ELSAM 2003; Linton 2004; Roper and Barria 2006; UN 2003; UN 2005a).

Indonesia managed to protect its own officers through a legal process that was 'intended to fail' from the start (D. Cohen 2003). Torture victims have commented that the process has reiterated previous repressive practices; it has been a shocking new presentation of power.

> This process has been terrible. The Indonesians made a mock trial, like they did with us. They made a process so that they can do whatever they want.
>
> Martinho

> We have seen it all before!
>
> Maria

Out of the 18 defendants brought to trial, twelve were acquitted and six convicted of crimes against humanity.[5] Following first appeals, five had their convictions overturned. In the end, just one individual, Eurico Guterres, the Timorese leader of the Aitarak militia, was sentenced to 10 years imprisonment in March 2006. This decision was overturned by the Indonesian Supreme Court in April 2008 and, on his release, Guterres, supported by relatives of the late President Suharto, declared that he would stand for a political position in West Timor.

Clearly, these court proceedings have demonstrated a wilful avoidance by the Indonesian government and judiciary of the matter of bringing any individual to account for any crimes. In an interview, Aniceto Guterres suggested that this situation has created further antagonism within Timor-Leste:

The process of the Ad Hoc Courts in Jakarta has made people even more upset. When you ask victims 'Has this process helped?' they say 'No, it's just made it worse'.

The Ad Hoc Courts have been a spectacle of Indonesian state power, a continuation of past injustices undertaken within the domain of a legitimate, seemingly progressive institution. Through a range of practices – from the political control of the mandate to judicial failings to military threats – this criminal justice institution was structured and operated to facilitate injustice. It has failed to change the lens of recognition regarding violations in Timor-Leste and has intensified status disparities between Timorese victims and Indonesian perpetrators.

Creating 'othering'

Transitional justice initiatives have also engaged misrecognition strategies of 'othering' in fundamental decision-making and practices. It is clear that states have the ability to hide their responsibility for violations through diverse 'othering' techniques. As previously detailed, state officials can minimize their involvement by distancing themselves from violations; alternatively, they can downgrade victims in ways that hide their victimization (by attributing them with guilt of some other crime) and place them outside of legal protection (Jamieson and McEvoy 2005). Of course, transitional justice mechanisms seek to counter these 'othering' techniques, to expose who was responsible, and to acknowledge victims *as* victims (Stanley 2002). Yet, the criminal justice institutions established for Timor-Leste have imitated these 'othering' strategies (Stanley 2008a).

Nowhere has this argument been clearer than in the proceedings of the Ad Hoc Courts. During trials, Indonesia was presented (by both defence and prosecutors) as a neutral force between clashing local groups. Caught between opposing Timorese sides, Indonesian officials were argued to have assisted Timorese civilians escape this violence. This myth, that the violence erupted without any 'organized support or participation by Indonesian military, police, or security units', was continually advanced by the regime during occupation (D. Cohen 2003: viii). The courts' acceptance of this misframing recreated the common assumption – widely held in Indonesia – that Indonesian forces were not involved in Timorese violence (Stanley 2008a). Thus, the culpability of the Timorese was amplified and Indonesian perpetrators were inoculated from criticism.

This technique was also illustrated in the general treatment of witnesses. Most witnesses were drawn from the Indonesian government, army, and police, and they focused on the involvement of Timorese in violence. The few Timorese witnesses did not have the opportunity to challenge this version of events as, lacking interpreters, they could not always understand proceedings (ibid.). These witnesses were also frequently subject to denigrating treatment from all court members. For example, witnesses were questioned for long hours without a break, court officials laughed at those with disabilities, and others were 'ridiculed and made the brunt of private jokes' (UN 2005a: s262–65). Through such techniques, the court controlled what was said and what was left unsaid.

In addition, there was consistent intimidation of victims and witnesses by judges, court staff, and defendants. Timorese participants were threatened by military officials who – sent to show support for accused colleagues – brought guns and knives to the courtroom (Amnesty International and JSMP 2004; Linton 2004; Roper and Barria 2006). Indonesian judges – having strong systemic links with the military as well as problems with corruption[6] – often failed to challenge such behaviours. Thus, Indonesian authorities engaged in a continuation of previous violence and fearful domination under the new dynamics of transitional justice. As Joao commented:

> Indonesian justice is bad. The victims have been intimidated and threatened. They have not been protected. There is no justice there. It is just like before.

Victim witnesses were devalued and traumatized through court proceedings (Amnesty International and JSMP 2004). Through official, legitimizing strategies, the courts ensured that they were prevented from operating on a par with others. These realities contributed to a situation in which other Timorese witnesses refused to attend.

Forms of 'othering' were also evident in the Dili-based serious crimes process. While these practices were not so overt, or hostile, the final outcome (in which most Timorese did not receive any legal protection and in which Timorese militia members were the only recognized perpetrators) has also enhanced Indonesian assertions that violence was fundamentally caused by the Timorese population (Stanley 2008a). Certainly, it appeared that any Timorese defendants coming before the Special Panels were almost automatically convicted, regardless of the strength of evidence against them.[7] Timorese defendants held a devalued identity within the Panels and, frequently, they did not enjoy legal protection. As shown in the following two case studies, Timorese defendants were not always given an opportunity to properly defend themselves and they could also face new violence from criminal justice officials.

Rusdin Maubere (*Maubere* (23/2003)) was charged with the torture and enforced disappearance of André de Oliveira. This crimes against humanity trial was beset with various injustices – no defence witnesses were called, the argument on crimes against humanity was not proven, and massive contradictions between prosecution witnesses were overlooked by judges on the basis that the witnesses were 'illiterate' and therefore apparently had 'a limited capacity for reasoning and memory' (D. Cohen 2006a: 78). However, the judges also argued that the initial charges could not stand. It was proven that Oliveira's injuries were so serious that he died on the night of the attack and that his body was buried in a shallow grave. However, his body was not found. The judges concluded that Maubere had intended to kill the victim – and they concluded that on that basis the crime of torture could not be upheld. Following this, they acquitted Maubere of the charges, but then 'requalified' the facts to find him guilty of murder; he was subsequently found guilty and sentenced to three years in prison (Stanley 2005a). This reclassification and conviction showed an ignorance of the SPSC regulatory definition of torture as a crime against humanity.[8] It violated international norms as well as the laws of the Special Panels (D. Cohen 2006a).[9] Moreover, it was undertaken without informing the defendant or his legal team; Maubere had no opportunity to defend himself. While the facts of the case were reconfigured to suit the Panel's imperative of a conviction, Maubere was not established as a full partner in legal proceedings. He had no opportunity to pursue his own claims for justice.

The 'othering' of Timorese defendants was also illustrated in the case of Beny Ludji (*Ludji* (16/2003)) who was indicted with the murder of a pro-independence supporter (Stanley 2005a). In 2002, Ludji was arrested by Timorese police, who were working under UN Civilian Police officers, on the border with West Timor. Following his arrest, he was detained and tortured over a period of two days. A leaked internal UN Police investigation found that he was beaten until he bled, defecated in his pants, and lost consciousness. In the end, he signed a confession and was then transferred to Dili to await trial. Ludji's defence counsel claimed that the SCU prosecutor used the confession during pre-trial detention hearings despite protests from the defence that this violated international law. The statement was also submitted for use at trial; however, following continued objections by defence counsel, the prosecutor stated that it would not be relied upon. Ludji was ultimately sentenced to eight years having been convicted of murder. The officers responsible for his torture were charged with 'light maltreatment' under the Indonesian Penal Code (Amnesty International and JSMP 2004) and fined US$15. Ludji's devalued status, as an ex-militia commander and serious crimes defendant, meant that his victimization was negated. The torture of Ludji was not subject to immediate condemnation from all court officials. The response of the court to his violation jarred against those sentences given to those convicted of similar acts by the Special Panels.

The general lack of judicial safeguards for defendants worsened with the UN's decision to end all trials by May 2005. At this point, defendants were often pressured to enter into plea bargains despite the fact that they 'did not understand that this entailed an admission of guilt' (Roper and Barria 2006: 56; Rapoza 2005). As they thought that defence counsel were being obstructive, some judges also began to cut short defence cross-examinations in the quest to resolve cases efficiently (D. Cohen 2006a). One defence counsel opined:

The Panels are conviction-centred. They are prepared to trample over the rights of the accused so it meets the deadline as laid down in the mandate.

A prosecutor commented:

I, for one, did not think that the process would be such a shambles – especially the situation where only East Timorese were convicted, and the internal inconsistencies in the various decisions that were handed down by the court ... really, nobody thought it would be this bad.

Certainly, the reproduction of 'othering' through this criminal justice measure has downgraded the officially recognized realities of repression in Timor-Leste. All too often, recognition was made to fit the institutional imperative of quickly convicting those who were pre-emptively deemed to be guilty. In these circumstances, Timorese individuals were prevented from participating on an equal footing – they were denigrated, subject to violence, and excluded from fair participation in judicial processes. In contrast, Indonesian leaders have evaded such devaluation or official censure.

Practices of exclusion

The techniques that have downgraded Timorese access to recognition-based justice have also been linked with practices of exclusion. The Ad Hoc Court, for instance, operated almost entirely without the involvement of Timorese people and, as detailed previously, those that did participate (as witnesses) were subject to intense pressure from the Indonesian military. The 'hybrid' serious crimes process in Timor-Leste was, however, established to work against such practices.

Hybrid courts have gained prominence in recent years as they are seen to combine the strengths of international tribunals with the benefits of local participation. 'These tribunals combine UN authority, funding, resources, judges, and prosecutors with local participation, creating a process that is potentially more meaningful to the victims, less politically divisive, and more effective in capacity building' (Kingston 2006a: 277). These mechanisms are seen as more attractive than international courts as they can have a direct impact on the population and on legal personnel development (Roper and Barria 2006; Tolbert with Solomon 2006). The inclusion of local people in providing justice for past crimes can have real 'political and symbolic significance' (Reiger and Wierda 2006: 12).

Despite the opportunities offered by hybrid courts, the Timorese experience has not been a happy one. As detailed here, the serious crimes process has suffered from institutional distancing, inadequate capacity-building, and the exclusion of prominent civil society groups.

Institutional distancing

A key problem was that the serious crimes process was established without 'sufficient or meaningful consultation with the East Timorese' people (Linton 2002: 106). Most negotiations 'occurred either within the Security Council or within the UNTAET' (Roper and Barria 2006: 51) and institutional bodies tended to distance themselves from local populations. Inevitably, the end result was that victims have been unable to participate in relevant processes.

Many Timorese people did not know that the serious crimes process existed – a point reflected in the lack of victim's testimonies in this chapter. The initial response of torture victims to this topic was instructive. While some responded by remaining silent and looking 'blank', others commented:

> What? I have never heard of it. There is a court, here, in East Timor?
>
> Alberto

> I can't say anything about this. I don't know what it is.
>
> Ana

> I live in a rural area and I don't have a radio or TV so I don't know about this. The bridges that link to Dili are also broken.
>
> Santa Isabel[10]

For a long time, serious crimes workers failed to communicate at all with the local population.[11] Outreach work was virtually non-existent; the SCU had one Public Affairs officer who had, in effect, no resources (Stanley 2008a). During 2005, Carl DeFaria, the then Deputy General Prosecutor, implemented a dozen district meetings to clarify the impending closure of the Panels. He was faced with angry locals who argued that they had not even known that the serious crimes process was operating and now they were told that it was to close (D. Cohen 2006a; DeFaria 2005). In these circumstances, one has to question, as Lino did, 'Who was this court process for? We know nothing about it ... yet you do!'

Limiting and ignoring local capacities

Despite the international proposals that the hybrid model would incorporate participatory principles, inclusivity was not necessarily applied in practice (Candio and Bleiker 2001). The serious crimes process regularly focused on the capacities of imported workers, rather than on building local skills and resources, and frequently excluded capable local actors.

Of course, the majority of Timorese did not have the capability to participate in legal processes. Maria Fatima remarked:

The people of East Timor are hungry for justice, they really want it. But, it is very difficult for a survivor to take a case through the courts. They have no money, so fighting a case would be very difficult. Also, people are illiterate, so of course they continue to be victims as they're easily cheated. They have no opportunity to pursue justice. So, finally, they get nothing.

The professionalization of legal processes excluded local victims from institutions of justice (as it does in so many other countries). However, even legally trained Timorese were missing from the picture. During 2004, for instance, there were no Timorese prosecution lawyers within the SCU, no Timorese defence lawyers, and only two Timorese judges in operation, the latter each working on a Panel with two international judges. This situation was not unusual and the intention to phase out internationals as Timorese staff gained experience did not happen.

Some local staff did build and refine their skills through the serious crimes process (and were often far more capable than their international counterparts), yet others were sidelined by internationals 'who were often too busy or disinclined to spend time mentoring and collaborating' (Kingston 2006a: 277). In addition, as Reiger and Wierda (2006) detail in their analyses of local judges, Timorese were regularly frustrated by the patronizing attitudes of their international colleagues. Some internationals would talk over local judges, ignore their dissenting opinions, and demonstrate a lack of cultural or historical awareness of the country they were working in.[12] Local workers did not always feel that they were 'treated as equals' (ibid.: 14); the lack of capacity-building re-emphasized patterns of uneven structural power.

This perception of differential status was also highlighted in the exclusion of other capable Timorese actors from work (Trowbridge 2002). Timor-Leste has a strong culture of local action, and church and non-governmental organizations (NGO) have provided a backbone for the monitoring of state activities and the provision of services. However, these capacities tended to be ignored by international serious crimes workers. As one Timorese NGO worker observed:

At the start, we tried to arrange meetings but they weren't interested. We have so many files, so much knowledge, but they didn't really want to know.

While a SCU investigator commented:

The former management [of the SCU] really didn't think that they needed them as well. I think they thought 'we've come in here, we're the experts, thanks, you've had your time, it's our time now' ... and, I think that was quite disastrous.

This approach created feelings of exclusion in local human rights groups and undermined confidence in the emerging legal system (Dickinson 2003).

While impairing the ability of internationals to efficiently conduct investigations, it further damaged public perceptions of this transitional justice process.

In conclusion, while the hybrid tribunal was established to encourage participatory processes, it tended to exclude local people from judicial activities and failed to build safety nets to address problems of participation. As a result, very few victims even knew that the process existed and those that did were often excluded on the basis that locals were seen to be 'incapable' or that 'internationals knew best'. Thus, the serious crimes process operated in a way that devalued the very victims it was established to serve; it closed representational justice down. The failure of the serious crimes process to provide participatory-based justice has undermined local perceptions of criminal justice processes. While the UN maintains that the project has been a success, it 'represents a virtual textbook case on how not to create, manage, and administer a "hybrid" justice process' (D. Cohen 2006b: 1).

Reflecting and deepening structural inequalities

The ability of these transitional justice mechanisms to provide redistributive justice has been hindered by institutional and political decision-making. While some of these problems are beyond the scope of court workers – as this process, like all legal procedures, is contextualized by external political and economic factors – it is clear that personnel have missed opportunities to present a challenge to structural inequalities within Timor-Leste.

For example, despite the fact that under international law, 'states are obliged to provide reparations for any harm or damage caused by a wrongful act or omission on the part of that state' (Sarmento 2005: 6),[13] neither criminal justice body implemented reparatory justice measures for victims.[14] Those who were legally designated as victims have not enjoyed any individual or collective restorative measures to improve their lives – for example, in terms of compensation, health assistance, counselling, the construction of memorials, and so on. The sidelining of redistributive justice in this regard means that economic or resource-based inequalities have not been addressed (UN 2006).[15]

Criminal justice personnel also failed to challenge structural difference. This was shown, for example, in their disregard for gendered relations of power. While at an international level significant progress has been made in thinking about the gendered experiences of crimes against humanity, and the subsequent need for gender sensitive court procedures and staffing (Oosterveld 2005), gender sensitive provisions did not always apply. The Ad Hoc Court, for instance, completely omitted rape or sexual violence charges. In Dili, while the SCU included rape within indictments, the Unit did not always manage staff to ensure positive outcomes. For example, one prosecutor who had spent the previous 13 years working on sexual offences cases in Canada was placed on generic cases in the SCU – her specialist training was completely overlooked by management. In the meantime, other staff struggled to deal with aspects of investigating this specific crime – that victims may be uncooperative, they downplay severity, they face embarrassment, trauma, and family exclusion in speaking out, and so on.

Such a lack of attention to the reality of sexual violations was also evident within the Special Panels. In an examination of the *Leonardus Kasa* (11/ 2000) case, Harris Rimmer (2004: 337) argues that:

> ... no knowledge of the international advances in the prosecution of gender-based crimes was discussed or applied in the judgement ... the trial proceeded without any reference to the context of systematic gender-based violence ... and ... the outcome for the alleged victim has actually been worsened, rather than improved, by ... the case.

Through such cases, criminal justice bodies failed to address structural differences – they inhibited recognition of gendered crimes and undermined the ability of women to participate in judicial processes. In doing so, they overlooked historical gendered injustice and failed to challenge the ongoing injustices and violence suffered by women in Timor-Leste.[16]

These serious crimes bodies neglected to connect recognition-based justice to measures that might overcome the inequalities that victims face in society. In situations where these institutions might have provided some element of redistributive justice – for example, by recommending compensation or by providing workers who could work against established power relations – they failed to do so. As a result, they did not establish victims as full partners in social life. While this has occurred for individual victims and local groups, it can also be identified as an issue at an international level.

Consolidating global inequalities of power

The dominance of Indonesia, a state that holds economic and strategic power, has been strengthened through the processes and end results of these transitional justice measures. This situation has been maintained by the way in which relevant actors have appeared unable or unwilling to 'own' the prosecutorial process. Indeed, key prosecuting parties have actively sought to distance themselves from court proceedings.

This distancing has been highlighted most clearly following the February 2003 release of the SCU indictment against General Wiranto, Abilio Soares (former governor of East Timor), and six senior military officials (see Stanley 2008a). Immediately, Indonesia declared that the UN had pushed a politically driven case (Hirst and Varney 2005). The UN, in response, insisted that the indictment had been formed and managed by Timor's prosecution service (De Bertodano 2004; Järvinen 2004) – this was technically correct although rather insincere as the UN had set up and run the judicial process. Shortly thereafter, Timorese politicians also dissociated themselves from the document.[17] President Xanana Gusmão publicly met and hugged Wiranto and stated that the implementation of the Ad Hoc Courts showed 'determination' and an 'attitude of political courage' (Järvinen 2004: 25–26). Then he wrote to the UN arguing that 'jail terms for senior [Indonesian] military officers would ... undermine stability' (UN 2005b). Hence, all the major 'players' distanced themselves, they legitimized Wiranto's high status position, and the 'hybrid' serious crimes process was an 'orphan ... fully owned by neither their international nor national progenitors' (Roht-Arriaza 2006: 10). Victims, like Maria Fatima, felt further antagonism at such impunity:

I was detained [by the Indonesian military] for no reason – there was no evidence for my crimes. However, Wiranto is charged with numerous crimes, of a serious nature. Yet he is still free. There is no equivalence here.

The Timorese government's distancing from the issues of criminal justice, in favour of economic development, trade, and bilateral reconciliation, is perhaps understandable. As shown in Chapter 8, economic survival remains a key concern – Timor-Leste is one of the poorest countries in the world and it is getting poorer (UNDP 2006). Given this, the new government of Timor-Leste has sought to build alliances with its more powerful neighbour. Some Timorese have been quite forgiving of these local political actions – after all, as Casimiro (cited in Stanley 2008a) says, 'What can they, who have nothing, do against these big powers?'

Despite the understanding shown by the Timorese people to this relatively powerless government, there is a common view that international actors have not fulfilled their legal and moral obligations to provide judicial redress. Impunity for Indonesian officials has emerged out of wilful avoidance on the part of the Indonesian government; however, it has been further entrenched by both the UN's and other relevant powerful states' (such as the US, UK, and Australia) failure to provide adequate resources, good management, or multilateral pressure on Indonesia. While the UN continues to maintain the need for justice (UN 2005a, 2006), and has recently re-established the Special Panels to complete outstanding investigations, its actions thus far have ensured that justice has been almost impossible to achieve. In other words, while the UN (among others) has managed a human-rights-conscious identity, it has not behaved in ways that encouraged or secured human rights standards. On the contrary, its actions have strengthened the legitimacy of a violating state.

Given these conditions, the failure to secure criminal justice is perhaps just a representation 'of the dominant-subordinate global North-South relationship' (Rae 2003: 177–78). That is, 'in this new era of international criminal justice, the law seems to be applied only to those who are defeated, disgraced or politically unimportant' (De Bertodano 2004: 926). Those who were most marginalized during repression continue to experience injustice, further harm, and denigration. These criminal justice mechanisms have not set the ground for structural change; rather, they have reiterated dominant power relations at every turn.

Conclusion: The continuation of injustice

The serious crimes process and the Ad Hoc Courts may be commended for providing some recognition of repression and violence during the Indonesian occupation. They have presented a challenge to the status of certain local perpetrators who have faced trial and conviction. However, in many respects, these institutions have fundamentally failed to fulfil a crucial role of justice – to bring serious human rights violators to account. Transitional justice bodies have been used as a way to entrench impunity, to prosecute the relatively powerless, while giving the appearance that justice is being done.

Additionally, these initiatives have provided a spectacle of Indonesian state power. This has been exemplified in the militaristic presence in the Ad Hoc Courts courtrooms, in the fact that no Indonesian officials have been subject to judicial scrutiny, and in the end result that Indonesia has been able to reconfigure itself as a good, global citizen. Shielded from criticism, the positive status of most Indonesian officials who were involved in violence has not been effectively dislodged.

At the same time, these bodies have placed low-standing Timorese individuals outside of legal protection. Through the Ad Hoc Courts, Indonesian officials have been able to reconstitute fear and intimidation among Timorese communities, to control what is said and not said, and to deter witnesses from coming forward. Within the serious crimes process, Timorese individuals have been marginalized in different ways – for example, in the omission of certain, less powerful groups from recognition *as* victims, in the ready attribution of guilt to those who have been produced as perpetrators, and in the exclusion of the local population from participation in legal practices.

As the 'owners' of these mechanisms distanced themselves from the processes when they became politically difficult, these criminal justice institutions have also failed to challenge the power imbalances within the country or the region. Dominant political, economic, and gendered agendas have been placed ahead of providing for the 'basics' of transitional justice – to establish the truth, to punish perpetrators, to provide reparatory measures – that might counter continuing redistributive injustices.

These injustices have led to negative perceptions of legal processes among local populations. For many victims, these bodies have reillustrated the international contempt or disregard for the Timorese population. However, they have also bolstered a continued campaign for prosecutions. Repeatedly during interviews torture victims continued to demand criminal justice. Antonio's thoughts were not exceptional in this regard:

There must be justice ... how can we make reconciliation without justice? ... There will only be good relations among the people if there is justice ... The peace can only be maintained if there is justice.

As shown above, the current administration does not favour this route and it does not appear, at present, that new initiatives have much international support.[18] For torture victims, justice is, at best, a distant possibility. But, what about the possibilities of official truth-finding? Can this provide a pathway to justice? It is to these questions that this book now turns.

7 Justice in Truth-telling?

This chapter assesses whether justice has been secured for Timorese torture victims through truth-telling mechanisms. It focuses particularly on the Commission for Reception, Truth and Reconciliation (CAVR); however, it also evaluates the ongoing Truth and Friendship Commission (CTF). The chapter shows that torture victims, like other survivors of serious violations, have had an opportunity to participate directly in CAVR practices – principally, they have given 'truth-telling' statements about their violations, but they have also engaged in community reconciliation hearings. These activities have led to a more complex recognition for torture victims and their perpetrators; they have culminated in a re-engagement between local people who were previously divided; and, on occasion, they have provided an opportunity for perpetrators to be shamed or punished.

Yet, victims could also be framed out of recognition practices as a result of the violence perpetrated against them, the limited opportunities provided to them to participate, and their need to protect themselves from further emotional harm and violence. In addition, a recognition-based justice has also been undermined by the activities of perpetrators and CAVR staff, as well as by institutional processes that narrowed and distorted the truths being told.

More significantly, however, the CAVR was undermined by its inability to deal with the status-based injustices that underpinned violations like torture. In many ways these shortcomings attributed to the CAVR are the problems of others – the failure of the Serious Crimes Unit (SCU) or the Ad Hoc Courts to prosecute Indonesian officers; the decisions by the Timorese government to forego claims for reparations or prosecutions; the stance of the CTF, to exchange truth-telling and prosecutions for 'friendship' with Indonesia; the determination of the United Nations and powerful states (such as the US, UK, and Australia) to distance themselves from justice provisions – nevertheless, they have cast a long shadow over Commission activities. The Commission began, then, to challenge misrecognition and non-recognition, but it has been downgraded by other transitional justice measures that have continued to devalue victims. And, in offering a participatory and recognition-based justice without a corresponding redistributive justice, the CAVR has contributed to feelings of marginalization among victims.

Connecting participation to recognition

From the start, the CAVR had wide public approval and was supported by Timorese political leaders, as well as the UN (Burgess 2004; C. Jenkins 2002).[1] The seven national Commissioners,[2] who were recruited through an open process, began work on 21 January 2002, and over the next four years the CAVR employed hundreds of people to operate its programmes.[3] The core mandate of the CAVR involved diverse tasks: to establish the truth regarding the nature, causes, and extent of human rights violations committed in East Timor between 25 April 1974 and 25 October 1999;[4] to restore dignity to victims; to reintegrate those who had harmed their communities through minor crimes; to promote reconciliation and human rights; to make recommendations to the government; and, to refer serious crimes matters to the SCU.

The final report, 'Chega!' (meaning 'no more', 'stop' or 'enough' in Portuguese), was published onto the internet in December 2005.[5] Extending to over 2,500 pages, it highlights the responsibility of diverse actors for repression and violence in Timor-Leste. Many of these 'truths' are detailed in previous sections of this book and will not be repeated here. Yet, overall, the report highlights that, although Timorese committed violations including torture, most responsibility lies with the Indonesian government, military officials, and their allies. This apportioning of blame is useful as these latter actors have started to 'whitewash' the past, by either hiding their involvement in violations or by framing events in a way that suggests that they were saviours of the country (see Nevins 2005[6]).

The report provides a contextualization of how violations in Timor-Leste were underpinned by global relations of power. This recognition exposes the identities of those involved in violations and illustrates how international routes of trade and the economy meshed with support for a violent regime. In addition, in highlighting that Timorese have been misrecognized as key perpetrators, the report acknowledges local victimization and positively revalues Timorese identities.

Alongside this recognition of historical truth, the report details the range of activities undertaken by the Commission: 7,669 victim statements, reporting 85,164 human rights violations, were recorded; 1,541 perpetrator statements were taken and 1,371 perpetrators engaged in community reconciliation hearings; public victims hearings were held in each of the 65 sub-districts; eight national public hearings were held in Dili to publicize key themes;[7] over 1,000 interviews to strengthen information on key themes were undertaken; six three-day healing workshops were held in Dili; death toll research that incorporated a graveyard census and a survey of 1,322 households across the territory was undertaken; and, large scale 'community mapping' exercises to produce local profiles of violations were carried out.

The CAVR encouraged a high level of participation from the Timorese population and their activities have encompassed the desires of many to be heard, to acknowledge past brutalities, and to move forward in building a new nation.

Encouraging participation has not been easy. Timorese people are not pro-lific consumers of printed material, and literacy rates are low. Hence, while the CAVR printed pamphlets, summaries of public hearings, and the report, it relied on posters, street banners, TV features, and, most importantly, radio programmes to inform most Timorese.[8] Even the most basic tasks were made difficult by the isolation of villages and the need to communicate across diverse languages.[9] These realities meant that CAVR success was heav-ily dependent on the ability of individual regional workers to connect with locals, build trust, and encourage community participation (Grenfell 2006).

Still, many people were compelled to participate in the CAVR venture. CAVR Commissioner Isabel Guterres noted that:

> This process has given people an opportunity to actually discuss events, to talk about what happened. It has provided a legitimate opening for people to discuss the past.

While Fransisco commented:

> I gave my testimony to the CAVR. I was happy with doing that. They must let everyone know what happened to people. Not just me but so many of us. So many people died and suffered for the independence.

For him, participation was specifically directed to the need to provide infor-mation about torture and other violence. These points were also picked up by Santa Isabel[10] who noted that the Commission was an opportunity to highlight hidden and diverse truths:

> The CAVR is good as it can show who was and who was not involved in violence. This is good for the Timorese because we are accusing each other. It's good too that people will be aware of women's suffering because women also suffered, they were tortured. Women lost their dig-nity because of the fight for independence.

The CAVR enabled participants to find out what happened to other people and to build a collective history of the region. The significance of this was reiterated by the fact that almost all interviewed victims argued that the CAVR report should be widely disseminated and that young people – the next generation – should learn from it.

Alongside educative outcomes, CAVR processes were also connected to opportunities for individuals, across the country, to realize that they are linked to others in their experiences. As Eduardo noted:

> I heard the story of a man, far away from here, on the radio. He had almost died after torture. I had suffered similar violence. I knew how he must feel.

Participation in the CAVR enabled a recognition of individual suffering and also led to a 'national consciousness' as disparate individuals could feel deeply linked to other victims (Grenfell 2006). Even the location of the Commission, the renovated building of the former Comarca prison in which hundreds were tortured, allowed reflection of this as some of the silent cells and the graffiti of former prisoners were retained. These features allowed individuals to reflect on their shared past while illustrating a symbolic transition to a new, more benign power (ibid.).

The collation and dissemination of individual truth-telling statements – and the related practices of public hearings – were important on personal, social, and symbolic grounds. They allowed individuals to be personally recognized as torture victims as well as connecting to the recognition of differential as well as shared experiences. Yet the CAVR also presented a chance for victims and perpetrators to face each other at separate community reconciliation hearings. These interactions, which this chapter now examines, were often regarded as a fundamental means to start 'social healing' and to strengthen local cultures of human rights and mutual respect.

Introducing Community Reconciliation Processes

The underlying purpose of the Community Reconciliation Process (CRP) was to reintegrate offenders back into their communities by undertaking a ceremonial practice that brought victims, perpetrators, and local residents together. This process was a crucial start in dealing with the conflicts that emerged following the involvement of local populations in intimidation, house burnings, beatings, lootings, minor assault, crop destruction, and the theft of livestock and property during the militia violence in 1998–99. The CRP was, then, focused on 'less serious crimes' and was not established to deal with violations of torture (although, as shown below, some torture cases did eventually progress through hearings). Still, many torture victims attended these hearings either as community bystanders or as direct victims if the hearings were in relation to non-serious crimes. Very occasionally, and albeit out of their remit, CRP hearings also dealt with claims of torture.

The CRP was a voluntary process[11] started at the request of a perpetrator who submitted a written statement to the CAVR. The statement[12] was initially reviewed by the CAVR and then sent to the Office of the General Prosecutor for a determination on whether the matter should be dealt with by the SCU (see below). Ensuing hearings were conducted in the affected community and led by a three- to five-person panel of local leaders and a Regional Commissioner. Following discussions, the panel established a Community Reconciliation Agreement (CRA), through which the perpetrator agreed to undertake certain actions such as making an apology, paying a fine, providing a symbolic payment of jewellery or *tais* (textiles), reconstructing property, or undertaking other community work such as cleaning or repairing public buildings. On the completion of these acts the perpetrator gained official reacceptance into the community as well as immunity, via the district courts, from civil or criminal action. If the perpetrator defaulted they could be liable to a sentence of a year in prison or a US $3,000 fine.[13]

The CRP offered a fast and cheap alternative to formal justice processes and it enjoyed relatively wide acceptance across Timorese communities. The hearings also incorporated long-established processes of *adat* or *lisan* to build local participation (Huang and Gunn 2004). These practices, which are variable across regions, are based on historical knowledge, ceremony, and customary belief. They are generally led by traditional, spiritual leaders who take a significant role in deciding right from wrong. In the past these measures have sometimes been harsh as wrongdoers have been beaten, ostracized, and even killed as a result. Within the CAVR, hearings incorporated rights-friendly customs – such as the chewing of betel-nut, the drinking of wine or blood, the rolling of the *biti* (the traditional mat used in local conflict resolution), chanting and dancing, the sprinkling of coconut water, the sacrifice of animals, or a celebratory feast (Babo-Soares 2004).

These practices revolved around community inclusion. As a result, while CAVR workers did have to initially 'sell' the hearings to traditional leaders – in terms of securing their involvement and indicating that the CAVR was not attempting to usurp their role (Pigou 2004) – they had significant success in attracting participants. The CAVR undertook 216 CRP hearings for 1,379[14] perpetrators and it is estimated that up to 40,000 people attended (CAVR 2005: Ch. 1.5.126).

At a personal level, CRPs provoked a re-engagement between distant parties and made individuals reconsider others in their communities. Aniceto Guterres, the CAVR Chair, explained:

> You can have a situation of two people who have become very distant from each other, and they don't have a proper look at each other anymore. So, we can create a context in which they sit across from each other, look each other in the eye and resolve their issues ... it's a process where you try to help to create a culture of talking together, of dialoguing and, slowly, in that way, accepting each other ... It's a process, a start.

These face-to-face encounters linked people together, often for the first time in years. For perpetrators, it was an opportunity to make themselves understood. Many perpetrators claimed that the CRP process had produced a significant positive effect on their day to day lives as it allowed them to state and close their case, to make amends, 'to work again and to interact with their neighbours rather than hide' (CAVR 2005: Ch. 1.5.127). In certain cases, perpetrators were able to show their diverse identities to illustrate how they were coerced or manipulated into offending or had been falsely accused (Burgess 2004, 2006; Grenfell 2006).

Similarly, victims have also been impressed by how hearings afforded them a better understanding of their perpetrator's actions, which helped to 'dissipate their anger' (CAVR 2005: Ch. 1.5.128). Further, following hearings, they experienced an elevated status in their community (Burgess 2004: 151).[15] Mariano commented:

> The hearing gave me a better idea of how he [the perpetrator] had been forced into the militia. He would not have done these things if the Indonesians were not here ... We were able to tell him how we had suffered and he apologized. This made me feel better.

These benefits were contingent on the openness of perpetrators to confess, apologize, and provide detail of their offending. Without full cooperation from perpetrators, the CRPs were devalued for victims (a point detailed further below).

Finally, in the practices of reintegrating individuals, remembering what happened, and clarifying events, the CRP set the ground for social reconciliation. While CRPs were intensely personal, they each contributed to a national attempt to come to terms with the past and move forward. As Jose reasoned:

> All of us have to accept and respect this process, as this is a national programme. With reconciliation, we can accept each other and work together to develop our nation ... otherwise we will never develop this country. And then what would happen?

Community reconciliation was seen as a continuing process that was vital to the growth and security of Timor-Leste as a whole.

Problems of participation

The CRP offered great potential in terms of identifying those involved in violations and setting a common ground for the future. However, during this research it became apparent that the CAVR was by no means a neutral process and a range of structural, institutional, and personal factors hindered victim participation. In addition, it was also clear that perpetrators, as well as CAVR staff, managed the process for their own ends. These factors ultimately led to complaints by victims that their needs had been downgraded in favour of smooth institutional processes regarding reconciliation.

Victim's capabilities

Many of the torture victims interviewed for this research had not given their testimony to the CAVR and most had not directly participated in a community reconciliation hearing. Of course, part of the reason for their non-participation, as discussed above, was that acts like torture were deemed to be too serious for community processes. However, other reasons for the lack of participation were that a number of victims knew little about the process and that the Commission had not reached their area to take testimony. For these reasons, victims had no capacity to remedy injustice. The following comments were not unusual:

> I know very little about this. I know that the CAVR went to collect testimonies from victims however no one came to see me about this.
>
> Ana

> I have heard about the CAVR, a bit, on the radio. I don't really know much about it. I didn't give my testimony.
>
> Martinho

> They didn't reach my village, only the town. I asked them and they said that they would come back later. But, they haven't returned yet.
>
> Eduardo

Added to this, victims did not always feel adequately supported by CAVR district teams and had not been briefed on what to expect during hearings (see also Pigou 2004). Victims had far less preparatory time than perpetrators, who submitted the initial request for a CRP, and they did not always enjoy full information before the event. In some circumstances, scared victims were taken from work to a hearing without any understanding of what was to happen (JSMP 2004b).

Victims' engagement with the process was also contextualized by their social status, and their related ability to participate 'as a peer' among others. For instance, some victims stated that they could not participate due to sickness or their lack of transportation. More often, victims could not participate as they could not take time off from working in the fields (also Pigou 2004); their economic problems surpassed those of individual conflict. Thus, Adelino explained:

> I couldn't get to the CAVR as I was working ... I went at night, they had a band and there was dancing. Although, by then, many people had gone home.

The issue of employment needs was also reflected in the comments – by numerous victims – that the CRP was dominated by young people who did not have deep family-support responsibilities. Health, ability, age, and economic responsibilities were, therefore, factors regarding who was able to engage with the CAVR.

This research also highlighted the dominance of gender in terms of participatory ability. Women were certainly hampered in their role as reconciliators as they had limited opportunity to work on hearings or to garner cultural support.[16] Alongside this it is evident that the majority of CAVR-identified victims and perpetrators were male. Part of the reason for this is that men were much more likely to have undertaken or suffered from acts of political violence (the civil and political violations) while women suffered greatly from the socio-economic violations of displacement, hunger, or poverty. However, regional workers struggled to access womens' stories of direct violence too. On arrival at villages they would be directed to male heads of households who would not discuss (and perhaps not know about) serious crimes undertaken by Indonesian occupying forces against female relatives or villagers. Similarly, it also seems that male perpetrators, who guided the CRP hearing through their initial statement, would tend to focus on male victims.

Women also discovered that their participation could face resistance from husbands or male family members, particularly if the topic was deemed to be sensitive (as torture violations often are). And, given that hearings 'could continue all day and into the night' (CAVR 2005: Ch. 9.1.1.5), women frequently faced difficulties in attending due to their home duties and childcare. Inacia commented:

> I didn't give my testimony to the CAVR people. I had different problems. First, they were working into the night and I could not get away from the children. I didn't want to take them so I stayed at home. Also, my husband was not happy that everyone would hear the detail about what happened to me. He thought it would be better if I kept quiet. I think that I would like to give my testimony.

Women were, then, regularly sidelined in reconciliation processes. CAVR staff commented that this was probably to be expected. After all, as Galuh noted:

> We are living in a patriarchal society so patriarchy is bound to be reflected in the collation of testimonies.

Operating in a society in which females are culturally devalued, the CAVR framed women out of stories. For a long time, the institution failed to build a safety net to pre-empt this problem of gendered participation and did not ensure that female victims could operate as peers alongside men. Consequently, the recognition of victims and their suffering is distorted.

Strategic decision-making by victims

Victims had their capacity to participate restricted by limited knowledge, economic standing, and social status. As a result, certain victims were excluded from this truth-telling process. However, victims also made their own strategic decisions to maintain a distance from the CAVR. In particular, some victims chose not to be identified as having suffered. For instance, Maria Fatima commented:

I have no need to be officially acknowledged as a victim.

While Agustinha[17] spoke about her desire to retain her privacy and dignity:

I was asked by CAVR to give a statement but I refused ... I said that God will know my suffering. I don't want to be presented like a doll.

Filomena took a political decision to not participate as she did not see the CAVR as the correct process to deal with perpetrators:

I thought 'What's the point? Why should I say what happened, release all this pain ... for what? What will I get? Be told that I am healed or reconciled?' That will not happen until they bring serious violators to account, to bring them before an international tribunal.

Victims made strategic decisions to place their own political and personal decisions ahead of CAVR objectives. In other circumstances, the issue was one of protection. For instance, victims discussed the stress of 'opening up' on demand and, on that basis, had made a decision not to engage with the CAVR. This combined with the real difficulties in talking about torture (discussed in Chapter 1). As Emilia responded:

No, I didn't talk about what happened. I'm not ready to talk so openly about what happened to me. I am still too upset, too angry.

While the Commission did make attempts to create a 'safe space' for individuals to speak, they did not have the power to protect victims or control events when CAVR staff moved to the next community. Besides, the CAVR did not provide extensive professional assistance to support victims, or other participants, suffering with trauma. As a result, while victims worried, had feelings of shame or embarrassment, or felt depressed, sad, angry, or withdrawn during proceedings or after them, there were very few trained counsellors or psychiatrists to assist – even in the short term, let alone in any ongoing way (Silove *et al.* 2006).[18] This created intense difficulties for victims who were 'exposing' themselves, which, in some circumstances, led to a 'worsening of symptoms of traumatic stress and grief' (ibid.: 1222). Given these realities, some victims chose not to engage.

The distancing from and the management of CRP

Thus, victims actively took pragmatic, personal decisions regarding their own well-being and the cost of giving their story. These choices were regularly linked to the political basis of CAVR activities. In particular, the ways in which victims engaged with the CAVR (and how they thought about it) connected directly to the ways in which other participants managed CRP hearings for their own ends.

For instance, CAVR staff were not always seen as efficient or neutral arbiters (Stanley 2008a).[19] In Baucau, for example, only 19 perpetrator statements were taken and just 13 CRPs completed. Part of the reason for this was that militia groups had not been well organized in that region; however, it also resulted from the fact that CAVR district workers did not work cohesively and had 'personality clashes' (CAVR 2005: Part 4.1.106). It was identified by several participants in Pigou's (2003: 36) study that in other circumstances 'the employment selection process had not been rigorous enough' and that workers undermined the CAVR process. It was felt that certain CAVR workers, or their family members, had been involved in wrongdoing and that this issue created a barrier to reconciliation. Staff members have also been blamed for closing or manipulating hearings in which their family members were present as perpetrators. Jose[20] remarked:

> ... those who were involved in the crime must confess to the community or the population that they have committed the crime against ... But in this situation, the family of the militia, who are also members of the CAVR, just closed the case. So, this is the weakness of the CAVR.

The actions of CAVR personnel could hinder participation. This was further intensified when it was clear to victims that not all perpetrators had come forward or that perpetrators were not being entirely honest or remorseful in their testimony (Pigou 2004). A number of torture victims also argued that the lack of Indonesian officials dealt with by the CRP undermined the whole reconciliatory project:

> I did not participate because the people who made me suffer were not there. They are in Indonesia.
>
> Joao

> I haven't participated in a reconciliation ceremony. Those who attacked me are in Indonesia. I don't know what will happen. I hope that the government will make something else happen. We seem to have been forgotten.
>
> Fransisco

> I have participated but I am upset with it. The people who are really behind the violence have not had to say anything. We know nothing more. We can understand a little about why some people acted as they did – because they were scared of more violence, and that makes it

better to reconcile with each other. But, the Indonesians have had nothing to do ... and, that is seen to be ok!

Alberto

The issue for these victims was that this process did nothing to bring torturers to account; these violators experienced no shaming or punishment for their actions.[21] In addition, when less serious perpetrators did participate, victims argued that they did so in a limited way and carefully managed their own involvement:

I attended a community reconciliation hearing. People were not very honest with themselves. I wonder about reconciliation when people are not open, they do not say what happened.

Emilia

Some of the perpetrators told lies. We all knew that they were lying. We know the truth but they still lied.

Lino

There was one man who had been incredibly vicious. I was so surprised when nothing came out of his mouth that was bad. He used to attack people in the street but you would never have known it!

Carla

While these limitations on shaming have been personally upsetting, they were also seen as a potential indicator of future conflict. The fact that some perpetrators did not make a meaningful commitment to the process was an indication, for some victims, that past concerns had not been fully reconciled and that status disparities had not been fully addressed (see also C. Jenkins 2002). This issue was seen to undermine the whole process of the CAVR, particularly as the Commission (see below) did not challenge dishonesty by investigating perpetrator testimonies.

Placing institutional mandates ahead of individual needs

It is clear that some victims did not necessarily want to be reconciled with individual perpetrators even though they participated in a CRP hearing. Some victims stated that they had a sense of obligation, to the CAVR Panel or to the *Chefe de Suco* (village head), to participate. Engagement was therefore subject to networks of power and victims did not always engage freely with the process.[22] Still, there was no obligation on individual victims to actually comply with the CRP hearing at all. Even if victims refused to participate in the process or did not agree with the proposed CRA, the hearing would continue and perpetrators could still 'be declared reconciled' or win 'immunity from prosecution' (Pigou 2004: 82). Thus, one of the consequences of the CAVR focus on the integration of perpetrators into communities was that the 'support' for individual 'victims was sometimes accorded a lesser priority' (JSMP 2004b: 35).

For such reasons, victims have suggested that the CAVR paid 'lip service' to their rights and needs. This argument also emerged in discussions about the leniency of acts of reconciliation, an issue that became particularly apparent when the CAVR began to rapidly process CRP applications.[23] With the impending closure of district activities, Commissioners began to run hearings with large numbers of perpetrators, which impacted on the length and depth of testimony.[24] Subsequently, panel members increasingly facilitated positive outcomes by 'manoeuvring victims and community members towards 'peace and reconciliation'' (JSMP 2004b: 37) and by setting up CRAs that only involved an apology from the perpetrator (Stanley 2008a). Hearings were streamlined for institutional ends and while the quantity of hearings increased, the quality of reconciliation practices was sacrificed. As Jose[25] observed:

> I saw a case in which people had had their mother killed and it was reconciled by giving a goat. That is not the right process.

While Alberto commented:

> There was a man who had burnt down so many houses and he just had to apologize ... while the people had nothing.

Despite the fact that thousands of individuals participated in the CAVR, the ensuing justice was inevitably skewed in favour of perpetrators as opposed to victims. Torture victims did not always have the capability to participate due to the seriousness of the violation against them, their lack of knowledge about the process, or the way in which they were institutionally 'framed out' due to their social and cultural status. Others chose not to participate. Some did not want to be identified as victims, some viewed the cost of telling their story as being too high, and others withdrew as a result of dissatisfaction with the actions of perpetrators and CAVR personnel. Finally, given that the engagement of victims with the CRP was not a vital element for its 'success', some victims argued that their redistributive needs were overtaken by an institutional remit to pursue fast reconciliation. Consequently, many victims took the view that perpetrators were not placed under adequate scrutiny. This issue was intensified by the fact that victims did not have an opportunity to address their torturers through the courts.

CAVR's connection to criminal justice

All CRP statements involving serious violations were to be retained by the SCU for investigation and indictment. Accordingly, while pursuing distinctly different ends, there was continuity between the SCU and CAVR. This relationship connected with the almost universally-held view that perpetrators of serious crimes should be prosecuted in the legal system. In reality, however, there has been a limited connection.

It is evident, for instance, that SCU staff did not have faith in the documentation emerging from the CAVR. Staff argued that summaries frequently missed key data and were poorly translated. This situation did improve as CAVR personnel gained further confidence, understanding, and experience, but, in the end, SCU staff simply checked the names of perpetrators on CAVR statements against their list of suspects. The problematic issue of names, detailed in the previous chapter, invariably meant that 'this was not a particularly reliable method' (Reiger 2006: 154). Ultimately, just 85 cases were retained by the SCU.[26]

Given that most statements were rejected by the SCU, the CAVR began to process CRP cases that constituted 'serious crimes' under UN Transitional Administration in East Timor (UNTAET) regulations. Crimes involving kickings and prolonged beatings with an iron bar would feature in SCU torture indictments yet they were also occasionally pursued through the CRP. This problem became more acute following the decision of the SCU to confine its prosecutorial mandate to events from 1999 because, for pre-1999 cases, the CAVR had to take the decision on whether a CRP would be better than the alternative – nothing.

The main problem, however, was that the SCU failed to indict and prosecute those whose statements had been retained. Few (possibly eight) of these 85 cases progressed to indictment stage. Yet the CAVR actively encouraged low-level perpetrators to participate in reconciliation hearings on the basis that all perpetrators of serious crimes would be prosecuted. Commission staff regularly warned those in attendance that if they hid their involvement, the formal system would 'catch up' with them (JSMP 2004b: 37). This has not happened. CRP referrals were not 'factored into the SCU's investigative policy' and, as shown in the previous chapter, the SCU failed to prosecute Indonesian officials (Hirst and Varney 2005: 14). As a result, there has been growing resentment towards the CAVR among participants. Victims see that while the 'little people' have progressed through the CRP, those involved in more serious events have enjoyed immunity. In short, the CAVR has been downgraded as a process of justice by the failure of the SCU to bring cases to court and there remains a considerable amount of 'unfinished business' – a significant caseload that falls in between the two procedures, 'more serious than those dealt with by CRP's and yet ... not dealt with at all' (Burgess 2004: 155).

The limits on recognition

Invariably, these limits on truth and justice have had an impact on how individuals come to be recognized as perpetrators or as victims. For instance, the gendered nature of data collation meant that women's stories have taken lesser prominence; in the same way, perpetrator's decisions not to attend CRPs or to provide a narrow testimony have also impacted on the process of official recognition; and, the way in which serious violations have fallen 'through the gaps' between transitional justice processes has meant that these cases have not been resolved. Yet, as detailed here, recognition has also been hampered by institutional foci and challenges regarding data collation.

CAVR documentation was, as shown above, of variable quality. This was a particular problem for report writers who realized, at quite a late stage, that statement-takers had recorded information without obtaining dealied versions of events. As one CAVR worker noted:

> We have statements in which people said that they were tortured but we don't know what was meant by it. The statement taker has not asked further questions ... they were not trained to take rich data The statements are very dry ... it's quite difficult to write a chapter on torture with so little detail.

Given this, while the naming of torture 'was accepted for statistical purposes' (CAVR 2005: Ch. 7.4.20), the CAVR counts of torture actually depict various mistreatments 'from light ill-treatment to severe torture' (CAVR 2005: Ch. 7.4.19).[27] Legalistic recognition was, therefore, subsumed under the attempt to give victims an institutional space in which to recount the past. Yet, in the end, this stance of participatory justice has undermined the true recognition of what individual victims have suffered.

Added to this, the CAVR's lack of investigations ensured that no account was ever verified.[28] All statements were accepted without reservation. As one Commissioner noted:

> Statement taking has been variable ... and we never know if someone is telling the truth. At first, statement takers were not critical of the information they heard ... I know that we had cases where individuals claimed that people were perpetrators when they weren't – just because they didn't like that person ... There was no challenge to this individual when they gave a false statement – the statement became part of the healing process.

Again, the 'healing' benefits of participation were viewed as more significant than a clear acknowledgement of who was involved in violations. Inevitably, this unconditional acceptance of statements meant that CAVR report writers could not always rely on the veracity of the information presented before them and a Commissioner detailed that it certainly impacted on the decision not to name individual perpetrators in the report.

For report writers, these issues of statement 'truthfulness' were compounded by the difficulties of working across languages. For instance, Sanne explained the process of writing the chapter on torture:

I work from the Bahasa [Indonesian] summaries then I go to the files. The statement will have been taken in Tetum or an indigenous language, and will be written in Tetum, sometimes Bahasa. I have problems when they are in Tetum, as I speak Bahasa. Then, I write it into English. It's a difficult process!

Thus, statements of varying quality would be subject to multiple translations before being finally written down in the report. Given this, it is inevitable that the CAVR recognition of who has perpetrated and who has been victimized, and in what way, has been structured by institutional problems of data collection. However, beyond this, it is clear that a recognition-based justice has also been dependent on an individualizing CAVR mandate that has narrowed debates on history and structure.

The first argument, here, relates to the CAVR's 'start of history'. Despite taking a 25-year mandate,[29] some commentators have argued that the Commission decontextualized violence between Timorese parties by ignoring historical divisions between villages (Rawski 2002). Inter-village conflict in Timor-Leste is, by no means, common. However, where it does exist, it can be the result of long-term divisions that emerged before the Indonesian occupation. Yet the CAVR – in promoting a narrative that Timorese violence was the end result of the Indonesian strategy to create local divisions – overlooked another local historical narrative: that violence could occasionally be an opportunity to settle old scores. In doing so, the CAVR simplified violence; the end result may be that the Commission may not have made the necessary challenge needed to propel significant reconciliation between antagonised parties (ibid.).

Similarly, as has been highlighted elsewhere (Stanley 2008a), the CAVR has been critiqued for being too narrow in its collation of truths. In a discussion of the coffee industry, Nevins (2003) proposes that the CAVR did not give adequate attention to the structural forces that contextualize life in Timor-Leste. The Timorese economy has been dominated by coffee production and, during occupation, the Indonesian military gained ownership of most plantations through the company P. T. Denok. In a bid to increase profits, they slashed sale prices to growers, which lead to extreme poverty. This situation worsened following the global fall of coffee prices due to the breakdown of the International Coffee Accord. Such global economic concerns continue – today about a quarter of the Timorese population are dependent on coffee farming and the average family makes an annual income of just US$200 for their efforts. The dramatic decline in coffee prices has resulted in a range of harms – from increased malnutrition to preventable death to a decline in school attendance due to the inability to pay 'modest' fees (ibid.: 694). These are concerns that will undoubtedly affect many Timorese for years to come; however this kind of 'violence' was not addressed by the CAVR that focused on individual acts of violence and individual responsibility (that is, the who did what, when, to whom, and why). This lack of attention to the conditions that may potentially create further harms and conflict in the future could also be cast as an 'othering' strategy as it hid the recognition of structural systems in the maintenance of violence and placed victims of such conditions outside consideration (Stanley 2008a).

While the CAVR has provided some recognition of torture and wider violence, the collated truth has been hindered by other factors, including: the CAVR reticence to examine the structural or historical basis to violations, institutional practices regarding statement collection and recording, as well as personal decisions – made by victims as well as perpetrators – on whether to participate and, if so, how much to say.

Setting the ground for redistributive justice

As previously highlighted, truth commissions cannot realistically solve wider status disparities on their own. Perhaps the most that can be asked of these bodies is that they set a firm ground for redistributive change. After that, redistributive achievements will rest on how transitional states respond to the status-based remedies that are often proposed by commissions. Some issues of redistributive justice through the CAVR have already been alluded to in previous sections of this chapter, principally with regards to the shaming and punishment of perpetrators through CRPs and the potential ability to direct cases through the serious crimes process. As detailed above, these processes have not always been successful. Here, two further aspects of structural justice are highlighted, reparations and recommendations.

The Commission did not have an extensive reparations programme. Urgent reparations were given to the 'most vulnerable' victims of serious crimes. These individuals, identified through the statement-taking process and often directed through a three-day healing workshop, were given a US $200 one-off payment. This payment was, as Aniceto Gurerres noted, an issue of levelling the status disparities between victims and perpetrators:

> We need to help to lift up victims to a place in which they have a better life, with dignity, so that they can participate fully in society, with their hopes ... We need to help victims improve their lives and create a balance between the lives of victims and perpetrators.

Yet while this sum proved vital for many to obtain medical assistance, purchase food, or establish work, there were just 712 recipients, including 196 women (Wandita *et al.* 2006). None of the victims interviewed for this research were recipients. These payments were not widely publicized and some victims complained about the lack of transparency in the process as they struggled to identify the difference between their situation and that of reparation recipients. Moreover, some victims also thought that individuals had lied to receive funds. Flisberto[30] noted:

I am not really satisfied with the CAVR because they gave good things to someone whose hand was fractured. He had fallen from a tree but he gave information to them that his hand was fractured because of torture. We who were in jail got nothing.

Given the limited funds available to the CAVR to engage in a more extensive programme of reparations, the issue became one of managing expectations. As Aniceto Guterres (cited in Stanley 2005b: 593) explained:

Sometimes when I respond to questions [about dealing with inequalities], I kind of laugh and say, 'Look, if you're really putting so much onto the CAVR then you don't need a Parliament, you don't need a Prime Minister, you don't need a Government. You don't need a President of Timor, you just ask the CAVR to do everything!' Because, only the CAVR is the one to do everything!

Certainly, the CAVR was in no position to deal with the poverty-wracked legacy of occupation and conflict. However, having taken statements on what victims wanted, CAVR Commissioners presented a wide range of recommendations relating to redistributive justice in the final report. Among other things,[31] Commissioners argued that external states that were involved in or supported violence (including Indonesia, Portugal, and the permanent members of the UN Security Council), as well as corporations who profited from weapon sales, should assist the Timorese government to provide reparations to victims (CAVR 2005: Ch. 11). They detailed that reparations should be targeted at the most vulnerable, namely: victims of torture; people with mental and physical disabilities; victims of sexual violence; widows and single mothers; children affected by the conflict; and, communities who suffered large scale violations (CAVR 2005: Ch. 11.12.9). They further argued that the international community, 'in particular the United Nations' should remain 'seized of the matter of justice for crimes against humanity in Timor-Leste for as long as necessary, and be prepared to institute an International Tribunal' for violations committed throughout the Indonesian occupation (CAVR 2005: Ch. 11.7.2.1).

The response from key Timorese politicians to these recommendations was uniformly negative. José Ramos-Horta remarked that the CAVR's recommendations were 'outlandish, with no connection to reality' (Powell 2006), while then President Gusmão (2005a), who officially received the report, stated that the Commissioners possessed a 'grandiose idealism' that went 'beyond conventional political boundaries'. President Gusmão further argued that the proposal to compel external states to fund reparations overlooked the fact that they had already paid for their mistakes via development aid. And, any further attempt to pursue criminal justice would mean that the population would be condemned for being 'brutal, violent and bloodthirsty' (Gusmão 2005b).

The response from Indonesia was one, perhaps unsurprisingly of denial and displeasure (Jakarta Post 2006). However, the UN also distanced itself from the Report. In early 2006, the United Nations Office in Timor-Leste reported that the 'CAVR Report is not a UN document', despite the fact that the CAVR was established under a UN Regulation, that it was heavily financed by the UN (as well as through bilateral funding), and that the Report had to be presented to the UN (UNOTIL 2006). The report was shunned from all sides.

In the wake of these developments, victims have continued to request reparations (Post-CAVR 2006: 2). For many victims, the giving of their story to the CAVR has a certain price. As highlighted in Chapter 1, stories are often given to effect change; as Maria commented:

> I wasn't going to give my story to the CAVR but they asked me and I thought that I could use the space to ask for a memorial for the Santa Cruz cemetery, for those who died.

The disconnection between testimonies and reparations has already begun to impact on victims. Bosco[32] explained:

> In my opinion, the victims are not happy because they came and took everything, so many stories. But, in fact, it ends with no justice, they have gained nothing in return and no facilities have been provided for them.

Connected to this are victims' perceptions of economic disparity between themselves and their perpetrators. There is a common view among victims that they, having struggled through repression, do not live well compared to perpetrators who have either secured positions in the new state administration or have continued their careers in Indonesia. These factors, connected to the overwhelming context of deprivation for many victims, have led to feelings of injustice. Testimonies to the CAVR cannot, then, be separated out from wider political and social processes. As Isabel Guterres, CAVR Commissioner, commented in interview:

> The Commission took testimonies but does it make people feel better? Is giving a testimony enough? Probably not if victims are struggling for work and food.

Given this context, the most that the CAVR could offer is that victims should hear the official truth. The dissemination process has now finished in all districts.[33] While certain aspects of this process are seen to have been successful – for example, a film *Dalan ba Dame* (*The Road to Peace*) was viewed as highly accessible and useful to propel community discussions – other aspects have been subject to criticism. JSMP (2006) argues that the dissemination of materials has, so far, been insufficient as only one copy of the final report[34] was given to each district and discussions on CAVR's findings have been limited to small numbers of people. The report has, therefore, been inaccessible to most Timorese (ibid.). In addition, there has been no official response to the Report; Parliament has not debated its content and no steps have been taken to implement any recommendations. This is perhaps indicative of the official distancing, highlighted above; however it also reflects the new agenda of the Timorese government to build strong political and economic alliances with the Indonesian government.

The turn to friendship

In March 2005, the governments of Timor-Leste and Indonesia established the Commission of Truth and Friendship CTF. This ten-person Commission, bearing equal representation from Indonesia and Timor-Leste, employs three ex-CAVR Commissioners.[35] Building on the findings from the previous transitional justice measures, the main objective of the CTF is to 'establish the conclusive truth in regard to the events prior to and immediately after the popular consultation in 1999' (CTF 2005: s12). Controversially, it has taken a mandate to 'heal the wounds of the past' through the recommendation of 'amnesty for those involved in human rights violations who cooperate fully in revealing the truth' (ibid.: s14c.i). The Catholic Church, local victims' groups, and the UN argue that this amounts to an official immunity for the prosecutions (Kingston 2006b; Stanley 2008a; UN 2006).

During interviews, torture victims highlighted a range of negative issues regarding this venture, particularly that: it was established without consultation; it has undermined attempts for 'truth' and criminal justice; and, it does not address grassroots reconciliation.

> How can we have friendship when they won't even admit what they've done? This Commission was established without consultation with the victims. And, they think that we should embrace it?!
>
> Santa Isabel[36]

> The CTF has impacted badly on the CAVR. The Truth and Friendship Commission seeks to freeze the past, to stop the truth being told. The CAVR has been put 'on ice'.
>
> Maria Fatima

> Those who worked for the CAVR left it and now work with the CTF ... this indicates that they don't have responsibility. I want them to be responsible, and to tell us about the CAVR report.
>
> Jose[37]

Who are friends here? How can I be friendly with those who refuse to accept what they have done? Why should that happen?

Martinho

We heard from the priest about the Truth and Friendship Commission, to eliminate justice. ... thousands of people were killed and their blood was shed throughout East Timor. Why should we eliminate justice and consider the traitors as heroes and, conversely, consider those who fought for independence as traitors?

Carla

For many victims the CTF has been structured to seal off justice and to institutionalize impunity. The Commission has provided further political protection for Indonesian human rights violators. In doing so it has consolidated the unequal power relations between the two countries and inhibited opportunities for redistributive justice.

Commentators have argued that this Timorese political response to Indonesia has been 'misjudged' and, moreover, it has begun to mask the true reality of Timorese experience for political ends. Aderito remarked:

We now have Xanana [Gusmão] claiming that we need friendship because our people are no longer victims, they are heroes. This is simply not true. There are people who have had their ears cut off, who scream all the time. These people *are* victims.

Timorese CTF Commissioners proposed that the ability to recommend amnesty does not mean that it will be implemented, particularly given the fact that (as the Pinochet case illustrated) crimes against humanity can be trialled anywhere in the world.[38] In their defence, they propose that the CTF will be able to highlight new truths about the Indonesian command and to illustrate the international involvement that supported the regime.[39] Moreover, they argue that victims groups do not necessarily represent those victims who see the potential of the new Commission. Dionisio Babo-Soares maintained:

These people [victims groups] want to monopolize the truth and impose their own views on the world, on what they think about justice. It is not democratic.

This comment reflects the broader political backlash against victims who continue to argue for prosecutions. Campaigners are increasingly stigmatized and represented as dissenting radicals, 'unwilling to bend to the good of the nation' (Wandita *et al.* 2006: 318). Justice has become politically untenable in the crafting of the new Timorese state.

Truth and friendship are, therefore, exchanged for justice. Yet, the truth that has emerged out of the CTF has been distinctly limited; indeed, some have argued that the CTF has just *'increased* the number of lies' about Indonesian occupation and violence (Hirst 2008: 32). While the final report is still to be published,[40] this issue has been illustrated in the CTF's public hearings, five of which were held in Indonesia and one in Timor-Leste.

CTF hearings drew on 56 witnesses, of which 13 were victims; from the outset, then, the CTF favoured an attempt to gather testimony from senior officials and alleged perpetrators (Hirst 2008). Contributing Timorese victims were treated poorly – they were laughed at by audiences during testimony and faced security concerns due to limited witness protection (ibid.). Moreover, it soon became apparent that at least three of the victims giving testimony had been chosen by Indonesian military authorities. For example, one victim, Domingos Alves, testified about his intimidation by pro-independence activists in 1999. He neglected to advise Commissioners of his militia involvement and his SCU indictments (*Mahidi militia* 6/2003 and *Da Crus et al. 4/2004*, see Appendix) for torture, murder and extermination (ibid.).[41] Needless to say, the Indonesian authorities directed that the victims of these alleged violations would not have the same opportunity to testify.

Given the dominance of witnesses from the Indonesian army, police, and government, it is perhaps unsurprising that the views presented also conformed to institutional truths. Certainly, the CTF provided an opportunity for Indonesian officials to repackage the past and hide their perpetrating identities in ways that contested CAVR findings. For instance, retired General Wiranto, appearing before an appreciative and applauding crowd at the CTF in May 2007, used the platform to argue that: the 1999 violence was attributable to Timorese people who enacted the 'age-old habit' of settling problems through violence; people burnt their own homes; there were no gross violations in 1999 (as evidenced through the Ad Hoc Human Rights Courts); there were no links between Indonesia and militia members; and, the UN was ultimately responsible for any violence as it placed too much pressure on Indonesia to leave in haste (JSMP 2007). Such testimonies were not unusual however; despite the reams of evidence that Commissioners held that disputed such claims, these versions of events went unchallenged and, in some instances, they were confirmed by Commissioners (Hirst 2008).[42] Thus far, there have been no official steps to challenge these misrecognitions. While the impending CTF report may yet present new truths about 1999, the Timorese government may find that it becomes complicit in misrecognizing the past.

Conclusion

The CAVR has provided a deep and complex recognition of violations in Timor-Leste. This has been a crucial step in providing individual acknowledgement, as well as a shared narrative for Timor-Leste. These processes of truth-telling have also engaged thousands of Timorese and begun a re-engagement between previous opponents. In this way the CAVR has made a vital contribution to peacemaking.

Of course, the provision of recognition and participatory justice has not been wholly successful. Justice has been hindered by a range of structural, institutional, and personal factors, including: victims' limited capability to participate; victims making strategic or protective decisions not to participate; the management of the process by CAVR staff and perpetrators; unreliable data collection; the CAVR pursuit of a narrowed, individualized mandate; and, the institutional focus on promoting collective reconciliation over individual needs. These participatory issues have undermined attempts for a fuller recognition of violations and their underpinnings.

The 'good' identity-based work of the CAVR has also been slowly eroded by the work of other transitional justice initiatives, particularly the SCU (and its limits on prosecutions) and the CTF. Already the CTF has been used by Indonesian officials to engage in misrecognitions, without challenge, and the Commission has undermined redistributive justice opportunities by promoting amnesty as a potential response to serious violators. In this light, the CAVR has been downgraded as a consequence of its inability to challenge Indonesian impunity or to provide redress for serious crimes.

Related to this, it is clear that redistributive justice remains an ongoing problem for victims. Torture victims, interviewed for this research, have not enjoyed assistance to overcome their subordination. Given the general exclusion of torture from the CRP, they not have experienced the shaming of their perpetrators. In addition, they have not received any reparations and their cases have not progressed to the courts. The cases of torture victims fall in-between institutions – too serious for the CAVR and not serious enough for the SCU – their structural disadvantage continues.

These factors have angered victims who feel that it is the Timorese who have had to 'pay' for violations (Le Touze *et al.* 2005) – they have been the ones prosecuted, and they have had to progress through the CRP – while principal violators go free. For many it has been another indication that their lives and the peaceful future of Timor-Leste are not of importance to those who wield economic and political power. As Amado opined:

> What this tells us is that justice doesn't belong to a small country like ours. It's only for the big countries ... for European countries, America, Australia ... for those who are seen to matter.

Justice is not, however, solely contingent on transitional justice mechanisms. As detailed previously, torture is just one aspect of violence for many victims; violence can also be seen as intrinsic to conditions of economy or human security. When talking about justice, therefore, it is imperative to also consider the concerns of social justice and how victims might be able to lead a 'good life'.

8 The Continuation of Violence and Insecurity

Courts and truth commissions are central to the attainment of justice for torture victims. The previous two chapters have described the 'successes' of such transitional justice mechanisms in Timor-Leste. For instance, through CAVR activities and serious crimes proceedings, the scale and depravity of violence during Indonesian occupation has been highlighted. These mechanisms acknowledged the physical and psychological suffering endured by victims and the CAVR, in particular, illustrated the range of perpetrators involved in violations. Such 'truths' provide a crucial first step in dealing with the past. For the CAVR, which also engaged thousands of Timorese in culturally inclusive practices, this recognition has underpinned a renewed social engagement between previous opponents. It has made a powerful difference to the lives of some victims.

These advancements have, however, been downgraded as a consequence of other justice failings. For instance, recognition-based justice has been undermined as a result of the restrictive mandates and policy decisions of transitional justice bodies. Recognition has also been limited by institutional incapacities to provide due process as a result of inadequate funds and staff, time constraints, structural 'blindness', or political reticence. For some torture victims, this has meant that they have been completely disqualified from programmes to shame or punish their perpetrators.

At the same time, transitional justice measures have often worked in exclusionary ways. Criminal justice bodies, even the 'hybrid' serious crimes process that was established around participatory ideals, operated without much Timorese involvement. While the criminal justice bodies regularly ignored local capacities, they also failed to build local skills. More broadly, victim's participation has been hindered by a range of factors, including institutional distancing and management; the minimizing behaviour of perpetrators; and, personal difficulties in accessing transitional justice events. These have combined to close down representational justice.

Human rights bodies have, then, perpetuated injustices with regards to recognition and representation. Ultimately, this has resulted in a situation in which Timorese people have been identified as 'the perpetrators' while Indonesians officials have circumnavigated official criticism. The culpability of Timorese individuals has been maximized, which is an issue exemplified by how Timorese witnesses and defendants lost protection within legal proceedings and faced devaluation, intimidation, and ill-treatment. In these instances, violence has continued under the new dynamics of transitional justice.

In this context it is clear that transitional justice bodies for Timor-Leste have also provided a limited form of redistributive justice. Notwithstanding the shaming and punishment of Timorese deponents, and the tokenistic reparations offered by the CAVR, these bodies have failed to challenge structural disparities. In the legitimizing maintenance of economic and political power for the principal Indonesian violators, and their international supporters, Timorese victims have not been established as full partners in social life. Moreover, those who have continued to demand justice – in the form of reparations or prosecutions – have faced official stigmatization. They are effectively denied the ability to make claims.

Of course, most aspects of redistributive justice lie outside the reasonable remit of transitional justice institutions. Their mandates and aims do not tend to reflect the structured injustices that underpin human rights violations. Yet to be truly effective, transitional institutions have to be connected to wider programmes of social change. After all, these bodies do not occur in a vacuum – truth and criminal justice cannot, by themselves, provide peace. With this in mind, this chapter turns to the wider social justice issues that contextualize victims' lives. It assesses whether, despite these institutional failings, victims might still be able to lead a 'good life' in Timor-Leste. To progress this evaluation, this chapter first returns to the idea of *statecraft*.

Crafting the state of Timor-Leste

Following the 1999 vote for independence – and the violent, destructive retribution from Indonesian officials and their militias – Timor-Leste was faced with the challenge of building most things again. The task has been made more problematic by poverty. With a population of just under one million, half of which are children, Timor-Leste is one of the poorest countries in the world and it is getting poorer (UNDP 2006). Life expectancy is 55.5 years, half the population cannot access safe drinking water, and two-thirds suffer food shortages. Almost 50 per cent of the population is illiterate, many adults do not possess work skills, and unemployment is high (ibid.). Basic health, housing, clothing, education, and transport needs are not met for most of the population. Children are particularly vulnerable: 1 in 10 will die before their first birthday; almost half are stunted and underweight; and nearly a third do not enjoy any education (ibid.). The situation for the poorest Timorese is beyond bleak. Against these socio-economic factors, the UN has engaged in a number of state-building missions.[1]

This international involvement reflects the wider emergence of state-building processes. Over the past decade, those ranked as 'failed' or 'weak' or 'fragile' states (including Bosnia-Herzegovina, Afghanistan, Iraq, and Kosovo) have been subject to significant international attention and intervention. International state-building measures – from peacekeeping operations to humanitarian assistance to the formation and governance of state institutions – are deemed necessary to protect populations from gross human rights abuses, as well as to maintain local, and thereby international, stability in states that 'are too weak to police their borders and enforce the rule of law' (Chandler 2006: 476). Thus, international interventions are generally underpinned by ideas that such areas are potential 'breeding grounds' for terrorism or 'dissidence' (Abraham and Van Schendel 2005; Charlesworth 2007).

In Timor-Leste, UN officials frequently proclaimed the new state to be a nation-building success (Chopra 2003). For a sustained period, Timor-Leste was something of a 'poster child'; perhaps because when the UN was first deployed the local population openly welcomed them, and Indonesian officials and supporters had largely withdrawn and there was no political struggle between different factions (Goldstone 2004). However, these proclamations of success can be critiqued.

As this chapter illustrates, Western models of statehood, presented as a default, have been superimposed over specific historical, social, cultural, and political contexts in Timor-Leste (Nixon 2006). Interventions have regularly been based on the premise that locals are 'unable' to help themselves and, in many instances, traditional structures have been overlooked and local histories and capacities have been disregarded. In this way, the international rebuilding of infrastructure or provision of services has impeded the development of local ability to create sustainable institutions and it has, in some instances, institutionalized conflict. Subsequently, new institutions have not garnered legitimacy from local populations and they have been more likely to fail (ibid.; Fukuyama 2006). One problem for Timorese people, then, is that internationals have failed to build the state in the 'correct' way.

However, the issue of state-building presents more than a technocratic problem to be solved by tampering with how institutions work. As, while state-building projects are commonly depicted as being short-term and benign, international actors can take the opportunity to embed dominant relations of power into new institutions and programmes.. In Timor-Leste, political, economic, and strategic priorities have been reconfigured so that local people – who have had little option but to concede – have become entrenched into the socio-economic frames established by the UN, international financial institutions, and/or more powerful neighbouring states. In this way, transitional state-building has led to a permanent embedding of a particular (Western) system. As shown below, the intended 'victories' (McCulloch 2007), or sometimes the unanticipated outcomes, for those who intervene have developed into longer-term problems of deepening inequalities or dependency for local people.

This chapter argues that, overall, international state-building has contributed to an insecure Timor-Leste. It has intensified divisions and conflict, deepened poverty, and encouraged a culture of dependency on external actors. It has also shaped conditions under which further harms and violations have and will occur. While these insecurities have been grounded in international, national, and community actions, they have had profound personal effects. As shown towards the end of this chapter, these insecurities have had a significant bearing on the lives of torture victims and they have also impacted negatively on how victims think about transitional justice measures.

Participatory injustices

Previous chapters have illustrated how Timorese were framed out as potential actors in transitional justice mechanisms. The UN and World Bank missions were, however, focused on developing capacity within Timorese systems of governance. The training and empowerment of local individuals, and the building of initiatives and structures that reflect the visions of local people, were viewed as essential in increasing the likelihood of sustainable structures and peace (Patrick 2001). Despite these participatory principles, local people have not always been engaged in social and political processes or had a stake in newly formed institutions (Candio and Bleiker 2001).

International workers regularly operated on the assumption that Timor-Leste was *terra nullius*, devoid of working institutions, a skilful workforce, or political structures (Chopra 2003). It was 'a place to be "invented" by the international community' (Järvinen 2004: 20). While certain aspects were correct – for example, many institutions had been completely destroyed in 1999 – there were strong social structures in place and a committed, eager population. For example, traditional structures had survived centuries of colonial rule and the return to 'normalcy' in Timor-Leste was due to the efforts of local people themselves; when internationals arrived in the region they found Timorese groups setting up schools, rebuilding homes, and providing health services (UNDP 2006).

Despite this, and as already highlighted, some internationals continued to work as if community structures did not exist or as if locals were completely incapable. Many internationals worked as if they were 'the experts' in the field and local groups often felt that they were patronized or 'reduced to being observers' (East Timor NGO Forum cited in Patrick 2001: 57). As Filomena remarked:

> These international bodies are treating us like children – internationals don't seem to understand that Timorese just need time and assistance to learn new skills and to be educated. There are no equal partnerships here.

Support structures, to ensure that Timorese people could participate, were often neglected (Chesterman 2004). Such inequalities were intensified by the propensity of the UN and World Bank to have meetings and documentation in English or with technical jargon, activities that excluded most Timorese (Pouligny 2006; Rawski 2005). In these circumstances, those who had returned from exile with new language and employment skills were often favoured, as were men, because women were less able to participate as a result of their illiteracy or other work duties (ADB and UNDFW 2005). This differential access to work has fed into unequal economic and power relations among local people and underpinned feelings of antagonism (particularly among independence fighters who spent years in the mountains). Antonio argued:

> Here we are, we sacrificed our lives in the struggle. We spent years fighting for independence. And, now, there is no work for us. The new jobs have gone to those who went to Australia, who went elsewhere, and who now fit with the new administrators. What did we fight for?! The UN has created new colonial conditions.

UN and World Bank officials did not always recognize fundamental community decision-making structures either. For instance, in 2000 the World Bank established the Community Empowerment and Social Governance Project (CEP) to kick-start the reconstruction of infrastructure; the commendable idea being that local people could identify their own needs and self manage allocated funds. The project was rolled out across 418 *sucos* (villages); however, administrators bypassed traditional leaders and implemented new community 'directors'. Inevitably, these appointees did not gain local support and projects regularly failed as a result, especially when internationals left (UNDP 2006). Further, by building new structures that 'challenged' traditional leaders, internationals created 'a locus of conflict – a new space in which power could be contested at the village level' (Rawski 2005: 947).

These modes of working, albeit well-intentioned, reflected Western cultures and short-term administrative priorities, and served to marginalize traditional, legitimate structures. Consequently, internationals were often charged with being more concerned with selling an image to the outside world and facilitating their own professional and political ambitions, rather than with addressing local needs (Pouligny 2006).

A limited recognition of historical conflict

Exclusionary practices have increased reliance on outsiders and led to local wariness about imposed and unreliable systems. International practices have also created new forms of conflict and insecurity within state institutions and local communities. In particular, the current 'problems' threatened by Timor-Leste are strongly connected to the UN's limited recognition of Timorese history in the construction of a new security sector. As detailed here, the recent breakdown in relations between the police and the military and the violence that has ensued have been an inevitable result of two institutions that were structured in opposition to each other.

In terms of policing, the UN recruited over 340 individuals who had served with the Indonesian Police during occupation. Despite the fact that these officers lacked legitimacy, were poorly trained, and frequently showed limited regard for the security of local citizens, they were placed on a career fast-track programme and entered the National Police of Timor-Leste (PNTL) at command levels (Hood 2006; Simonsen 2006). This situation was made worse by the UN's approach to the creation of the new Timorese army, *Falintil-Forças de Defesa de Timor Leste* (F-FDTL). Here, and without consultation with local leaders, the UN recruited staff from the reserves of *Falintil*, the armed resistance group that fought for independence (Neves 2006). Moreover, once F-FDTL was established, the UN 'essentially absconded' (Hood 2006: 61) – no defence policy or management plans were established, recruits did not receive training, and there was no clear delineation of roles between the military and the police (Amnesty International 2003; Rees 2006). Internal divisions within the F-FDTL were also apparent and some soldiers, particularly those from the west of Timor-Leste, campaigned for better pay and conditions, and an end to alleged widespread discrimination in the force.

This UN-led approach, which politicized security institutions, created significant tensions within a society attempting to make the transition to peace (Huang and Gunn 2004; Rees 2006). From their inception, clashes regularly occurred between the two forces and further violence was seen, by many, to be inevitable. For example, during a 2004 interview, one police investigator commented:

> Internal security is a real concern. There are significant problems between the military and the police. They are basically head to head. It's going to kick off again in the near future.

Serious violence erupted in May 2006. The aftermath was devastating: at least 37 people were killed, hundreds injured, homes and cars were torched, over 100,000 people were displaced and a humanitarian crisis evolved within new, crowded refugee camps. The nascent justice and security systems also collapsed – at the start of 2007, just 160 Timorese, out of a previous 3,000, remained on duty in the Police; prosecutorial archives were destroyed; the courts were placed out of action; and, prisoners were released. The government was thrown into disarray and Prime Minister Mari Alkatiri was replaced by José Ramos Horta in June 2006. Over 2,200 international troops (principally from Australia, New Zealand, Malaysia, and Portugal) were sent in to calm the situation, as well as to provide a long-term security presence. Following elections in 2007, a coalition headed by Xanana Gusmão's CNRT (National Congress for the Reconstruction of East Timor) party took power and Ramos Horta became President. Disputes about the constitutionality of this arrangement renewed violence across the country and, in February 2008, the two leaders were attacked by Major Alfredo Alves Reinado, the ex-head of the military police, and his supporters. Ramos Horta, seriously wounded, was airlifted to a hospital in Darwin. While Reinado was killed in the crossfire, his supporters are, at the time of writing, negotiating their surrender (Stanley and Marriott forthcoming).

In most media and political statements the responsibility for this resurgence of violence and destruction is placed squarely at the feet of the Timorese (Curtain 2006). Discussions have brewed on whether the failures of the local population have contributed to a 'failing' state (BBC 2006). Certainly, this violence was bolstered by past antagonisms that were fuelled by supposed distinctions between those from the east (*lorosa'e*) and those from the west (*loromunu*) of Timor-Leste, and inflamed by disaffected young people frustrated with rising poverty (Curtain 2006). It is also clear that the first *Fretilin*-led government of Timor-Leste bears some responsibility for institutional divisions. For instance, the decision to sack 593 soldiers (almost half of the military) following their strike regarding pay and conditions indicates a government unable to listen to grievances (Kingsbury 2006).[2] Such events – in addition to the fact that certain politicians, such as Rogerio Lobato, then Minister of Interior, used the police and military as their personal armies – did little to build a culture of trust and democratic participation.

Despite these local antagonisms and failings, the UN's building of state institutions in ways that disregarded historical conflict has also contextualized Timor-Leste's current troubles. This approach decreased local trust for international interventions, undermined the legitimacy of new state institutions, and fostered new conflicts. For victims who were already struggling with desperate living conditions, it has made the situation worse.

Institutional incapacity and further violations

State-building 'failures' may also be connected to the inadequacy of institutional resources, management, and training programmes. This has been particularly apparent with the international building of domestic criminal justice institutions. For instance, following six years of domestic court operations, there were still no fully qualified Timorese judges, prosecutors, defence counsel, or other court personnel (JSMP 2005b). For many years, Timorese trainees were not supported to develop vital administrative skills and, as a result, numerous problems emerged with regard to filing, recording, communications, finance, and managerial practices (ibid.; Marshall 2005).[3] Out of four district courts, three were prevented from functioning for most of the time as a result of insufficient funds for staff, vehicles, generators, and other basic resources. Given these conditions, court processes have rarely met standards of fairness and due process. Public confidence in the court system has gradually dissolved and villages have depended on *lisan* or *adat* (traditional dispute mechanisms) to settle problems (JSMP 2005b).

Problems of violence within the Police have emerged out of similar deficiencies. Most new recruits received limited training and the fast recruitment process led some to argue that the 'emphasis has tended towards quantity rather than quality' (Amnesty International 2003: 1). The vast majority of UN Civilian Police officers had no institutional development experience and none were specifically recruited for training (Hood 2006). Nor did the UN necessarily 'select trainers with sustained experience in human rights standards' or community policing – for instance, training officers came from Zimbabwe and Brazil (Amnesty International 2003: 4; Hasegawa 2003). As a result, in force and firearms sessions, trainers did not teach the basic principles of restraint or proportionality (HRW 2006), an issue made more concerning given that few trainees have experienced democratic policing during their lifetime. Neither did trainers have sufficient knowledge of local law, which meant that they continually imported 'their own [domestic] law, procedure and practice into training' (McDonald 2001: 13). This was profoundly damaging, not least because trainers came from over 30 countries and new recruits had to wade through conflicting information from one session to the next (HRW 2006).[4]

The establishment of the PNTL was, therefore, lacking in effective management, planning and policy development. This culminated in a police force that lacked critical skills and proficiency. While some officers had a degree of professionalism, UN police advisors detailed that over half of the new recruits were incompetent (HRW 2006). The inability of the PNTL to maintain law and order in a democratic way has been identified in various events: in the inappropriate treatment of women, children, and other vulnerable groups; in situations where police have fired live rounds into crowds in an attempt to quell protests; and in the marked increase in alleged cases of professional misconduct, arbitrary detention, mistreatment, rapes, and torture (Hasegawa 2003; HRW 2006; UN 2005c). The continuation of past brutality was an issue consistently raised by interviewees:

> An incident took place in Maubara. There was fighting between local people. When the police arrived, they beat a man up ... The man fainted because he was hit and kicked ... This is not good. It is like the past.
>
> Alerico[5]

> Not long ago, police officers beat a disabled boy, he couldn't speak. He was young, perhaps twelve. They tied him to a tree and burnt him with cigarettes. It was so open. They didn't hide it!
>
> Maria Fatima

> The National Police mimic POLRI [Indonesian Police] in almost every manner from the vehicles they drive, they way they swagger around ...

One of the biggest problems is that they don't have the skills to conduct investigations to a successful outcome, so they resort to violence through frustration and lack of control, to achieve results.

Dave

With a low priority given to bodies of oversight or accountability (HRW 2006; Stanley 2005a; UN 2005c), the police have often been identified as a continuation of the old regime, albeit with different uniforms and badges.[6] In short, the ways in which new state institutions have been built have contributed to further violations in Timor-Leste. For torture victims, these issues have led to continuing feelings of fear regarding those officials who have a remit to protect them.

Embedding global economic inequalities

A great amount of resources and money has been spent in Timor-Leste – UN budgets have totalled over US$1.7 billion and international aid donations have surpassed US$2 billion since 1999 (Neves 2006). Yet most skill and economic benefits have flowed to the hundreds of highly paid international consultants involved in the rebuilding process. Most development assistance has gone to international staff, many of whom are part of 'a new elite cadre of state-building experts who move on to new conflict situations' at the end of their short-term contracts (Charlesworth 2007: 10). Filomena observed:

So, it looks like we are getting lots of money. But, it's a worry economically as most of it is going out of Timor Leste.

The development system followed in Timor-Leste has focused on imported capital and skills rather than on building local talents and resources (George 1995).[7] Similarly, most international aid and loans have reflected Western models of economic development. No more is this apparent than in the actions of the World Bank.

Notwithstanding the history of the World Bank in Timor-Leste (highlighted in Chapter 1), it has assumed a central role in Timor-Leste's economic development. In particular, it supervised the Trust Fund for Timor-Leste (TFET) which was established to corral and distribute money from international donors, it administered the European Commission's donor fund, and it reviewed government planning and expenditures (Bello and Guttall 2006).

While, as detailed above, the World Bank can be charged with implementing reasonable projects in an inappropriate way, it has also embedded structures that are likely to reiterate structural inequalities. Specifically, the World Bank has geared the new economy of Timor-Leste along free-market principles that promote private expansion, foreign investment, and export production.

For instance, in the agricultural sector (that sustains income for 80 per cent of households), farmers have traditionally engaged in bartering or non-monetary exchange of their produce and services. Under the Pilot Agricultural Service Centres (PASC) project, the World Bank encouraged business expansion and monetary profit. Under PASC, farmers pay market prices for equipment and seeds, and are encouraged to increase their yield, for example through the use of high maintenance equipment, hybrid seeds, chemical fertilizers, and pesticides (La'o Hamutuk 2002a). Yet, problems – such as the fact that Timorese terrain that does not suit new technologies, irrigation difficulties, fluctuating market prices, the poor quality of storage facilities, the inability to transport surplus produce (ibid.) – have all made farmer's livelihoods extremely vulnerable.[8] Moreover, cheaper food imports, such as Vietnamese or Thai rice, have flooded local markets and priced out local producers, driving them further into poverty (Bhatia 2005). As Lino lamented:

> We used to be able to sell our rice at the market but that has changed now. Foreign rice is much cheaper, and people couldn't afford to pay our prices. We sold it cheaper but it didn't work out. We are struggling with money now.

The free market model of development has, therefore, made living conditions more difficult for Timorese and food insecurity has become increasingly common (UNDP 2006).

Further problems of Western modes of development can be gleaned from the World Bank's implementation of its CEP scheme in which, as detailed above, sub-districts could decide on their own development priorities. While this scheme had some real successes, and many villages enjoyed new access to quality infrastructure (Moxham 2004), its implementation could undermine principles of participation and transparency. For instance, in Iliomar, in Lautem district, village consultation found strong support for a clean-water system. Yet CEP staff argued that the project was too small and that a larger initiative was required to comply with CEP rules. Staff subsequently suggested, and commenced, a project to repair the main road. Villagers, who argued that they had no need for the road (as they walked between their homes, school, fields, and church), refused to work on the project and the project stalled (La'o Hamutuk 2002b). CEP rules did not, therefore, allow for genuine community consultation and implementation of local demands.

In addition to this, it is evident that the hasty delivery of CEP meant that the political, social, and economic contexts in which projects were implemented were ignored. For example, the scheme also offered micro-credit loans for individuals wishing to establish businesses and thereby invigorate local, rural economies. In reality, as Moxham (2004) identifies, villagers acquired loans to establish their only business option: kiosks to sell small household items (Stanley 2007a). The difficulty was that village kiosk owners could only source similar goods, creating a surplus of products, which village customers did not have the money to buy. World Bank researchers concluded that in 70 per cent of cases, those taking out loans would not make enough money to pay back the original debt (ibid.). Inevitably this will compound a local culture of dependency on international financial institutions.

In summary, the World Bank has engaged in market-led policy making that has intensified the economic-based suffering and insecurities of the Timorese people. While these hastily implemented policies have not necessarily intended to create harms, they have eroded traditional structures of decision-making and labour, and failed to consider the local context of economy and employment. As a result of non-participatory approaches and the limited local access to decision-making, economic structures that are bound to produce financial vulnerability have been rooted within Timor-Leste. Uncertain economic structures, *ad hoc* food access, and unemployment have created new insecurities and violations within villages.

For the Timorese, of course, the choice of whether to engage, or not, with international financial institutions has been limited. In this way, the discourse of state-building (that frequently revolves around ideas of empowerment, development, and human rights) hides structural relations of power and institutionalized subordination.

Strategic state-building: In whose interests?

The building of the new Timorese state has illustrated how neocolonial standards and ideals are employed by international organizations within emerging democracies (Grenfell 2004; Whyte 2007). It is also clear that state-building measures have centralized the power priorities of third-party states, and that certain states have successfully used the state-building context to bolster their own strategic, political, and economic interests. This has been especially apparent in the actions of the Australian government.

Australia was the only country to ever officially recognize Indonesia's annexation of Timor-Leste. Part of the prize for doing so was the Timor Gap Treaty, signed in 1989, in light of which Australia reorganized international maritime boundaries and took control over most oil fields in the Timor Sea. This has become the principal economic issue affecting Timor-Leste. The opportunities for economic reconstruction of Timorese society have rested heavily on negotiations regarding oil reserves between the Timorese and Australian governments.

Timor-Leste argues that the maritime boundary is the midpoint between Timor-Leste and Australia, a claim supported by international law (Bugalski 2004), while Australia argues that the boundary exists at the edge of Australia's continental shelf, approximately 50kms off Timor-Leste's shoreline. In March 2002, shortly before Timor-Leste's independence, Australia withdrew from the International Court of Justice (ICJ) case on the matter and the disagreement remains unresolved. If the ICJ rules in Timor-Leste's favour, as is widely expected, most oil fields would belong solely to Timor-Leste (ibid.; Ishizuka 2004; Schofield 2005).

A number of oil fields have been subject to bilateral negotiations. The biggest, the Bayu-Undan and Greater Sunrise fields, have exemplified the struggle Timor-Leste has faced to secure a sound economic future. Negotiations over the former fields (undertaken through the Timor Sea Treaty signed on 20 May 2002) shifted from an initial Australian offer of an 80:20 split in favour of Timor-Leste to a 90:10 settlement. The agreement was argued by Alexander Downer, then Australia's Foreign Affairs Minister, to be a generous, early 'Christmas present' for the Timorese people (Schofield 2005: 272). The Greater Sunrise field was subject to further intense and protracted negotiations. In 2003, Australia offered Timor-Leste an 18:82 split in favour of Australia. By December 2005, the Greater Sunrise field was settled with an agreement of a 50:50 split. The subsequent Certain Maritime Arrangements in the Timor Sea (CMATS) Treaty, signed in January 2006, prevents any further maritime boundary discussions for fifty years (La'o Hamutuk 2006). However, and perhaps more significantly, Australia appears to have secured all future on-shore processing. It is anticipated that the Australian company, Woodside Petroleum, that has the license to develop the field will pipe all gas to Darwin for processing. This will create an estimated 1,000 new jobs in construction and liquefaction, and will provide significant investment in the Darwin region (Grenfell 2004; Ishizuka 2004).

Resistance from Timorese actors to Australia's actions was quickly suppressed. Accusations from Timorese politicians that Australia was 'stealing oil' were met with Canberra trimming its development aid budget to the country (Schofield 2005). Similarly, local NGOs who were calling for Australia to act according to international maritime principles were faced with AusAid withdrawing all funding from certain groups (Stanley 2007a). Criticisms of the Australian government were therefore subject to economic punishment. One NGO worker commented:

> We've spoken out too. We signed the letter highlighting Australia's position on the oil. We're waiting to see what our punishment will be – hopefully it will not be like 'Forum Tau Matan'.[9] That would be really bad for us.

At the same time, the Australian government has made political capital out of its involvement in Timor-Leste. Involvement in state-building presents a good marketing strategy as countries can bask in the glow of a human rights conscious identity while simultaneously ensuring that their contributions protect and consolidate state power in the region. Thus, Australia has provided between AU$300–400 million in development aid between 1999 and 2005 (Bugalski 2004; Schofield 2005). Yet, during recent negotiations, the Australian government was taking in between US$700,000–US1 million per day from disputed oil reserves (Nevins 2005) and has taken over US$2.1 billion since 1999 (Bugalski 2004; Timor Sea Justice Campaign 2005).

The strategic nature of Australia's 'generosity' to its neighbour has not gone unobserved by victims. As Aderito remarked about the Australian government:

> Well, we saw [during occupation] that they would do anything to access the oil. We see it again now. They happily take our resources even when they know the development of this country is dependent on it.

Income from oil production is key to the development of Timor-Leste. For many Timorese victims, it represents the main route to a peaceful, secure state. Without economic security, many victims contend that the aftermath of torture will be more difficult to cope with.

The personal realities of surviving torture

In Timor-Leste, as Galuh observed, 'You don't have to go very far to see that people are bottled up, twisted'. It is clear that individual victims suffer high levels of post-traumatic stress and severe mental health disorders (Modvig *et al.* 2000). For example, in a study of 48 case notes from the Timorese organization PRADET (Psychosocial Recovery and Development in East Timor), Silove *et al.* (2004) highlighted that almost all service users met the criteria for having an extreme social and mental health need, meeting at least one of five indicators – self harm or being a danger to others; being incapable of self-care; exhibiting bizarre, extreme, or culturally inappropriate behaviour; suffering incapacitating distress and agitation; or having such severe mental incapacity that family or caregivers could not provide adequate care or protection.

During interviews, victims often displayed strong feelings of anger or powerlessness alongside their physical injuries. Eduardo, for instance, commented:

> It makes me feel so bad when I think about what has happened to us. And that nobody really helped us. It hurts me here [here, he pointed to his heart and scrunched his fist]. Things are a bit easier now. I'm not hiding in the mountains but it's still tough.

While Isabel detailed:

> We struggled then. We really suffered. But now, it goes on. Nothing has really changed. But it seems that there is nothing we can do.

Victims also demonstrated intense feelings of fear. Many victims remained anxious about the intentions of Indonesian perpetrators. Given that these perpetrators had not been challenged or devalued, and that they had not acknowledged their previous violations, many victims felt that Indonesian officials might reinvade. As Alberto reflected:

> We lived in fear, especially at night, as that was when they would come to detain you. Every noise that we heard, we wondered if they were coming to get us. I still don't sleep very much at night, it's very difficult to change this behaviour … I am still worried that Indonesia will invade again.

None of the interviewed victims had previously received any assistance for their psychological suffering. The vast majority of victims, with trauma or mental health difficulties, are unable to access the rare (and underfunded) services of PRADET. Most Timorese do not have much choice but to cope with their reality by themselves or with church or community support. As Lino highlighted about dealing with his own suffering:

> I feel bad when I think about it, I feel like I'm going mad. But, there is not much I can do. Who can help me? My suffering is in God's hands.

The fact that victims consistently downplayed their pain and minimized their trauma might be viewed in this light of limited practical support. What choice do victims have but to get on? For example, during interviews, torture victims constantly compared their own personal suffering to that of others – it was not unusual to hear statements like 'I'm lucky to have survived, others didn't' or 'I was beaten but not as severely as [someone else]'. Thus, individual victims downplayed their own individual trauma by linking it to wider social and political experiences.

Despite this, it appeared that most victims continued to struggle with the trauma bubbling away under the surface. Thus, one PRADET worker noted:

> Sometimes, people come [to Timor-Leste] and think that everyone is OK, that people don't look too stressed or hurt. But, trauma is simmering underneath. It emerges in alcoholism, domestic violence and the continued sense of struggle. It is simmering and it may well bubble over when hope begins to dwindle. So far, many victims have been given nothing – there are not enough services, they have not been acknowledged … How long will that last out?

For this worker, past trauma and current social conditions must be understood and addressed if further social problems are to be avoided. Violence, for example, has not magically disappeared from independent Timor-Leste. As detailed above, it has emerged within recent 'troubles' and has remained a significant problem for women and children. For example, Hynes *et al.* (2004) have highlighted that women continue to face regular physical and sexual violence from those known to them.[10] Moreover, the majority of these victims do not seek assistance on the basis that they would be stigmatized and that nothing would be done. In such situations, violence is normalized.[11]

Of course, legacies of violence have intertwined with social conditions of poverty, unemployment, poor housing, limited education, and ill-health. In the wake of independence, Timorese people are faced with 'an unending contest' of development (Fanon 1963: 74). For many victims, their daily realities have deteriorated.

> Victims do not have enough work. They do not have money to send their kids to school. They have no food – it is very difficult for them to get a sack of rice or cooking oil. These people were at the frontline of the Timorese struggle but now their daily life is worse than before.
>
> Maria Fatima

> Now, we continue to suffer. Ex-prisoners cannot afford to send their children to school, some are now handicapped and cannot find work ... some only have broken corrugated iron roofing for shelter, their life conditions are worse than before ... we sacrificed our life for the independence.
>
> Isabel

> Life has not changed much for me. The house is still in disrepair and getting work is even more difficult. We need more jobs.
>
> Alberto

> In the districts, people are starving because the rain hasn't come. The government doesn't want to know about it ... Lots of times, we say we are independent but if you look at the economy or the justice system, then we are not independent.
>
> Maria Afonso

Timor-Leste does not currently have the economic, political, social, psychological, or medical infrastructure to address these problems. In this context, Manuel[12] forcefully argued that assistance had to be viewed as an international responsibility:

> We are disabled, we have poor eye sight, and some people can't walk, all because of the invasion. They made us disabled. Many of us go through pain, and we can't work ... Those who created this war must take responsibility, especially those people that allied with Indonesia to destroy Timor-Leste ... We didn't use guns to fight but we sacrificed our physical bodies to be beaten dreadfully, even to vomit blood.

For him, powerful states have a moral responsibility to provide long-term assistance to the Timorese people. This is a matter of justice.[13]

Evidently, the ongoing social and economic violations experienced by torture victims, and others, in Timor-Leste are a long-term issue. Redistributive justice requires an enduring commitment from a large number of actors. For example, employment skill shortages demand education and training over numerous years. Changes will not occur overnight. Despite the dire conditions in which they live, and the tiredness that they feel in facing these difficulties day after day, this truth is understood and accepted by many victims. At the same time, victims want to see some international and governmental attempt to rectify redistributive injustices. Thus, Martinho stated:

> We don't expect everything to be perfect. We don't expect that we will live like you do overnight. We know it will take time. We have to be patient. But, we want to see some change!

The uncertainties about structural justice in Timor-Leste impacted heavily on victim's thoughts on transitional justice. Social and economic conditions sometimes overshadowed the limited successes of transitional justice bodies, and they often re-emphasized their failures.

> We will get to know more [through the CAVR] but the 'big fish' have not been prosecuted and we live like this. Where is justice? I cannot see it.
>
> Emilia

> How can we feel satisfied with the CAVR or with the courts when we continue to face violence from the police, or when so many people are hungry?
>
> Maria Afonso

> We need justice. We need to find out more about what happened to us. The courts have not done this, and we are waiting for the report from the CAVR. We wait and wait. And, we still need help … our children are not being educated, my roof is broken …
>
> Fransisco

While status disparities remain entrenched, transitional justice bodies (that failed in their limited way to provide or set the ground for redistributive justice) are devalued. It appears that transitional justice 'success' is deeply contextualized by social and political conditions. These injustices, or rights claims, bundle together. If people continue to live with fear, economic insecurity, or violence, the use value of truth commissions or courts is called into question.

Conclusion

This chapter has illustrated that recognition-based injustices have persisted through state-building processes. Timorese people have continued to face denigration, 'othering', and subordination. This has been particularly apparent in their exclusion from democratic activities on the grounds that they are totally 'incapable' or do not fit neatly with the state-builder's *modus operandi*. International attempts to address local issues of capability – for example, through strategic education and training – have been woefully inadequate (and, in the case of the PNTL, they have led to further torture). Ultimately, misrecognitions have dovetailed with participatory injustices. Most Timorese have been 'framed out' as a result of their cultural devaluation; they have not been established as full partners in social life.

It is clear, too, that Timor-Leste was viewed by many 'state-builders' as a blank landscape, a place where new, ahistorical structures and institutions could be built and would thrive. Of course, the UN and World Bank's lack of recognition regarding previous conflicts and traditional decision-making structures culminated with institutions and programmes that were unsustainable. The end result has been catastrophic: from 2006, victims faced further violence and upheaval and Timor-Leste has had to effectively start the process of state-building again. Despite the role of internationals in this 'collapse', their involvement has been hidden and responsibility has been attributed to local failures.

Alongside these recent 'troubles', victims continue to cope with the daily realities of social and economic violations of rights. These redistributive injustices permeate every aspect of life for Timorese people. Torture victims suffer various degradations – they cannot access appropriate health or psychological services; they endure poor housing and sanitation; their children often do not receive education; they struggle to find and maintain employment; they continue to face interpersonal violence; and so on. While these injustices are intensely personal, they have their basis in regional and global structures. As this chapter argues, the continuing injustices experienced by torture victims cannot be explained without regard to the detrimental actions of other powerful actors, including the UN, the World Bank, and external states.

International state-building in Timor-Leste has eroded the legitimacy of new state institutions and intensified divisions within local communities. This has occurred for two main reasons. First, internationals have been negligent in the processes and practices of state-building. International actors have imposed Western 'one size fits all' models of development, overlooked capacities, excluded locals from participation, and created unsustainable institutions. Second, international actors have reconfigured social, economic, and political priorities in terms of their own interests rather than local needs. Individual state-builders have benefited from short-term, high pay contracts; international financial institutions have embedded market-led economic programmes; and Australia has ensured its access to oil reserve production and profits in the Timor Sea.

The end results of these practices are already becoming apparent. Together with the emergence of conflict in the country, there has been a deepening of inequalities and the population has become more socially and economically insecure. Moreover, the limited successes of transitional justice bodies have been further downgraded. It would seem, then, that the positive discourse on state-building (that emphasizes human rights, sustainability, and empowerment) has not been reflected in practice. The building of the new state in Timor-Leste has ultimately reiterated dominant structural relations of power. In this context, torture victims have limited opportunities to live a 'good life'.

9 Looking to the Future

Torture victims in Timor-Leste have experienced forms of violence that, for those of us fortunate to live in less repressive states, is unimaginable and incomprehensible. For many victims, fear and brutality have dominated their lives and torture has been just one part of a wider repression; victims have been made vulnerable to a spiral of victimization – for instance, they have watched as their loved ones were killed, their homes have been destroyed, they have continued to endure societal and interpersonal violence, and they have lost opportunities to gain an education or to work.

Torture has intertwined with other forms of physical and structural violence, leaving a wake of problems and injustices. Torture is traumatizing on personal and secondary levels and its physical, psychological and societal legacy continues to impact on individuals, their families, and communities. Most interviewees for this book downplayed their violation, arguing that they were often the 'lucky ones', yet they also exposed their anger, sense of powerlessness, continuing fear, and the lack of support for their mental and physical health. These victims do not occupy a 'safe space'. While they have had little choice but to cope with such sequelae themselves, trauma bubbles away and intensifies with deteriorating social conditions.

Against these realities of life, this book has provided a (limited) space for some victims to speak about the injustices against them. Building on the arguments from Fraser (1997, 2003, 2005), these experiences have been identified under three main tenets. First, that torture victims are often subject to a lack of recognition or to harmful misrecognitions, and subsequently they are placed outside of general concern or protection. Second, that victims are commonly excluded from democratic legal and political processes. These limits on interventions can occur due to lack of capability (such as poverty or limited education or societal disadvantage) or as a consequence of being excluded from claims-making processes. And, third, that victims will regularly have a bundling of rights claims linked to their direct suffering of violence and to their disadvantaged structural location. These injustices may be connected to localized relations of power, but they also reflect wider conditions that cut across national borders.

In dealing with such injustices, torture victims frequently pursue acknowledgement; they want their identities to be upwardly revalued and made respectable or given authority and, simultaneously, that their perpetrators be culturally devalued. Further, victims want to be represented and able to take part in democratic decision-making. They seek the availability of institutions that enable rights claims to be met and that offer 'real' protection and access for victims. Finally, torture victims also want to be established as full partners in social life. They want the arrangements of structural and institutional disadvantage, within and across diverse societies, to be addressed. The question for this book has been: might transitional justice mechanisms provide such just measures for victims?

Transitional justice 'from below'

There remains something of a feel-good factor about truth and justice bodies. The dominant account of transitional justice mechanisms are that they are fundamental to the progress of peace and reconciliation; these bodies are presented as being benign, profound, much needed, and undoubtedly progressive. Consequently, transitional justice ideas, notions, and practices are now promoted across the globe as part of the 'toolkit' to deal with past violence in varied countries – there is something of a 'mini-industry' emerging around these norms – and transitional justice bodies are now almost a compulsory response to any country emerging from conflict.

This is, perhaps, because they are connected to all kinds of positive outcomes including exposing denials, shaming and holding perpetrators to account, deterring future offenders, healing victims and their families, reforming institutions, and redefining societal norms and conditions around respect and dignity for all. On paper, they offer many of the things that torture victims want. Given such potential outcomes, these bodies have found ready support from the UN, powerful states, non-governmental organizations, academics, practitioners, and many victims.

In the case of Timor-Leste, just one transitional justice mechanism – the Commission for Reception, Truth and Reconciliation (CAVR) – has contributed to certain aspects of 'doing justice' for victims. This truth commission worked hard in difficult social conditions to communicate and engage with thousands of people. Its culturally resonant practices, operating from the bottom-up, made sense to Timorese communities. As a result, many victims view that the CAVR was able to highlight hidden truths, to provide acknowledgement, and to begin building a national history contextualized by global relations of power. At a more local level, these processes encouraged Timorese people to identify and re-engage with others; to better understand how local victims suffered and why local perpetrators acted as they did. These face-to-face encounters linked people together, sometimes for the first time in years.

Yet, these instances of recognition and participation have been undermined by a range of injustices associated with this transitional justice body. Victims found that they were framed out of recognition as a result of: the CAVR's mandate, rules, and institutional deficits; their limited capacity to participate (due to their lack of awareness about the institution; the limited support offered to them in relating their experiences; or their structural location that made participation difficult or impossible); and, their belief that perpetrators were being 'protected' while their needs were accorded a lesser priority. In these ways the Commission did not ensure safe access to justice for victims. Besides, any advances of truth-telling, acknowledgement, or reconciliation sustained through CAVR practices have been dramatically undermined by the distancing response by local politicians and international actors to the CAVR report.

This situation has been made worse by the failings of all other transitional justice mechanisms to provide justice. The Ad Hoc Court in Jakarta, the serious crimes process in Dili, and the Truth and Friendship Commission have each been condemned by victims.[1] These bodies were, to a greater or lesser extent, associated with a range of injustices, including that they:

- implemented overly restrictive mandates and rules (that did not recognize the vast majority of victims and thereby placed them outside legal protection);
- closed representational justice down by excluding local populations from participation (these bodies were established without local consultation; many victims did not know that these processes existed; and local workers were often ignored);
- maximized the culpability of the Timorese population and shielded Indonesian officials from criticism (offering the latter an opportunity to reconfigure a new, positive global identity);
- failed to provide conditions of legal protection or due process for Timorese participants either as victims (who were placed in situations in which they were subject to further myth-making, denigration, intimidation, and violence) or perpetrators (who experienced inadequate defence standards);
- offered no opportunities for redistributive justice measures for victims (they failed to offer reparations or other institutional changes).

Taken together, these transitional justice bodies were frequently damaged by the lack of political will to cooperate with procedures, provide sufficient funds or respond to recommendations. As a result of time limitations, mandate, powers and skewed practices, they failed to recognize most victims and most perpetrators (and they almost wholly ignored the historical, social, institutional, and structural conditions through which violations emerge). Complex experiences of victimization and perpetration were sidelined in favour of individualistic, smooth, and fast processes that were dominated by

'professionals' and associated simplified, individualistic categories of violence and suffering. Through this approach, transitional justice was severely
undermined among local populations.

The discourse and practice of transitional justice was also co-opted by
powerful actors to pursue strategies of dominance. While these mechanisms
made little challenge to the institutionalized and structural relations of marginalization and deprivation that give rise to human rights victimization,
transititional justice institutions were often manipulated by those who enjoyed
most power and influence and who sought to advance their own myths,
rather than truths, about conflict. In this way, these transitional justice institutions have not set the ground for emancipatory conditions; rather than
enabling victims to express their needs or to live a 'good life', they have further
constrained victims (Young 1990). Quite simply, with the exception of the
CAVR which has provided some positive outcomes, these transitional justice
measures have become part of the problem faced by Timorese populations

Reflecting torture

Indeed, it could be argued that these transitional justice mechanisms have
engaged in a continuum of injustices that reiterates many of the underpinnings of torture. For instance, it is clear that transitional justice processes
have been used to consolidate the domination of the Indonesian state,
undermine due process for Timorese victims, and, in some instances, spread
fear, terror, and a sense of hopelessness among victims and the wider
Timorese population. These mechanisms have placed most Timorese victims
in a space of 'bare life' in which they enjoy no legal or political protection
(Agamben 1995). The previous repression – reflecting the contempt, dehu-
manization, and vulnerability of the Timorese people – has progressed into
new injustices that are based on impunity, disregard and 'othering'.

Moreover, injustices have evolved with the continued management over
victims' language and 'truth'. Most torture victims have not been offered a
space to communicate their pain and, as a result, no one will know about
their violation. Through court processes, victims' talk has also been controlled by principal perpetrators. In other circumstances, victims have been
denigrated by the new Timorese elite who have criticized claims for justice
amid attempts to foster friendship initiatives with their old opponents. As a
group, torture victims have been repeatedly silenced.

Of course, albeit with some exceptions (such as the *Ludji* case), these justice responses have not been directly violent and the majority of transitional
justice workers have been well intentioned and have worked against the odds.
However, the psycho-social underpinnings are on the same continuum. The
structures, policies, and practices of these transitional justice institutions
have re-established injustice in Timor-Leste. Further, this injustice has been
met with indifference and a lack of firm action from powerful international
institutions and states.

This situation is made worse by the fact that these actions have been undertaken in the spirit of human rights, and a discourse that emphasizes the welfare and interests of victims. Past injustices have continued and consolidated within the domains of legitimate, seemingly progressive institutions. Yet, when victims raise their concerns – that transitional justice institutions have become part of the problem rather than the solution of injustice – they are depicted as needy, too demanding, or unreasonable. Alternatively, their claims just go ignored. Thus, transitional justice is used to hide violations and injustice and to isolate victims, while demonstrating an apparent compliance with human rights norms. In this sense, it reflects the foundations of stealth torture techniques.

The convergence of injustices

These injustices of transitional justice have, of course, been dovetailed with those of social injustice. The legacy of violence endured by victims has intertwined with social conditions of poverty, insecurity, unemployment, poor housing, limited education and ill-health. And, the uncertainties about these conditions have impacted heavily on victims' thoughts on transitional justice.

The lack of transitional justice attention to issues of social justice has been consistently criticized by victims. With the exception of limited actions – such as the reparations offered by CAVR or the prosecutions within the serious crimes process – these mechanisms have missed many opportunities to challenge redistributive injustices or to prime states for change. In this way, they have not addressed the social, institutional, or structural factors that are so often conducive to violations of torture in the first instance.

This is not to say that victims contend that transitional justice mechanisms should be responsible for dealing with all redistributive problems. That is by no means the case, and victims are quite aware that these are political problems. However, victims make clear that any transitional justice success is drastically undermined when social and economic conditions are not improved. For them, transitional justice has to be dovetailed with institutional and redistributive change (Boraine 2006). For this to occur, the Timorese state and international actors must create new programmes that will establish victims as full partners in social life and that will prevent future violence.

The signs for the future, however, are not particularly hopeful. As highlighted in the previous chapter, the international state-building interventions in Timor-Leste have not tended to reflect the interests and priorities of the Timorese population. Western models of statehood have been superimposed over the specific historical, social, cultural, and political context in Timor-Leste. Internationals have frequently excluded local populations, overlooked traditional structures, and disregarded local capacity. As a consequence of international distancing, interventions have also structured local organizations in non-democratic or unsustainable ways. Further, despite the rhetoric of state-building that connects projects to notions of rights, sustainability, and development, interventions have tended to embed dominant relations of power into newly constituted structures. Thus, international workers have benefited from short-term contracts; international financial organizations have pursued strategies and programmes that have not reflected local needs for sustainable development; and certain states, such as Australia, have continued to enjoy the benefits from local oil reserves.

These social, economic, and political frames of state-building, albeit sometimes well-intentioned, have reflected Western systems and hasty, short-term administrative procedures. In marginalizing the context of local structures and needs, they have already begun to develop into long-term problems of deepening inequalities, financial vulnerability and dependency, as well as increased insecurity and violence among the Timorese population. They have shaped conditions under which further harms and violations have and will occur. Against this setting of injustices, the usefulness of truth commissions or courts is, again, called seriously into question.

Rethinking transitional justice

In detailing this 'view from below' in Timor-Leste, this work raises significant questions about how transitional justice – that stands for something beneficial and protective – can be applied in such harmful or distressing ways. The experiences of Timorese torture victims have highlighted that transitional justice measures, implemented and managed with strong international backing (and, in some instances, coercion) have not just fallen short of the ideal. Rather, they have recreated the divisions and inequalities that led to harms like torture. In such circumstances, when the discourse of transitional justice is articulated to provide a cover for further violence, the whole value of democratization, the rule of law, and human rights is called into question. In these terms, transitional justice is just another cynical tool for powerful actors to maintain their dominance.

As highlighted in Chapter 4, these critiques and fundamental concerns can be linked to other case studies of transitional justice. Yet, the fact that truth commissions and trials often fall way short of the ideal has not prevented their global growth and popularity; the knowledge of these deficiencies has not challenged the belief in their fundamental efficacies. Moreover, they are continually implemented as the sole official response to past violence. In these respects, the dominant view is that transitional justice mechanisms have just suffered from 'teething problems' and that all that is required is to readjust how truth and justice is done, and to implement the right institutions at the right time. It is, perhaps, just an unfortunate issue of experimentation in the *realpolitik* domain of transitional justice.

At the centre of that 'experiment', however, stand the victims – individuals who suffered brutal violence, who endure a multitude of social inequalities, and who, now, face new harms in the name of justice. Not surprisingly, many victims argued that injustice is intensified by transitional justice done badly – that is, it would have been better if these institutions had not existed at all. For any participant or bystander these realities are disconcerting. If transitional justice causes more problems rather than solving injustices, then should we just abandon the transitional justice project altogether?

For this author, the answer to that question is 'no'. This book has not set out to undermine the pursuit of transitional justice altogether, rather it has worked to acknowledge the deep structural difficulties that must be challenged to ensure that victims of torture, alongside other victims, receive the recognition, participation, and redistribution that they crave. It has sought to raise questions about where the transitional justice project is going – and how practitioners, both locals and internationals, need to think in 'a more nuanced way' about their own role as well as the nature of programmes they pursue (Lutz 2006: 335).

The issues raised, then, are that those who implement truth commissions or courts need to do far more to ensure that these limited institutions are: (i) devised and operated in ways that ensure that recognition and participatory injustices are significantly challenged – that is, they undertake their limited tasks in a decent, thorough and inclusive manner; and, (ii) dovetailed with other programmes that implement redistributive change – future transitional justice mechanisms must be implemented alongside a firm economic, political, and strategic commitment to see justice done. Without attempts to address these multiple layers of justice, transitional justice is, at best, a sop, and, at worst, a tool of domination.

The responsibility to support transitional justice has to go further. In particular, it is evident that future initiatives must do more to critically engage and include local people – whom they serve – in their planning and programmes. The mechanisms for Timor-Leste frequently operated in exclusionary and impositional ways and led to deep dissatisfaction among victims. The issue, therefore, is to ask: who are these institutions for? And, what do local people require in terms of justice? These questions must be clarified at every stage of transitional justice programmes. The answers will, inevitably, make processes much harder for workers – for instance, it is more difficult and time consuming for institutions to follow culturally relevant, inclusive practices; or for programmes to ensure access to vulnerable or hard-to-reach groups; or for international workers to engage in deeper capacity-building to support and develop local skills.

It may sometimes mean that local models of justice – that include traditional processes of dealing with conflict or unrest at community levels – take prominence while Western models – such as the use of individualized prosecutions or legal classifications – become less dominant. Whatever the particulars of such specific models, the role of internationals should revolve around reacting to, and supporting, local requirements in ways that enhance human rights ideals. How these inclusionary practices might be undertaken will vary from country to country; they will require long-term, truly hybridized ventures; and they will often require a challenge to dominant global relations of power.

Related to this, it is clear that transitional justice initiatives must be addressed in context. That is, these measures cannot be operated in isolation from other initiatives of development and social justice. The success of transitional justice initiatives is dependent on and contextualised by other institutions, programmes, and interventions (Orentlicher 2007). In order for justice to emerge, there has to be different opportunities for victims (Roht-Arriaza 2006). This requires the development of new democratic institutions and groups, locally and internationally, to build the diverse elements of justice.

This point is reflected in the fact that victims often participate in these ventures because they want to effect a response: they seek acknowledgement; they want to upwardly revalue their status or downgrade the status of their perpetrators; they want compensation, financial assistance, or medical or social help; they want to find out where their loved ones are buried; they want to establish memorials or days of remembrance; or they want assistance to gain employment, training, or education. Thus, if victims are engaged, we must also prepare for their demands and bear responsibility to effect action. It cannot be expected, for instance, that allowing them to tell their story will be enough.

In short, in implementing transitional justice mechanisms, we must be attentive not just to from where the transition is going, but also to where the transition is going, and how we might build a more democratic situation (Stanley 1996). Transitional justice institutions operate as a fulcrum between the past and the future. This is a vital issue for consideration since if victims continue to live with fear, economic insecurity, or violence, truth commissions and courts will have lesser value. Thus, we need to prepare for a long-term commitment to justice – one that does not just provide partial recognition, but also sets the ground for just institutions that provoke deeper social transformations.

Towards social change

In building these arguments, the value of this book is that of a 'deep' recognition; it is an act of solidarity. It attempts to bolster the idea that we are implicated in each others lives (Butler 2004) and to progress the stance that the first act to take against human rights violations is one of identification – with those who have been victimized and with the broader social and structural contexts in which violations are allowed to thrive. This approach reflects the degree of hope, espoused by Giroux (2002: 160), that:

> Pedagogy, economic justice and cultural recognition are central to the
> goal of creating a world in which democratic principles provide fertile

ground for spreading the values of human rights, the rule of law, and social justice as a way of connecting people of all cultures and places, not merely through the abstractions of theory but through the everyday, place-based experiences that shape their lives.

The recognition of commonalities, as well as a critical consciousness, are what enable individuals to take what may be construed as bold steps to progress social, political and economic change, and to take actions that demonstrate care for others (S. Cohen 2001; Giroux 2002).

Accordingly, this book demonstrates the complexities of human rights perpetration and the diverse forms of suffering that ensue. In doing so, it makes clear that those who suffer human rights violations have the right to both truth and justice. This is a stance based on a transformative recognition (Butler 2004), not just for the struggles that continue in Timor-Leste, but also to those that will duly 'flourish' in future 'brutal regimes' (Huggins *et al.* 2002: 18).

Thus, this book, albeit limited, has been an attempt to stand on the side of victims, to challenge the disengagement of onlookers, and to highlight that we are each implicated in the lives of others. Timorese victims continue to demand justice for the brutalities inflicted against them – their ongoing struggles expose profound injustices. In a period in which internationals continually demand accountability for gross human rights violations, they have to be prepared for all of the consequences that this position might entail. If powerful states and mainstream international institutions wish to create a global human rights culture they cannot continue to renege on the issue of preventing violations from occurring in the first instance; nor can they ignore these flaws of contemporary transitional justice practice.

Appendix
Recognizing Torture in the Serious Crimes Process

This appendix lists the 26 Serious Crimes Unit (SCU) indictments containing torture and illustrates their progression, or otherwise, through the Special Panels. Key points:

- There are 121 individuals are connected to torture in SCU indictments. Of these, eight feature as torturers in more than one indictment.
- The indictments listed here focus on acts of torture and those indicted for torture. However, these torture charges were entwined with a range of gross human rights violations, and often linked to murder. Consequently, some indictments charged numerous men with a range of offences, of which torture formed a part. For instance, in the indictment against Siagian *et al.* (18/2003), 57 defendants were charged with a range of violations. Of these 57, just five defendants were charged with torture.
- Some individuals were initially indicted for torture and then the charge was 'dropped'. This occurred for various reasons including that counts were withdrawn by prosecutors or there was a 're-evaluation' of charges by judges. These cases are included here in order to illustrate the impact of prosecutorial and court practices on torture charges.
- There have been 17 individuals prosecuted and convicted for torture. One of these, Pereira (*Pereira* (34/2003)), was convicted for persecution however this charge revolved around torture and other violations.
- Torture has been proven in just five of the eleven cases that came before the Panels – *Marques et al.* (09/2000), *Lolotoe* (04/2001), *Soares* (11/2003), *Mesquita et al.* (28/2003) and *Pereira (34/2003)*.
  Of the remaining six cases: Pedro (*Pedro (01/2001)*) had his count of torture, as well as a murder charge, dropped by prosecutors; Correia (*Correia (19/2001)*) pleaded guilty to inhumane acts and the prosecution team, sensing that the prosecution evidence was inadequate, withdrew the charges of murder and torture; the court intervened at a preliminary stage

in *Sufa* (4a/2003) stating that the facts alleged in the indictment 'did not sufficiently support the charge of torture' and that the seven accused should instead be charged with inhumane acts; *Morreira* (29/2003) culminated in a complete acquittal of the defendant as two key prosecution witnesses were declared by the court to be 'completely unconvincing'; Maubere (*Maubere* (23/2003)) was acquitted of charges of torture and forced disappearance although the material facts were 'requalified' in court by the judges and he was subsequently found guilty of murder; and Soares (*Soares* (7a/2002)) was similarly acquitted of a torture charge, but convicted on a second count of murder.

With regards to 15 other torture cases, no one was brought before the Special Panels. Most torture indictees remain at large and are presumed to be in Indonesia.

(9/2000) *Marques* et al. *(Los Palos)*

Torture indictees: Joni Marques; Joao da Costa; Mautersa Moniz; Gilberto Fernandes.

Outcome: The first two indictees were convicted on a range of violations and were each sentenced to 33 years and 4 months (this was later reduced to 25 years in line with local law); the latter two received four years and five years respectively for their involvement in torture (judgement, 11 December 2001).

This indictment charged 11 men with seven counts (encompassing 13 murders, deportation, persecution, and torture). The specific count of torture related to the activities of four men in the torture and subsequent murder of Evaristo Lopes. The victim was beaten with iron rods, punched, kicked, stamped on, stripped to his underwear and an iron rod was pushed into his genitals as he was being questioned. He was then hit with an electrical cable, stabbed with a knife, had parts of his body mutilated, and his hair was cut. Finally, his throat was cut and, thereafter, he died. While the violence was brutal, the court also made the point that the cutting of hair was an act of psychological torture.

(1/2001) *Pedro aka Geger*

Torture indictee: Francisco Pedro.

Outcome: Pleaded guilty and convicted on counts of inhumane acts, murder, and attempted murder. Sentenced to eight years (judgement, 14 April 2005).

Pedro was initially indicted on two counts of murder, one attempted murder, one torture, and one inhumane act. The torture count related to the alleged involvement of the accused in the torture of eight individuals at Balibo Fort. Pedro, and others, had kicked, punched, and beaten the victims with sticks for about 30 minutes. Over four years (2001–5), prosecutors continually amended the indictment and eventually withdrew the count of torture and one count of murder.

(4a/2001) *Da Silva, (4b/2001) Leite (4c/2001) and Fereira (Lolotoe)*

Torture indictees: Joao Franca da Silva; Sabino Gouveia Leite; Jose Cardoso Fereira.

Outcome: The first two indictees pleaded guilty to torture and imprisonment charges and subsequently received sentences of five and three years respectively (judgements, 5 and 7 December 2002). The last indictee received a sentence of 12 years for his involvement in imprisonment, torture, inhumane acts, rape, and murder (judgement, 5 April 2003).

The *Lolotoe* case illustrates the experiences of four torture victims. Bendito da Costa was detained and severely beaten; Adoa Manuel suffered severe beatings and had his ear cut; Jose Gouveia Leite was cut and beaten over a period of weeks; Mario Goncalves was beaten by over 30 militia members, attacked with a machete, and forced to eat his ear. Prosecutors charged this latter event as two counts – of torture and inhumane acts – to make a point about severity. At trial, the judges agreed and it was held that the act of cutting off an ear was torture while forcing a man to eat his own flesh was an inhumane act.

(19/2001) *Correia*

Torture indictee: Abilio Mendez Correia.

Outcome: Correia pleaded guilty to inhumane acts and was sentenced to three years. Having served over two years awaiting trial, he was immediately granted conditional release.

Correia was initially indicted with murder, torture, and inhumane acts. The murder count was withdrawn by prosecutors due to lack of evidence. The torture count relates to Correia's alleged involvement in the beating of Mariano da Costa. Torture was not substantiated and this count was also withdrawn (judgement, 29 March 2004). Despite the severity of the charges against him, Correia progressed through a community reconciliation process in the CAVR.

(7/2002) *Sutrisno* et al. *and (7a/2002) Soares*

Torture indictees: Lt Sutrisno; Asis Fontes; Joao Baptista; Vitalis Fernandes; Marito LeloBere Moreira; Jose Soares; Humberto Lopes; Martinho Afonso; Manuel [last name unknown]; Salvador Soares.

Outcome: The first nine indictees are at large, presumed in Indonesia. Salvador Soares was found guilty of two murders and sentenced to ten years and six months.

All 10 men were indicted on the torture and murder of Reuben Soares and the murder of Domingos Pereira, both UN workers. Following the arrest of militia member Salvador Soares, the charges were separated. Salvador Soares was found not guilty on the charge of torture. The court declared that torture had to 'be accompanied by an intention ... to torture'. As such ... 'an action primarily aimed at causing the death of a person cannot be regarded as torture' (judgement, 9 December 2003, s222). This judgement works against the definitions of torture in Special Panels for Serious Crimes (SPSC) regulations.

(8/2002) *Gonsalves* et al. *(Atabae)*

Torture indictees: Paulo Gonsalves; Marcelino Leto Bili Purificasao; Rosalino Pires.
    Outcome: At large, presumed in Indonesia.
    The three indictees were charged with 14 counts of multiple rapes, torture, and persecution. Over months, the 11 female victims suffered abduction, illegal detention, rapes, and beatings. Prosecutors argued that this was undertaken systematically as part of the interrogation and punishment of the women. Prosecutors charged torture and rape together as a way to test the connection between torture and sexual violence.

(11/2002) *Sarmento* et al.

Torture indictees: Vidal Doutel Sarmento; Filomeno Brito; Antonio Doutel Sarmento.
    Outcome: At large, presumed in Indonesia.
    This indictment accuses five commanders responsible for hundreds of militia members. Together, they face 38 counts of murder, attempted murder, torture, persecution, imprisonment, inhumane acts, forcible transfer, and deportation. The torture charges, directed against the three men, relate to the restraining, beating, electroshocking, and burning of three victims.

(2/2003) *Siagian* et al. *(Cailaco)*

Torture indictees: Burhanuddin Siagian; Lt. Sutrisno; Joao da Silva Tavares; Mahalan Agus Salim; Paulo Gonsalves; Francisco Viegas Bili Ato; Feliciano Mau Bere; Manuel Mali Lete; Gustavo Soares; Arlindo Bere Dasi; Yeohanis Loe Dasi.
    Outcome: At large, presumed in Indonesia.
    This indictment charges 32 defendants with 16 counts including abduction, imprisonment, torture, persecution, forcible transfer and murder. Eleven men are charged with six counts of torture for the severe beatings of 13 individuals, three of whom were killed as a result.

(4/2003) *Cloe* **et al.,** *(4a/2003) Sufa, (4b/2003) Beno and (4c/2003) Metan*

Torture indictees: Anton Lelan Sufa; Agostinho Cloe; Agostinho Cab; Lazarus Fuli; Lino Beno; Anton Lelan Simao; Domingos Metan; Lazarus Tael.

Outcome: Charges withdrawn against Lazarus Tael. The remaining men were convicted on inhumane acts and murder charges, and received sentences of between four and seven years.

All eight were initially indicted with the murders of Anton Beti and Leonardo Anin and the torture of Fransisco Beto. Beto had been tied to a bamboo tree and beaten and kicked for approximately 30 minutes by militia members. The Panels found that these acts did not sufficiently support the charge of torture. Following this, the prosecutor amended the indictment and charged the indictees with inhumane acts. Three indictees – Cab, Simao, and Metan – were not eventually indicted or convicted for this new charge although they were convicted of murder (judgements, 16 and 25 November 2004).

(6/2003) *Lopes de Carvalho* **et al.** *(Mahidi Militia)*

Torture indictees: Cancio Lopes de Carvalho; Vasco da Cruz; Marcelino Beremali; Domingos Alves.

Outcome: At large, presumed in Indonesia.

This indictment contains 27 counts (including murder, persecution, imprisonment, disappearances, inhumane acts, and torture) against 22 accused. Three counts of torture are recorded, detailing prolonged detention, severe beatings, and the burning of five victims. One victim, Alviro Tilman, was shot dead while trying to escape.

(9/2003) *Manek* **et al.** *(Laksaur militia)*

Torture indictees: Egidio Manek; Maternus Bere; Pedro Teles; Henrikus Mali; Cosmas Amaral; Alipio Gusmao; Domingos Mali; Joaquim Berek; Olivio Tatoo Bau; Americo Mali; Zito da Silva.

Outcome: At large, presumed in Indonesia.

In this indictment, 14 men are charged with 51 counts in relation to murder, attempted murder, disappearance, torture, rape, persecution, and deportation. Of those counts, 12 relate to the torture of 45 victims by 11 indictees. Described torture includes severe beatings, stabbings, suffocation, cuttings, the pulling out of fingernails, starvation, and death threats. The indictment also charges indictees with the rape of four women. In these events, female independence supporters were questioned and then raped. The victims allegedly wanted a torture charge to be brought but the SCU did not progress the claim.

(11/2003) *Marcelino Soares*

Torture indictee: Marcelino Soares.

Outcome: Convicted on charges of torture, persecution, and murder. Sentenced to 11 years.

Soares was charged and convicted on three counts of murder, torture, and persecution. The torture count relates to the torture of three detainees who were severely beaten, cut, and burnt. One victim, Rafael de Jesus Arnaral, managed to escape through a window; a second, Felipe de Sousa, was released with the assistance of his soldier cousin; the third, Luis Dias Soares, was beaten to death and buried in an unmarked grave. The judgement (11 December 2003: 4) details that Marcelino Soares 'was aware that the death of Luis would occur in the ordinary course of events as a result of the severe injuries inflicted'. This runs against the *Soares* (7a/2002) judgement that argued that knowledge of impending death would rule out a conviction of torture.

(14/2003) *Sedyono* et al. *(Second Covalima)*

Torture indictees: Lt Col. Achmad Mas Agus; Lt Col. (Pol.) Gatot Subiyaktoro; Lt Sugito; Lt Widodo; Lt Supoyo; Leonito Cardoso; Lt Col. Lilik Koeshardianto.

Outcome: At large, presumed in Indonesia.

This indictment details 31 counts against 16 individuals and, among other violations, encompasses the massacre on the Suai Church and the Laktos Massacre. There are six counts of torture that affected 46 listed victims. Torture is linked to severe beatings, suffocation, cuttings, mutilation, extraction of fingernails, forced nakedness, death threats, and forcing victims to violate each other. It is also connected to mass tortures – such as the attack on villages with machetes and swords – as well as the murder of individual victims. The violation of torture is presented as one element of broader systematic violations undertaken against whole communities.

(15/2003) *Ermelindo Soares* et al.

Torture indictees: Ermelindo Loeasa Soares; Albino Da Cruz; Yohannes Loe Dasi; Frederico M Pires; Agustino Manu Bere.

Outcome: At large, presumed in Indonesia.

There are seven counts against the indictees, including five counts of rape, one of torture, and one of deportation. The indictment revolves around the extensive rapes, over prolonged periods of time, of five women. Each indictee is charged with the rape and torture of an individual victim. SCU prosecutors argued that the indictment was built as a test case.

(18/2003) *Siagian* et al. *(Maliana)*

Torture indictees: TNI Sgt Domingos dos Santos; TNI Sgt Juliao Lopes; Sgt Mau Buti; Antonio de Jesus; Inacio De Concencao.

Outcome: At large, presumed in Indonesia.

This indictment presents 14 counts (11 murder, two persecution, one torture) against 57 defendants. The torture counts, involving five defendants, refers to the beating of two victims, Manuel Pinto Tilman and Abilio Cardoso. This is also linked to a murder charge in which the victims were taken to a gully, shot, and then stabbed.

(23/2003) *Maubere*

Torture indictee: Rusdin Maubere.

Outcome: Convicted of murder and sentenced to three years.

Maubere was initially indicted for the torture and forced disappearance of André de Oliveira. In court it was proven that Oliveira's injuries were so serious that he died on the night of the attack and his body was buried in a shallow grave. For unknown reasons, the body was not found when an exhumation was conducted. The judges found that the perpetrator had beaten the victim in a way that would inevitably cause death from injuries. Following this, they acquitted Maubere of torture and forced disappearance but then 'requalified' the material facts and found Maubere guilty of homicide. As they argue (judgement, 5 July 2004: 17), 'the norm that punishes homicide … consumes the protection that is sought after in the crime of torture'.

(24/2003) *De Carvalho* et al.

Torture indictees: Lt Agus Yuli; Antonio Pinto; Mario Malekat; Mateus de Carvalho; Mateus Guterres; Manuel da Silva; Lino 'Watulari'; Gaspar da Silva; Florindo Malimeta; Domingos Beremau; Pedro Sousa; Domingos Teebuti; Mateus Malimeta.

Outcome: At large, presumed in Indonesia.

Four, out of 18, counts relate to torture. The first is based on the torture of Luis Dias Soares, Rafael de Jesus Amaral, and Felipe de Sousa, as featured in the *Soares* (11/2003) indictment. The second count, of the torture of Thomas Ximenes and Sebastião Gusmao, also forms the basis of the *Mesquita* (28/2003) prosecution. A third count relates to the torture of Mantus de Araujo and Martinho Vidal, which underpins the *Morreira* (29/2003) prosecution. The final count relates to the torture of Estevao Pereira and Agostinho Carvalho, who were interrogated, beaten, and killed. Despite their bodies being recovered, their deaths were not recognized in a count of murder.

(28/2003) *Mesquita* et al.

Torture indictees: Alarico Mesquita; Florindo Morreira; Domingos Amati; Fransisco Matos; Laurindo da Costa; Laurenco Tavares; Mateus Guterres; Angelino da Costa.

Outcome: All men were convicted on torture charges. The first four indictees were also convicted on persecution charges. Sentences ran from five years to six years and eight months.

The eight defendants were charged with beating Thomas Ximenes, 'until blood came out of his mouth and nose' and Sebastião Gusmao, until he fell unconscious. The judges concluded that the collective force of the beating ensured that it reached the torture threshold (judgement 6 December 2004). Defence counsel and some court observers argued that this violence, while undoubtedly traumatic for victims, did not reach this threshold.

(29/2003) *Morreira*

Torture indictee: Florindo Morreira.

Outcome: Acquitted on torture and murder charges.

Morreira (who was convicted in the *Mesquita* (28/2003) case) was indicted with two counts of murder and torture which were related to the beating and stabbing to death of Martinho Vidal and Mantus de Araujo. The case culminated in a complete acquittal of the defendant as two key prosecution witnesses were declared by the court to be 'completely unconvincing' (judgement, 19 May 2004). The prosecution team had previously tried to withdraw the case, a request that had been rejected.

(33/2003) *Hutadjulu* et al.

Torture indictees: Richard Hutadjulu; Karel Polla; Irwan (last name unknown); Igidio Sarmento; Manuel Ariate; Faustino dos Santos; Domingos Alaguia; Adelino Freitas; Domingos Filipe.

Outcome: At large, presumed in Indonesia.

There were 17 men indicted on 14 counts (of murder, inhumane acts, torture, and persecution). The two counts of torture relate to the arrest, interrogation, kicking, beating, crushing, cutting, electroshock, burning, intimidation, and shooting of five victims.

(34/2003) *Pereira*

Torture indictee: Francisco Pereira.

Outcome: Pereira was sentenced to three years for the crimes of attempted murder and persecution.

Pereira was indicted with murder and persecution charges. The persecution count reflected the detention, assault, torture, and murder of five victims in

Covalima. Pereira was found to have arrested, beaten, cut the hair, kicked, and blinded victims with chemicals. The court held that the 'prolonged unjustified beatings, humiliations, threats and abuses amount to torture' (judgement, 27 April 2005)

(3/2004) *Soeharsoyo* et al.

Torture indictees: Lt Col. Djoko Soeharsoyo; Lt Minton; Lt Yusuf Tandi; Sgt Andreas Prawin; Martinho Fernandes; Emiliano Joaquim Gomes.
   Outcome: At large, presumed in Indonesia.
   Seven men were indicted for seven counts of murder, torture, deportation, forcible transfer and persecution. The torture count, against six of the men, relates specifically to the abuse and murder of Domingos Soares Aparicio. Aparicio was arrested, questioned, and repeatedly beaten, punched, kicked, and burnt. Blindfolded, he was then placed into a grave and stabbed to death.

(4/2004) *Da Crus* et al.

Torture indictees: Vasco da Crus; Domingos Alves; Napoleon dos Santos; Lino Barreto; Cancio Lopes de Carvalho.
   Outcome: At large, presumed in Indonesia
   This indictment charges seven men with 20 counts of persecution, imprisonment, torture, murder, extermination, and deportation. Regarding torture, five indictees had detained and questioned over 70 pro-independence civilians. During these arrests, civilians were beaten, burnt with cigarettes, made to perform sexual acts, bitten by animals, crushed, and whipped. Detainees also suffered death threats, limited food and water, and were forced to dig graves and watch the executions of others.

(5/2004) *Gonsalves* et al.

Torture indictees: Ruben Gonsalves; Ruben Tavares; Joao Oliveira; Joaquim Maia Pereira; Joao Tavares.
   Outcome: At large, presumed in Indonesia.
   In this indictment, five men face 11 counts of murder, torture, and persecution. Numerous victims were also said to have been detained and severely beaten. Longuinos Pereira was arrested, restrained, stabbed, beaten, punched, kicked, slashed with razors, and eventually stabbed to death and dumped out at sea. Carlito Constantion and Cesar Soares were arrested, severely beaten, burnt, and electrocuted. Cesar Soares' body has not been found.

(6/2004) *Tallo*

Torture indictee: Frans Tallo.
   Outcome: At large, presumed in Indonesia.

Frans Tallo was indicted with four counts of murder and one of torture. The torture charge relates to the torture and murder of Longuinos Pereira (as detailed in *Gonsalves 05/2004*).

(12/2004) *Nur* et al.

Torture Indictees: Lt Col. Muhammad Nur; Lukas Martins.
    Outcome: At large, presumed in Indonesia.
    This indictment charges six men on 16 counts of murder, torture, and rape. The torture charges, against two indictees, relate to the torture and murder of two men, Jose Martins and Sabino da Lus. Martins was arrested, beaten, and stabbed to death. Da Lus was arrested and beaten to death.

Notes

1 Introduction

1 At the end of the nineteenth century, Portugal instigated attempts to strengthen its empire and a labour programme, to build infrastructure as well as to cultivate crops and coffee for export, was forced onto the Timorese population (CAVR 2005: Ch. 3.8). Such impositions resulted in political instability and strong resistance from the indigenous population. Eventually, with assistance from the indigenous elite and the Catholic Church, the Portuguese authorities consolidated their position in the region (Jardine 1997).

2 This coup, the Carnation Revolution, overthrew the authoritarian regime of Marcelo Caetano. It was forced by the Armed Forces Movement, 'a group of left-leaning military officials dedicated to democracy within Portugal and the decolonization of all its overseas territories' (Jardine 1997: 13).

3 Initially named the Association of Timorese Social Democrats, Fretilin based their programme on socialism, democracy, and a rejection of colonialism. They envisaged a decade of decolonization processes, giving time for the Timorese to develop their own political and social structures. UDT represented Timor's wealthiest citizens, and had conservative and pro-Portugal policies, while *Apodeti* (often regarded to be a 'product of Indonesian intelligence') favoured integration with Indonesia (Jardine 1997: 14).

4 Official Indonesian press releases portrayed the invasion as a successful coup undertaken by *Apodeti*, UDT, and other smaller parties. This contributed 'to the myth that Indonesia was not invading but rather it was the integrationist East Timorese parties who were regaining control of their territory with the assistance of a small number of Indonesian "volunteers"' (CAVR 2005: Ch. 3.242).

5 These included: (i) *Operasi Seroya* (Operation Lotus) launched at the time of invasion and concluded in March 1979, which sought to quell Fretilin resistance to Indonesian presence; (ii) *Operasi Keamanan* (Operation Security or Operation 'Fence of Legs'), employed between April to September 1981, in which thousands of civilians were deployed in human 'fences' to flush out Fretilin forces; and (iii) *Operasi Sapu Bersih* (Operation Clean Sweep) commenced in August 1983, which was aimed at eliminating Fretilin.

6 The 'Balibo Five' consisted of five journalists – two Australians (Greg Shackleton and Tony Stewart), two Britons (Brian Peters and Malcolm Rennie), and a New Zealander (Gary Cunningham). They were killed on 16 October 1975 by Indonesian troops as they attempted to report on the Indonesian incursion into Timor-Leste; their bodies were later buried in Indonesia. Indonesian officials claimed that the men were Fretilin members. Remarkably, international governments downplayed and 'covered up' the event (Retboll 1987). Following years of

campaigning from victims' families and friends, a 2007 inquest was opened into the death of Brian Peters. The New South Wales coroner held that the Balibo Five were deliberately shot and stabbed by members of the Indonesian special forces, and that the killings were undertaken to silence the journalists so that they could not expose the Indonesian invasion.

7 These Ploughshares activists subsequently successfully argued in court that their actions were in fulfilment of the UN Genocide Convention, as the Hawk Jets were being used by Indonesia to bomb the East Timorese population.

8 The terms 'survivors' and 'victims' are used interchangeably in this book. The term 'survivor' defines an individual who has been subject to past state violence, while 'victim' denotes someone who continues to suffer violence or harm, either directly or in their inability to move forward.

9 In recent work on the Chilean Commission on Torture, Bacic and Stanley (2005) show that many torture victims continued to sustain their silence despite the apparent benign attempts by the government to expose testimonies of torture. While this occurred three decades after most violations, victims continued to remain fearful about the repercussions of speaking out. Some felt that government officials could still not be trusted to represent their needs.

10 See, for example http://badgas.co.uk/lynndie.

11 Of course, such data belies the messy reality of actually *doing* the research. The issue of getting victims and transitional justice workers to tell their stories was by no means straightforward. There were practical issues such as the expense of actually travelling to and around Timor-Leste, as well as health concerns (dengue fever, for instance, affected many workers and victims; and the author was frequently ill from unclean water). However, the biggest issue was around access to respondents, especially in terms of accessing victims. This was principally undertaken via introductions from friends and local organizations; however, building trust with victims was often a slow process. The status differential between the author and the respondents meant that many individuals were curious and suspicious of the author's intentions. There were also difficulties in communicating across diverse languages. For example, while hired translators often worked brilliantly, there was an occasion when one attempted to subvert the victim's testimony so that I was not hurt by their criticisms of British policies.

2 Contextualizing Torture

1 The Rome Statute of the International Criminal Court (ICC) presents a wider definition of torture as a crime against humanity (Art. 7.2.e). Here, the ICC forgoes the public status of the torturer. In doing so, it allows a consideration of torture by other actors such as militia members, paramilitaries, private contractors, or resistance groups. Of course, as a crime against humanity, this torture would need to be part of a widespread or systematic attack directed against a civilian population.

2 The European Convention on Human Rights, the American Convention on Human Rights, and the African Charter on Human and Peoples' Rights.

3 The proposition that torture is capable of extracting the truth or proof has always been debatable. The Romans, for instance, accepted that any retrieved evidence was weak and acknowledged that those who were subject to torture would either remain silent or lie rather than endure pain (Lea 1878).

4 For example, the rules of *lex talionis* (where any accuser who failed to prove the charge became liable to be tortured with the same severity) provided safeguards from the eager overuse of torture.

5 There were, of course, ruptures to this 'rule' – highlighted most clearly in the torture used by Nazi officials and their allies. Nonetheless, the reaction to these

atrocities, that included UN Conventions on human rights, confirmed the position that 'civilized' countries viewed that they had a 'duty ... to foster, nurture and cherish life' (Pratt 2002: 29). This stance led to the abolition of the death penalty as well as to new initiatives on the treatment of prisoners (ibid.).

6 Similarly, the forced standing and hooding depicted in the photographs that emerged from Abu Ghraib prison in Iraq can be linked back to methods undertaken by the British Army, the French Legionnaires, and the US police in the early twentieth century (Rejali 2004). In 1956, the CIA noted the painful physiological effects of forced standing – that ankles and feet swell to twice their normal size in 24 hours, that blisters develop, that heart rates increase dramatically, and that kidneys cease to function (ibid.).

7 The proposition that powerful states are *always* at the forefront of torture technologies and techniques cannot, as Rejali (2007) highlights, be sustained. Certainly, there have been occasions when states like the United States and the Soviet Union have shaped torture in external states – and there are plenty of examples when these powerful states have provided military and economic support to other torturing states – however the relationships between states may be overstated. The techniques of torture do not always follow routes of trade and power. That is, torturing states will often develop their own techniques, and 'most torture instruments are local and homemade' (ibid.: 28). Thus, we also need to pay attention to the agency of local torturers and to the differences between states.

8 These victims often received special treatment that reflected their high status – they slept on beds, ate the same food as staff, and received medical treatment. Nonetheless, they were still tortured and usually killed (Chandler 1999).

9 Kois makes the point that classifying the event as rape opens the victim up to allegations that she is also blameworthy. Blaming the victim is a dominant response to rape survivors (see Jordan 2004). Calling the event 'torture' will protect the victim from this rhetoric, as 'few would question whether the victim consented to torture' (Kois 1998: 91).

10 Feitlowitz (1998) shows how torturers incorporate everyday items (such as forks, irons, and kettles) into their methods so that, on release, victims find it difficult to function normally. In this way, torture's pain is remembered well after the physical attacks have stopped.

3 Introducing Justice

1 As detailed further in this chapter, Fraser (1997, 2003, 2005) proposes a focused socio-economic justice. This does incorporate aspects of wider discrimination – including those related to racism, neocolonialism, patriarchy, and heterosexism – however she gives primacy to the economic structures that facilitate such oppression.

2 The definition of the state applied throughout this book is of a 'public power' that holds a claim to the monopoly of legitimate force, and that enjoys legitimacy on the basis of some level of support from the population (Green and Ward 2004; Held *et al.* 1999).

3 Of course, in 'places like Somalia, Afghanistan, West Africa and parts of the former Soviet Union', states have completely lost their power to protect their populations to warlords, drug cartels, and other small groups that control through force (Hogg 2002: 197), making it impossible for states to direct their fate. However, most states are able to command and regulate the activities of non-state actors.

4 Mackenzie (2006: 175) makes a persuasive argument that the omissions of international organizations and companies to 'provide poor countries with fair access to determining the rules of international trade' are examples of criminal negligence.

5 There may be exceptions to this rule. For example, the recent killing of Jean-Charles de Menezes in London provoked public outrage and placed the London Metropolitan Police into a position of defence. Nonetheless, at the time of writing, no one within the Met Police has been made accountable for the shooting.

6 The boundaries of 'appropriate victimhood' are further skewed by how powerful groups permeate discourses that emphasise their own risk of violation. For instance, within liberal democracies, the theme of dangerous outsiders is consistently percolated through official and media discourse. This is an issue that has intensified post 9/11; however it has a longer history. In terms of asylum and immigration, for example, such states have readily drawn attention to the risks posed by the 'unknowable' populations that arrive at borders, and states have spent vast amounts of money in attempts to deter such individuals from claiming refuge (Malloch and Stanley 2005). The principal human rights threats in these instances are derived from demonized groups who, while often fleeing violations themselves, hold limited cultural value. These individuals are, instead, represented as threats to security, the economy, cultural cohesion, and so on.

7 This book takes the definition of a 'good life' from Iris Young (1990: 37) who notes:

> The values comprised in the good life can be reduced to two very general ones: (1) developing and exercizing one's capacities and expressing one's experience ... and (2) participating in determining one's action and the conditions of one's action ... To these two general values correspond two social conditions that define injustice: oppression, the institutional constraint on self-development, and domination, the institutional constraint on self-determination.

> For her, the practical realities of oppression include material deprivation, maldistribution, the inhibition of play or communication, or the prevention of learning, while domination relates directly to the institutional or structural conditions in which some persons or groups determine the actions of others – for example, in preventing people from determining their actions or the conditions in which they live (ibid.: 38).

8 Young (1997) rightly proposes that Fraser's argument here is misplaced. She argues that those involved in recognition politics do simultaneously pursue a mandate to improve material lives. Thus, feminist, anti-racist, or gay liberation movements do not just call for recognition rather ' ... they are better understood as conceiving cultural recognition as a means to economic and political justice'. Simply put, such movements are not as one-dimensional as Fraser makes out.

9 Invariably, gender status also interacts with other attributes such as nationality, religion, or political standing. Thus, Muslim women in Bosnia-Herzegovina were held in rape camps on the basis that they were female and Muslim. The mode of violation does however directly link to the gendered status of the victim. To attack a woman in this way is often seen as a way to emasculate the opposing male force, on the basis that they have been unable to protect 'their' women.

10 For instance, Angela Davis (2005) notes that most Western attention on the recent US-led torture has focused on those detainees who hold citizenship in liberal democracies such as Britain or Australia. While not downplaying their victimization, it is clear that other detainees – for example, victims from Iraq, Afghanistan, or Pakistan – have had far less attention and subsequent support. For Davis (ibid.) this focusing reflects the racism inherent in media reporting and public concern. Similarly, as detailed in other parts of this book, it is evident that women are often not seen as torture victims at all – their violations are often downplayed when compared to the suffering of their male counterparts.

11 There are, however, textual differences in international human rights law. Under Art. 2.1 of the Covenant of Economic, Social and Cultural Rights, rights may be

progressively realized according to the maximum available resources. This tempering of obligations is not evident in the Covenant of Civil and Political Rights.
12 Pogge (2002) presents a strong argument that even a small reduction in the income of economically powerful countries (eg. 1.2 per cent of annual gross income) would make a huge impact to 'third world' countries.
13 Chossudovsky (1997: 37) argues that this restructuring, while commonly displayed as a neutral interplay of market forces, is a form of 'economic genocide'.
14 Nussbaum (1999) establishes a list of central human capabilities: life; bodily health, and bodily integrity (includes free movement); senses, imagination, and thought (includes education, training, producing works, and free speech); emotions (includes love and care, and not to be fearful); practical reason (includes engaging in critical reflection and planning of life); affiliation; ability to live with other species; play; and, control over one's environment. She (ibid.) argues that a capabilities approach is not tied to any particular historical, economic, or cultural tradition and, thus, it provides a more culturally sensitive forum for discussing human needs and functions.

4 Transitional Justice

1 In some circumstances of transition, it can be argued that representational justice should be shut down due to the *realpolitik* of local power relations and the quest for stability. The negotiated transfer of power in South Africa, for example, underpinned the provisions of amnesty for perpetrators; similarly, in Chile, amnesties were identified as necessary to facilitate the move to democracy. Nonetheless, it is clear that, in such situations, the issue of representation never goes away. Decades after violations, victims and their advocates continue to campaign for prosecutions and further truth-telling, and with some success. Thus, while the issue of representation may be postponed, experience tells us that it cannot be cancelled.
2 Institutions such as the International Center for Transitional Justice (in New York and Paris) and the Transitional Justice Institute (in Northern Ireland) have begun to offer short courses on transitional justice; and relevant debates can now be aired in the *International Journal of Transitional Justice* and the *Journal of International Criminal Justice.*
3 In countries that have limited legal resources, the involvement of 'outsiders' can become a perceived necessity if international law trials are to be undertaken 'correctly'. In such circumstances, local workers are squeezed out or become dependent on internationals to take action.
4 Evidently, some victims will have more capacity (in terms of education, skills, legal knowledge, financial ability, or media 'friendliness') than others to represent themselves and to attain acknowledgement or redress.
5 Individualism can sustain repression in the first instance. In relation to the 'dirty war' in Argentina, Phelps (2004: 49) states that the 'goal of oppressors' was to produce 'social fragmentation … passivity and learned helplessness' and to 'reduce society to a set of separate individuals living their atomized lives'. This kind of isolation made violations easier to commit as few would 'stand up' for the 'targets'. Isolationism is not challenged by transitional justice measures that present 'problems' as being solely individualistic (rather than, also, societal or institutional) in nature.
6 Byrnes (1988–89: 218–19) shows that the historically male membership of the UN Committee against Torture resulted in a situation in which the UN compiled reports that made 'no reference to the fact that women suffer not only many of the same violations as men but different ones as well'. Discussions on torture neglected to discuss sexual violence, and the UN Committee did not uncover the

gender dimension of torture as it failed to 'ask states to provide data about detainees disaggregated by sex' (ibid.: 233).

7 Women who have suffered specific victimization, such as sexual torture, are likely to remain silent about their suffering. This silence is consolidated by investigators who ignore or lack understanding of such issues, or who have limited skills to retrieve information in a sensitive way. It is also sustained through court processes that offer no protection for, and sometimes harm, women – for example, by inappropriate cross-examinations (Byrnes 1988–89; Franke 2006).

8 There have been exceptions: the Salvadorean commission identified more than 40 officials for their involvement in atrocities (Hayner 2001); the truth commission in Chad published pictures of perpetrators; and, the South African commission was able to entice a small number of perpetrators to appear in public hearings (Stanley 2001).

9 Bell *et al.* (2007) argue that the US administration used the discourse of transitional justice to legitimize their violating actions under the rubric of building peace. The discourse of transitional justice – shaped by Western values on transition, democratization, and the rule of law – was useful to build the US identity as a progressive, rather than occupying, force. In this way, transitional justice operated to build the US's hegemonic status (ibid.).

10 For example, amnesty provisions and pardons have been employed in Argentina, Chile, Colombia, El Salvador, Mozambique, South Africa, Sierra Leone, Uganda, and Uruguay.

5 Torture in Timor-Leste

1 The CAVR (2005: Ch. 7.4.33) named the UDT as responsible for 3.8 per cent of torture and ill-treatment cases. Commissioners also found that the UDT (along with other political parties such as *Apodeti, Klibur oan Timor Asuwain* (KOTA), and Trabalhista) helped to provide a 'veneer of legitimacy to the illegal Indonesian occupation and annexation of the territory' (CAVR 2005: Ch. 8.10).

2 'Rehabilitation' centres or 'Renals' (Campo de Rehabilitação Nacional) were an essential part of *Fretilin*'s social and political strategy. These centres focused on disciplining 'wayward' *Fretilin* or *Falintil* members and civilians in need of 're-education'. Many people were indefinitely detained for criticizing *Fretilin* leadership, breaching party rules, or for suspected collaboration. If held in a Renal, individuals would work in the fields during the day and have lectures on politics and literacy in the evening. Food was often scarce and there was widespread cruel treatment and torture (CAVR 2005: Ch. 7.4.266–68).

3 The CAVR (2005: Ch. 7.4.33) found *Fretilin* responsible for 11.5 per cent of reported torture and ill-treatment cases.

4 Individuals had to obtain 'clearance certificates' relating to PKI involvement. Certificates were required for those applying for government jobs or employment in big corporations. Eventually, a clearance certificate was needed to install a telephone, see land records, or be admitted to universities (van der Kroef 1976–77). King (1987) argues that this 'tagging' was used by the Indonesian government to facilitate widescale economic restructuring – for example, security authorities would fire thousands of workers on the basis of accusations that they were 'Communist-affiliated'.

5 In the 1990s, more than 70 torture photographs circulated in Australia. A few appeared in the mainstream press and an exhibition was held in Darwin – this was closed down on the grounds of being offensive (McCosker 2004). The images were consistently questioned in terms of their authenticity. Furthermore, their purchase (from Indonesian soldiers by human rights workers) was argued to have created a 'pornographic' market, thus making the purchasers complicit in torture.

6 Manuals also detailed that torture was not a useful tool to gather 'true' information as 'the person being interrogated under duress confesses falsely because he is afraid and, as .a consequence, agrees to everything the interrogator wishes' (Amnesty International 1985: 54).

7 The state philosophy of Pancasila, which incorporates a belief in God, humanitarianism, nationalism, democracy, and social justice, was developed in 1945 by Sukarno to bind the diverse Indonesian state together. It was subverted to 'justify depriving Indonesian citizens of their ... rights to freedom of expression, religion, assembly, and association, as well as the right to choose their government' (Lawyers Committee for Human Rights 1993: 5).

8 By July 1998, 6,097 East Timorese were serving in the Armed Forces (ABRI), mostly in the army but with over 500 in the police. They tended to occupy the lower ranks (CAVR 2005: Ch. 4).

9 There were various civil defence organizations, the most well known being 'Hansip', 'Wanra', and 'Ratih'. Unlike others, Hansip members were salaried and by the end of the 1970s, there were almost 5,900 Hansip in East Timor (CAVR 2005: Ch. 4.94). Some Hansip were sent to Indonesia for further training and, on their return, would join the ABRI.

10 In Hynes *et al.*'s (2004) study of 288 women, one in four East Timorese women reported being exposed to violence during 1999.

11 The CAVR (2005: Ch. 7.7.7) recorded 853 incidents of sexual violence. Wandita *et al.* (2006) detail that women faced distinctive repercussions of victimization. In particular, if male others were killed, they became particularly vulnerable to abuse from civilians or military. Following sexual violation, they were also likely to be socially excluded or marginalized. Victimization had long-term social repercussions.

12 Prisoners were held across military sites, including the headquarters of Korem (regional command) in Dili, Kodim (district command) and Koramil (precinct). The Special Unit Kopassanda (RPKAD) also had interrogation houses, many of which had a fearsome reputation (Amnesty International 1985).

13 For example, as a child Maria Fatima fled to the hills with her family of 14. Within months, only three had survived the Indonesian onslaught.

14 In interview with Judicial System Monitoring Programme (JSMP) outreach staff, 19 February 2006.

15 In interview with JSMP outreach staff, 19 February 2006.

16 While the Vatican remained largely silent on the issue of East Timor, Pope John Paul II was the only world leader to visit the territory in 1989, during occupation. For Timorese people, the Catholic church provided a sense of sanctuary and many people joined the Church as a result.

17 In interview with JSMP outreach staff, 22 November 2005.

6 Entrenching Criminal Justice

1 In interview with JSMP outreach staff, 22 November 2005.

2 Generally, rape featured as a separate count within indictments and was not often subsumed under a torture charge. The decision on whether to connect rape with torture rested on the discretion and politics of individual prosecutors. During interviews some prosecutors argued that rape should always be 'separated out' from torture, while others proposed that torture and rape were intertwined. As shown in the Appendix, in the *Atabae* (8/2002) and *Ermelindo Soares* (15/2003) indictments, prosecutors defined the same events with both torture and rape. The female victims had each been systematically raped and had suffered questioning, beatings, and intimidation. The prosecutors involved claimed that these elements constituted torture as well as rape. Conversely, in the *Laksaur Militia* (9/2003)

case, in which four female victims suffered similar rape and violence, the events were charged solely as rape. The prosecutor, here, argued that rape should always be distinct from torture. The lack of a clear prosecution strategy may have meant that some women were not recognized as torture victims at all.

3 The serious crimes process had an annual budget of less than US$6 million (JSMP 2004a). Compared to other initiatives – the Extraordinary Courts in Cambodia (US$19 million annually); the Special Court in Sierra Leone (US$16 million per year); the International Criminal Tribunal for Rwanda (a 2008 budget of US$277 million); the International Criminal Tribunal for the Former Yugoslavia (with total costs, thus far, of US$1.6 billion) – the Timorese prosecutions were relatively cheap (UN 2004, 2005a).

4 This is where one individual translates from, say, Tetum to Bahasa Indonesia, then another translates from Bahasa Indonesia to English, and so on (D. Cohen 2006a).

5 The following defendants were acquitted: Timbul Silaen, Herman Sedyono, Liliek Kushadianto, Ahmad Syamsudin, Lieutenant Sugito, Col. Gatot Subiyaktoro, Asep Kuswani, Adios Salora, Leoneto Martins, Endar Priyanto, Tono Suratman, and Yayat Sudrajat. The following were convicted (with the sentence indicated in brackets) and then acquitted on appeal: Abilio Soares (three years), Lieutenant Col. Soedjarwo (five years), Adam Damiri (three years), Nuer Muis (five years), and Hulman Gultom (five years). Eurico Guterres served less than two years before being released on appeal.

6 The UN (2005a: s240) details that judges are continually compromised and that: the Ministry of Justice exercises excessive power over judicial appointments; there is no transparency within court proceedings; there is no effective accountability mechanism; corruption is systemic; and, there is a lack of public confidence in the system. It must be noted, however, that some judges did try to uphold the rule of law and they convicted in the face of severe harassment, including death threats (D. Cohen 2003; UN 2005a).

7 In interviews, defence counsel strongly argued that torture defendants were convicted on evidence that could only sustain simple assault charges. The offences of some low-level perpetrators (see *Mesquita et al.* (28/2003) in Appendix) fell 'far short of the threshold for crimes against humanity' (Open Society and CIJ 2004: 37).

8 In line with the Rome Statute of the International Criminal Court (Art. 7(2)(e)), the SPSC definition of torture as a crime against humanity did not require that torture be conducted for a specific purpose, or that the perpetrator has official standing or support (UNTAET 2000: s5.2(d)). Of course, to prove this charge, the act must qualify as a crime against humanity – the conduct must be knowingly committed as part of a widespread or systematic attack directed against a civilian population.

9 UNTAET Regulation 2000/30 (s 32.4) states: 'The accused shall not be convicted of a crime that was not included in the indictment, as it may have been amended, or of which the accused was not informed by the judge.'

10 In interview with JSMP outreach staff, 21 February 2006.

11 It is possibly more appropriate to say that serious crimes workers failed to communicate with anyone outside their immediate sphere. For example, the SCU only established an internet site containing press releases and some indictments at the very end of the serious crimes process and the Special Panels would not give out copies of transcripts or court decisions. A key reason for this is that they could not trust the quality or the veracity of the information contained in documentation and databases. Of course, this made the collation of information very difficult – for instance, while much data was collected by JSMP staff, and published on their website (www.jsmp.minihub.org/), most of the information contained in

the appendix is the result of tracking down individual staff to gain hard copies of indictments and judgements. Thankfully, these are now available at: socrates.berkeley.edu/~warcrime/ET.htm#SeriousCrimesUnit.

12 This lack of local knowledge was perhaps inevitable given that many internationals lived completely separate lives from the population they were to assist. The enormous salary differences between international and local staff ensured non-integration as internationals would eat, socialize, and sleep in places that were inaccessible to the Timorese.

13 This right is enshrined in the UN's Basic Principles and Guidelines on the Right to a Remedy and Reparation for Victims of Gross Violations of International Human Rights Law and Serious Violations of International Humanitarian Law. Resolution 60/147 of 16 December 2005.

14 The Special Panels had no mandate to provide reparations. The Ad Hoc Courts did have such provision, but judgements did not request any reparatory measures.

15 Redress (2003) details that two Timorese plaintiffs filed and won claims for torture damages in the US. These claims against Indonesian generals, made under the 1991 Torture Victim Protection Act, resulted in awards of US$14 million and US $66 million respectively.

16 Although not covered here, it is also worth mentioning that these serious crimes bodies failed to address other inequalities of power. For example, children and young people tended to be excluded from judicial processes. Indeed, one prosecutor informed me that children were not a priority for the SCU as 'their testimony was not often reliable' and, besides 'the crimes against them were not of a serious nature'. Of course, as highlighted previously, children were often tortured during occupation. This viewpoint reflects a lack of commitment to really understand or address the injustices faced by vulnerable groups.

17 Following a recommendation from the Timorese General Prosecutor, Dr Longuinos Monteiro, Judge Philip Rapoza issued an arrest warrant against General Wiranto in May 2004. Dr Monteiro was then called to President Gusmão's office, after which he stated that the warrant was a 'stupid move' and subsequently refused to ask Interpol to issue the warrant. Illustrating the political pressure brought to bear over the serious crimes process, this underpinned the complete breakdown between the serious crimes bodies and the government (D. Cohen 2006a; UN 2005a).

18 The possibility of pursuing judicial accountability was made more difficult by the May 2006 destruction and looting of SCU records and evidence in Dili. Looters were reported to have ransacked and scattered evidence, and to have stolen 138 computers that stored vital information (ABC Online 2006). While copies of records were taken by the UN in 2006, it is thought that original records were destroyed.

7 Justice in Truth-telling

1 Funded entirely by 'outsiders' – notably from Japan, the UK, New Zealand, Sweden, Ireland, US, Australia, the European Community, and the UN (as well as funds from other states, NGOs and the World Bank) – the total budget of the CAVR was approximately US$6.147 million, plus 28 international advisors, equipment, technical, management, and translation assistance (CAVR 2005: Annex 4). In terms of monetary value, total CAVR funds equalled the annual budget of the serious crimes process.

2 Aniceto Guterres Lopes (Chair), Father Jovito Rêgo de Jesus Araújo (Deputy Chair), Maria Olandina Isabel Caeiro Alves, José Estévão Soares, Isabel Amaral Guterres, Rev. Agustinho de Vasconselos, and Jacinto das Neves Raimundo Alves.

3 At the peak of operations, between 2002–03, there were 278 staff including commissioners, international advisors, finance officers, administrators, archive workers, translators, regional commissioners, regional coordinators, truth-seeking statement-takers, victim support outreach staff, community reconciliation officers, and logistics officers. Over 90 per cent of staff members were Timorese; however internationals took a prominent role in CAVR design, operations and report writing (CAVR 2005: Ch. 1.6). During informal discussions with Timorese CAVR staff, the control that internationals held was continually mentioned and often subject to criticism.

4 The former refers to the date of the Lisbon coup that gave rise to Portuguese decolonization practices while the latter is the day when the UN finally took control of the territory.

5 It can be found at www.ictj.org/en/news/features/846.html or www.etan.org/news/2006/cavr.htm.

6 Nevins (2005) highlights how third parties (particularly Australia, the US, and the UK) have begun to downplay their own involvement in providing economic, military, or political support to the Indonesian government. Post-occupation, these states have focused on highlighting their own involvement in challenging repression and getting the Timorese 'back on their feet', and have begun to erase their own complicity in brutal crimes.

7 Themes included: victims; political imprisonment, detention and torture; women and conflict; self-determination and the international community; forced displacement and famine; massacres; internal political conflict 1974–76; and, children and the conflict.

8 While TV is almost entirely absent in rural districts, communities will often have a radio.

9 The CAVR worked with Tetum, Portuguese, Indonesian, English, and a range of indigenous languages. However, there was little language-correlation between different activities: field activities were carried out in indigenous languages and Tetum, statements were written in Tetum or Indonesian; the database was written in Indonesian; statements to the SCU were translated into English; and the Final Report was written in English, Indonesian, and Portuguese (CAVR 2005: Ch. 1.4).

10 In interview with JSMP outreach staff, 21 February 2006.

11 While some perpetrators participated voluntarily, others experienced community pressure and did not have 'much choice to refuse' (JSMP 2004: 18). The CRP was also undertaken without the victim's consent.

12 This included a full description of 'political conflict' crimes and those involved, an admission of responsibility and a renunciation of violence.

13 Despite this 'stick', there does not appear to have been any formal punitive actions against those that did not comply.

14 At another point, the Report (CAVR Ch. 9.4.1) contradicts this figure by stating that 1,371 perpetrators participated.

15 Sometimes victims had to demand attention from their listeners. For example, Wandita *et al.* (2006: 295) detail the case of a victim of sexual slavery who was faced by a laughing group of men during her testimony. She responded ' ... you in the back there, who are laughing and judging me. You who call me "whore" behind my back. Today I will speak about what happened to me and maybe you will stop judging me'. The men immediately fell silent.

16 At the start of the reconciliation programme, in June–July 2002, there was only one woman working for the CRP hearings. Following a United Nations Development Programme (UNDP) appraisal, a further 13 workers were recruited. All of these new recruits were women and, starting in September 2003, they worked across the regions until March 2004. Some female commissioners found it

difficult to build trust with community leaders and to fully participate as, traditionally, conflict resolution was undertaken by male elders (Pigou 2004).

17 In interview with JSMP outreach staff, 23–24 February 2006.

18 Each district team had two victim-support staff however they did not have professional expertise. A respected local NGO, Fokupers, also provided occasional services to support victims. However, staff were greatly outnumbered by the number of victims to support.

19 Zifcak (2004) shows how village chiefs also used their status to direct hearings, for example by stating that perpetrators were not guilty of charges.

20 In interview with JSMP outreach staff, 22 November 2005.

21 During interviews, victims continually argued that the distancing of Indonesian torturers from any forms of accountability – including prosecutions, lustration, community reconciliation practices, compensation, and apologies – was fundamentally unjust. Many victims were also explicit about the difference between 'big fish' (those individuals who gave the orders) and 'little fish' (local perpetrators as well as low-level Indonesian perpetrators). They argued that 'little fish' could be made accountable through local reconciliation practices, while 'big fish' should face official sanction.

22 There was also a tendency for victims to defer to the CAVR panel in discussions and some victims remained silent on what they knew or chose light punishments as they were fearful of the repercussions if they acted differently (JSMP 2004b).

23 Given the number of perpetrators coming forward, the CAVR quickly accrued a backlog of CRP hearings. From October 2002 to December 2003, the Commission had processed 600 cases, yet, with a deadline to complete field operations by March 2004, there were almost 900 cases to deal with in the space of three months. Between 'January and March 2004, 887 cases were processed in over 100 hearings run in all districts across the country' (Pigou 2004: 23).

24 For example, the CRP dealt with 55 perpetrators over a period of four days in Passabe (Pigou 2004).

25 In interview with JSMP outreach staff, 22 November 2005.

26 There were also 32 cases in which hearings were adjourned as the perpetrator was deemed responsible for serious crime, or the community had refused to accept them (CAVR 2005: Ch. 9.4.1).

27 Torture counts exclude violations of rape, sexual violations, and ill-treatment. In the CAVR's 2003 database table, ill-treatment was illustrated by the example that '*Falintil* soldiers chop off the ear of a person suspected of being a traitor'. As shown in the Appendix, this activity constituted torture in the *Lolotoe* (04/2001) case.

28 This brought concerns regarding the legal basis of statements, particularly as CRP statements could be used by the SCU to propel further legal action (Burgess 2006).

29 It is thought that approximately 90–95 per cent of all statements taken by the CAVR focused on the 1998–99 period.

30 In interview with JSMP outreach staff, 19 February 2006.

31 Recommendations also encompassed issues of: memorialization; providing rehabilitation support for severely affected communities; facilitating an exhumation programme; establishing a register of those who 'disappeared'; recording sites of detention; developing a human rights curriculum in schools; promoting media freedom; and establishing a national commitment to non-violence.

32 In interview with JSMP outreach staff, 21 February 2006.

33 Dissemination was undertaken by the Post-CAVR Technical Secretariat (STP-CAVR) that spent a month in each district. They undertook an initial meeting with community leaders at which an executive summary of the report, a CD-ROM of the report, and a book containing victim's photos and statements were

handed out. Following this, they showed a video and then held a seminar and a workshop.

34 The report is not currently available in Tetum.

35 These are Aniceto Guterres, Jacinto Alves, and Olandina Caeiro. Their incorporation into the CTF was particularly painful for other CAVR workers who argued, to me, that the situation had been very difficult. These other staff argued that the CTF would undermine opportunities for justice.

36 In interview with JSMP outreach staff, 21 February 2006.

37 In interview with JSMP outreach staff, 22 November 2005.

38 Indeed, by July 2008 the CFT had not granted an amnesty to any individual.

39 During interviews CTF Commissioners stated that, in a situation in which the Indonesian and Timorese Commissioners could not agree, they could see the possibility of hatching two different reports.

40 In July 2008, at the time of the final editing of this book, the CTF report was released to, and accepted by, the governments of Timor-Lests and Indonesia. Although the report (entitled *Per Memoriam ad Spem*, Through Memory Toward Hope) has not been made publicly available, some of its contents were leaked to the media. This publicized information has shown that the CTF concludes that Indonesia bore 'institutional responsbility' for the violence in 1999 (ICTJ 2008). Although welcoming of this outcome, victims' groups have argued that this information is not new. Further they maintain that the CTF report draws attention away from the CAVR's recommendations which remain unaddressed (ANTI 2008).

41 Of the CTF witnesses, 22 had been previously indicted by the SCU for a range of crimes against humanity (six on torture counts); only one, Joni Marques (*Joni Marques* (09/2000)) had faced trial and conviction. The others were all at large. Nine of these witnesses had also been acquitted by the Ad Hoc Human Rights Courts. Having already benefited from legal protection, these individuals did not request a CTF amnesty.

42 Issues here included: Commissioners were ill-prepared to undertake intensive questioning; they asked leading questions that minimized Indonesian responsibility for violations (e.g. by building statements about the apparent involvement of UN staff in torture into questions); they provided positive verbal and visual cues (e.g. nodding heads) during myth-making testimony; and they competed to establish their own national, historical view (Hirst 2008).

8 The Continuation of Violence and Insecurity

1 These have been: (i) UNAMET (UN Assistance Mission in East Timor), established on 11 June 1999 to oversee the consultation process on independence; (ii) UNTAET (the UN Transitional Authority in East Timor), established on 25 October 1999, and bearing a mandate to provide security and maintain law and order; (iii) UNMISET (the UN Mission in East Timor), started in May 2002 and coinciding with the formal independence of Timor Leste, and which sought to provide interim law enforcement and public security and to assist in the development of key institutions; (iv) UNOTIL (the UN Office in Timor Leste), formed in May 2005 with a year-long mandate to develop capacity within state institutions; and, finally, (v) UNMIT (the UN Integrated Mission in Timor-Leste), established in August 2006. This ongoing mission focuses on restoring public security, electoral support, and democratic governance.

2 Similarly, the 2004 Law on Freedom, Assembly and Demonstration, which prohibits actions that are contemptuous of 'the good reputation and respect due to the Head of State and other officeholders of the State institutions', shows a lack of tolerance for criticism or dissent that is not conducive to developing democratic

practices (Simonsen 2006: 583). The government has also pushed an agenda that has undoubtedly benefited the country's elite. For instance, the decision to adopt Portuguese as the official working language, a language that over 90 per cent of the population cannot fluently speak, reflects its use by local politicians, many of whom were exiled in Mozambique and returned in 1999 to dominate the principal political party, *Fretilin* (Kingsbury 2006).

3 These included reports that: thousands of cases were lost due to poor case management; telephone and electricity lines were cut off due to late bill payment; final written judgements were not recorded; and international judges implemented new court systems without informing national staff.

4 This problem was compounded by constant interpretation, which slowed training sessions 50 per cent, and the production of regulations in Portuguese which meant that most trainees could not understand them (Hood 2006).

5 In interview with JSMP outreach staff, 18 February 2006.

6 A survey on public perceptions of the PNTL found, however, that almost 70 per cent of 230 respondents still trusted and respected police work (Saldanha *et al.* 2004).

7 A 'dual economy' emerged in Timor-Leste from 2000. In Dili, this was identified by the floating hotels, numerous restaurants, hotels, and car-hire offices, all of which were far beyond the means of Timorese. Most of these services collapsed when the majority of internationals left the region (Bhatia 2005). International salaries also pushed up prices for food and housing thus making survival more difficult. Devereux (2005) argues that these differential wage structures, and differential working conditions, created a 'credibility gap' for the UN. Issues of credibility were also related to the ways in which UN workers, who had been allegedly involved in human rights violations, were treated in non-transparent ways. Violators were dealt with through 'secret' processes and were not subject to punishment (although some were sent home).

8 These market approaches to development have also traditionally disadvantaged women who spend more time on subsistence farming to ensure that family members are fed. The limits on women's involvements often links into perceptions that they are not contributing to a market economy and are, therefore, undeserving of grants or aid. When women do participate in market-led agriculture, they inevitably end up working a double day (Charlesworth 1988–89).

9 The NGO 'Forum Tau Matan' had an Australian government grant revoked after signing the same letter that questioned Australian actions on oil in the Timor Sea.

10 This research highlights that, in the year before the 1999 crisis, 47 per cent of women reported intimidation, verbal abuse, physical abuse, and sexual coercion. In the year before the interview, this figure had only dropped to 43.2 per cent. Rates had remained, therefore, relatively consistent. Despite this, the general perception among women was that violence had decreased. This was probably due to the fact that collective violence had declined.

11 This issue is also apparent in the widespread acceptance of corporal punishment in the rearing of children.

12 In interview with JSMP outreach staff, 22 November 2005.

13 Of course, to attain this justice there needs to be a second realization: that powerful states also identify that this is their duty (Fanon 1963).

9 Looking to the Future

1 While the serious crimes process in Dili was successful in terms of providing some recognition of previous suffering and perpetrators, this was not often identified by victims – mainly because victims did not know that this institution even existed.

Bibliography

ABC Online (2006) *The World Today – Serious Crimes Unit Office Looted in Dili*, 31 May 2006. Online. Available at www.abc.net.au/worldtoday/content/2006/s1652102.htm (accessed 2 June 2006).

Abraham, I. and van Schendel, W. (2005) 'Introduction: The Making of Illicitness', in W. van Schendel and I. Abraham (eds) *Illicit Flows and Criminal Things: States, Borders, and the Other Side of Globalization*, Bloomington, IN: Indiana University Press.

ADB and UNDFW, Asian Development Bank and United Nations Development Fund for Women (2005) *Gender and Nation Building in Timor-Leste: Country Gender Assessment, November 2005*. Online. Available at www.adb.org/Documents/Reports/Country-Gender-Assessments/cga-timor-leste.pdf (accessed 13 February 2006).

Agamben, G. (1995) *Homo Sacer: Sovereign Power and Bare Life*, trans. D. Heller-Roazen, Stanford, CA: Stanford University Press.

Agger, I. and Buus Jensen, S. (1996) *Trauma and Healing Under State Terrorism*, London: Zed Books.

Alasuutari, P. (1998) *An Invitation to Social Research*, London: Sage.

Allodi, F., Randall, G., Lutz, E., Quiroga, J., Zunzunegui, M., Kolff, C., Deutsch, A. and Doan, R. (1985) 'Physical and Psychiatric Effects of Torture: Two Medical Studies', in E. Stover and E. Nightingale (eds) *The Breaking of Bodies and Minds*, New York: Freeman and Company.

Amaral, F. (2003) *Prospects for Coffee Development in East Timor*, Dili: Timor-Leste MAFF. Online. Available at http://www.gov.east-timor.org/MAFF/English/Coffe.html (accessed 11 January 2004).

Amnesty International (1968) *The Condition of Political Prisoners in Indonesia: International Conference on Torture, Inhuman and Degrading Treatment, Stockholm, August 1968*, AI Index ASA 21, London: Amnesty International.

—— (1977) *Indonesia*, London: Amnesty International.

—— (1983) *Troops in East Timor Given Secret Manual Permitting Torture*, News Release 10/83, AI Index ASA 21/06/83, London: Amnesty International.

—— (1985) *East Timor Violations of Human Rights: Extrajudicial Executions, 'Disappearances', Torture and Political Imprisonment 1975–1984*, London: Amnesty International.

—— (1987) *Indonesia / East Timor: Further Releases of Political Prisoners*, AI Index ASA 21/24/87, London: Amnesty International.

—— (1989) *Amnesty International Statement to the United Nations Special Committee on Decolonization*, AI Index ASA 21/11/89, London: Amnesty International.

—— (1991) *Statement to the United Nations Special Committee on Decolonization August 1991*, AI Index ASA 21/14/91, London: Amnesty International.

—— (1993) *Indonesia / East Timor: A New Order? Human Rights in 1992*, AI Index ASA 21/03/93, London: Amnesty International.

—— (2000) *Take a Step to Stamp out Torture*, London: Amnesty International.

—— (2001a) *Stopping the Torture Trade*, London: Amnesty International.

—— (2001b) 'The Torture of Children: The World's Secret Shame', *Amnesty Members Magazine*, January/February, pp 16–18.

—— (2001c) 'Crimes of Hate: Conspiracy of Silence', *Amnesty Members Magazine*, July/August: 4–7.

—— (2003) *Timor Leste: Briefing to Security Council Members on Policing and Security in Timor-Leste*, AI Index: ASA 57/001/2003, London: Amnesty International.

Amnesty International and Judicial System Monitoring Programme (2004) *Indonesia. Justice for Timor-Leste: The Way Forward*, AI Index: ASA 21/006/2004, London: Amnesty International.

Anderson, B. (2000) 'Petrus Dadi Ratu', *New Left Review*, 3: 7–15.

Anderson, T. (2001) *Aidwatch June Briefing Note: The World Bank in East Timor*. Online. Available at www.aidwatch.org.au (accessed 14 March 2005).

ANTI, *Nasional Timor-Leste ba Tribunal Internasional* (2008) *An Open Letter in Response to the CTF Report*, 15 July 2008. Available http://laohamutuk.org/Justice/ TFC/ANTIonCTFEn.pdf (accessed 16 July 2008).

Arcel, L. T. (2002) 'Torture, Cruel, Inhuman, and Degrading Treatment of Women: Psychological Consequences', *Torture*, 12, 1: 5–16.

Babo-Soares, D. (2004) '*Nahe Biti*: The Philosophy and Process of Grassroots Reconciliation (and Justice) in East Timor', *The Asia Pacific Journal of Anthropology*, 5, 1: 15–33.

Bacic, R. and Stanley, E. (2005) *Dealing with Torture in Chile*, Nuremburg Human Rights Centre. Online. Available at www.menschenrechte.org/beitraege/lateinamerika/ Dealingwithtorture.htm (accessed 1 October 2005).

Bagaric, M. and Clarke, J. (2005) 'Not Enough (Official) Torture in the World? The Circumstances in Which Torture is Morally Justifiable', *University of San Francisco Law Review*, 39, 3: 581–616.

Bauman, Z. (1995) 'The Strangers of Consumer Era: From the Welfare State to Prison', *Tijdschrift voor Criminologie*, 3, 3: 210–18.

—— (2001) 'The Great War of Recognition', *Theory, Culture and Society*, 18, 2–3: 137–50.

BBC (2006) *Australia Seeks E Timor Support*. 5 June 2006. Online. Available at www./news.bbc.co.uk/1/hi/world/asia-pacific/5047272.stm (accessed 6 June 2006).

Becker, D. (2005) 'Dealing with the Consequences of Organised Violence in Trauma Work', in M. Fischer and B. Shmelzle (eds) *The Berghof Handbook for Conflict Transformation*. Online. Available at www.berghof-handbook.net (accessed 14 December 2006).

Becker, D., Lira, E., Castillo, M., Gómez, E. and Kovalskys, J. (1990) 'Therapy with Victims of Political Repression in Chile: The Challenge of Social Reparation', *Journal of Social Issues*, 46, 3: 133–49.

Bell, C., Campbell, C. and Ní Aoláin, F. (2007) 'The Battle for Transitional Justice: Hegemony, Iraq, and International Law', in J. Morison, K. McEvoy and G. Anthony (eds) *Judges, Transition, and Human Rights*, Oxford: Oxford University Press.

Bello, W. and Guttall, S. (2006) 'The Limits of Reform: The Wolfensohn Era at the World Bank', *Race and Class*, 47, 3: 68–81.

Berrington, E., Jemphrey A. and Scraton, P. (2003) 'Silencing the View from Below: The Institutional Regulation of Critical Research', in S. Tombs and D. Whyte (eds) *Unmasking the Crimes of the Powerful: Scrutinizing States and Corporations*, New York: Peter Lang.

Bhatia, M. (2005) 'Postcolonial Profit: The Political Economy of Intervention', *Global Governance*, 11: 205–24.

Birch, M. L. (2003) 'Torture, Identity, and Indigenous Peoples: Individual and Collective Rights', *Albany Law Review*, 67, 2: 537–44.

Blaauw, M. (2002) 'Sexual Torture of Children – An Ignored and Concealed Crime', *Torture*, 12, 2: 37–45.

Blau, J. and Moncada, A. (2005) *Human Rights: Beyond the Liberal Vision*, Oxford: Rowman and Littlefield.

Boraine, A. (2006) 'Transitional Justice: A Holistic Interpretation', *Journal of International Affairs*, 60, 1: 17–27.

Boraine, A., Levy, J. and Scheffer, R. (eds) (1994) *Dealing With the Past: Truth and Reconciliation in South Africa*, Cape Town: Institute for Democracy in South Africa.

Breytenbach, B. (1994) 'Dog's Bone', *The New York Review of Books*, 41, 10: 3–6.

Brody, R. (2005) 'The Road to Abu Ghraib: Torture and Impunity in U.S. Detention', in K. Roth, M. Worden and A. Bernstein (eds) *Torture: Does it Make Us Safer? Is it Ever OK?*, New York: The New Press.

Budiardjo, C. (1974) 'Political Imprisonment in Indonesia', in British Indonesia Committee (ed.) *Repression and Exploitation in Indonesia*, Nottingham: Spokesman Books.

Bugalski, N. (2004) 'Beneath the Sea: Determining a Maritime Boundary between Australia and East Timor', *Alternative Law Journal*, 29, 6: 290–95.

Burgess, P. (2004) 'Justice and Reconciliation in East Timor. The Relationship Between the Commission for Reception, Truth and Reconciliation and the Courts', *Criminal Law Forum*, 15: 135–58.

—— (2006) 'A New Approach to Restorative Justice – East Timor's Community Reconciliation Processes', in N. Roht-Arriaza and J. Mariezcurrena (eds) *Transitional Justice in the Twenty-First Century: Beyond Truth versus Justice*, Cambridge: Cambridge University Press.

Butler, J. (2004) *Precarious Life: The Powers of Mourning and Violence*, New York: Verso.

Byrnes, A. (1988–89) 'Women, Feminism and International Human Rights Law – Methodological Myopia, Fundamental Flaws or Meaningful Marginalisation?', *Australian Year Book of International Law*, 12: 205–40.

Cabral, E. (2000) 'The Indonesian Propaganda War against East Timor', in P. Hainsworth and S. McCloskey (eds) *The East Timor Question: The Struggle for Independence from Indonesia*, London: I. B. Tauris Publishers.

Campbell, T. (1999) 'Human Rights: A Culture of Controversy', *Journal of Law and Society*, 26: 6–26.

Candio, P. and Bleiker, R. (2001) 'Peacebuilding in East Timor', *The Pacific Review*, 14, 1: 63–84.

CAVR, Comissão de Acolhimento, Verdade e Reconciliacão de Timor-Leste (2005) *Chega! The Report of the Commission for Reception, Truth and Reconciliation in Timor-Leste*, Dili: CAVR.

—— (2003) *Violations Table*, 21 August 2003, Dili:CAVR (not publicly available).

Chadwick, K. and Scraton, P. (2001) 'Critical Research', in E. McLaughlin and J. Muncie (eds) *The Sage Dictionary of Criminology*, London: Sage.

Chan, J. with Devery, C. and Doran, S. (2003) *Fair Cop: Learning the Art of Policing*, Toronto: University of Toronto Press.

Chandler, D. (1999) *Voices from S-21: Terror and History in Pol Pot's Secret Prison*, Berkeley, CA: University of California Press.

—— (2002) *From Kosovo to Kabul: Human Rights and International Intervention*, London: Pluto Press.

—— (2006) 'Back to the Future? The Limits of Neo-Wilsonian Ideals Exporting Democracy', *Review of International Studies*, 32, 3: 475–94.

Charlesworth, H. (1988–89) 'The Public/Private Distinction and the Right to Development in International Law', *Australian Year Book of International Law*, 12: 190–204.

—— (2007) *Building Democracy and Justice after Conflict*, Cunningham Lecture 2006, Occasional Paper No 2, Canberra: The Academy of the Social Sciences in Australia.

Chesterman, S. (2004) *You, the People: The United Nations, Transitional Administration, and State-Building*, Oxford: Oxford University Press.

Chinkin, C. (1998) 'International Law and Human Rights', in T. Evans (ed.) *Human Rights Fifty Years On: A Reappraisal*, Manchester: Manchester University Press.

Chomsky, N. (1996) *Powers and Prospects: Reflections on Human Nature and the Social Order*, London: Pluto Press.

—— (1998) 'The United States and the Challenge of Relativity', in T. Evans (ed.) *Human Rights Fifty Years On: A Reappraisal*, Manchester: Manchester University Press.

—— (2000) *A New Generation Draws the Line: Kosovo, East Timor and the Standards of the West*, London: Verso.

Chopra, J. (2003) 'Building State Failure in East Timor', in J. Milliken (ed.) *State Failure, Collapse and Reconstruction*, Oxford: Blackwell.

Chossudovsky, M. (1997) *The Globalisation of Poverty*, London: Zed Books.

Christie, N. (1977) 'Conflicts as Property', *The British Journal of Criminology*, 17, 1: 1–15.

Clough, P. and Nutbrown, C. (2002) *A Student's Guide to Methodology*, London: Sage.

CODEPU, Comité de Defensa de los Derechos del Pueblo (1989) 'The Effects of Torture and Political Repression in a Sample of Chilean Families', *Social Science Medical Journal*, 28, 7: 735–40.

Coffey, A. and Atkinson, P. (1996) *Making Sense of Qualitative Data*, London: Sage.

Cohen, D. (2002) *Seeking Justice on the Cheap: Is the East Timor Tribunal Really a Model for the Future?*, Asia Pacific Issues No 61, Honolulu, HI: East-West Center.

—— (2003) *Intended to Fail: The Trials before the Ad Hoc Human Rights Court in Jakarta* New York: International Center for Transitional Justice.

—— (2006a) *Indifference and Accountability: The United Nations and the Politics of International Justice in East Timor*, Special Report Number 9, Honolulu, HI: East-West Center.

—— (2006b) *'Justice on the Cheap' Revisited: The Failure of the Serious Crimes Trials in East Timor*, Asia Pacific Issues No 80, Honolulu, HI: East-West Center.

Cohen, S. (1985) *Visions of Social Control*, Cambridge: Polity Press.

—— (1993) 'Human Rights and Crimes of the State: The Culture of Denial', *Australian and New Zealand Journal of Criminology*, 26: 97–115.

—— (1996a) 'Government Responses to Human Rights Reports: Claims, Denials and Counterclaims', *Human Rights Quarterly*, 18: 517–43.

—— (1996b) 'Crime and Politics: Spot the Difference', *British Journal of Sociology*, 47, 1: 1–21.

—— (2001) *States of Denial: Knowing about Atrocities and Suffering*, Cambridge: Polity.

Coleman, R. (2003) 'CCTV Surveillance, Power, and Social Order: The State of Contemporary Social Control', in S. Tombs and D. Whyte (eds) *Unmasking the Crimes of the Powerful: Scrutinizing States and Corporations*, New York: Peter Lang.

Coleman, R. and Sim, J. (2005) 'Contemporary Statecraft and the 'Punitive Obsession': A Critique of the New Penology Thesis', in J. Pratt, D. Brown, M. Brown, S. Hallsworth and W. Morrison (eds) *The New Punitiveness: Trends, Theories, Perspectives*, Cullompton: Willan Publishing.

Connell, R. W. (1995) 'Sociology and Human Rights', *Australian and New Zealand Journal of Sociology*, 31, 2: 25–29.

Conroy, J. (2001) *Unspeakable Acts, Ordinary People*, London: Vision.

Crelinsten, R. D. (1995) 'In Their Own Words: The World of the Torturer', in R. D. Crelinsten and A. P. Schmid (eds) *The Politics of Pain: Torturers and their Masters*, Boulder: Westview Press.

—— (2003) 'The World of Torture: A Constructed Reality', *Theoretical Criminology*, 7, 3: 293–318.

Cribb, R. (2001) 'Genocide in Indonesia, 1965–66', *Journal of Genocide Research*, 3, 2: 219–39.

—— (2002) 'Unresolved Problems in the Indonesian Killings of 1965–66', *Asian Survey*, 42, 4: 550–63.

CTF, Commission of Truth and Friendship (2005) *Terms of Reference for The Commission of Truth and Friendship Established by The Republic of Indonesia and The Democratic Republic of Timor-Leste*. Online. Available at   http://www.ctf-ri-tl.org (accessed 13 March 2007).

Cunneen, C. (2008) 'Understanding Restorative Justice through the Lens of Critical Criminology', in T. Anthony and C. Cunneen (eds) *The Critical Criminology Companion*, Sydney: Hawkins Press.

Curtain, R. (2006) *Crisis in Timor-Leste: Looking Beyond the Surface Reality for Causes and Solutions*, paper presented at State, Society and Governance in Melanesia Project Seminar, Australian National University, 27 July 2006.

Das, V. (1997) 'Language and Body: Transactions in the Construction of Pain', in V. Das, A. Kleinman and M. Lock (eds) *Social Suffering*, Berkeley, CA: University of California Press.

Das, V. and Kleinman, A. (2001) 'Introduction', in V. Das, A. Kleinman, M. Lock, M. Ramphele and P. Reynolds (eds) *Remaking a World: Violence, Social Suffering and Recovery*, Berkeley, CA: University of California Press.

Davidson, J. S. (2001) 'East Timor: Human Rights at the Edge of Destruction', *Human Rights Law and Practice*, 6, 1: 5–22.

Davis, A. (2005) *Abolition Democracy: Beyond Prisons, Torture and Empire*, San Francisco, CA: Seven Stories Press.

Davis, M. (2001) 'The Flames of New York', *New Left Review*, 12: 34–50.

De Bertodano, S. (2004) 'Current Developments in Internationalized Courts', *Journal of International Criminal Justice*, 2, 3: 910–26.

De Faria, C. (2005) *ET's Quest for Justice: The Serious Crimes Files*, Dili: Office of the Deputy General Prosecutor for Serious Crimes in Timor-Leste.

De Saussure, F. (1974[1959]) *Course in General Linguistics*, trans. W. Baskin, London: Fontana.

Dershowitz, A. (2002) *Why Terrorism Works: Understanding the Threat, Responding to the Challenge*, New Haven, CT: Yale University Press.

Devereux, A. (2005) 'Searching for Clarity: A Case Study of UNTAET's Application of International Human Rights Norms', in N. D. White and D. Klaasen (eds) *The UN, Human Rights and Post-Conflict Situations*, Manchester: Manchester University Press.

Dickinson, L. A. (2003) 'Notes and Comments: The Promise of Hybrid Courts', *The American Journal of International Law*, 97: 295–310.

DuBois, P. (1991) *Torture and Truth*, London: Routledge.

Dunn, J. (2003) *East Timor: A Rough Passage to Independence*, 3rd edn, Double Bay: Longueville Books.

Dunne, T. (1999) 'The Spectre of Globalization', *Indiana Journal of Global Legal Studies*, 7: 17–33.

ELSAM, Institute for Policy Research and Advocacy (2003) *The Failure of Leipzig Repeated in Jakarta: Final Assessment on the Human Rights Ad-Hoc Tribunal for East Timor*, Jakarta: ELSAM.

Evans, M. and Morgan, R. (1998) *Preventing Torture: A Study of the European Convention for the Prevention of Torture and Inhuman or Degrading Treatment or Punishment*, Oxford: Clarendon Press.

Evans, T. (1998) 'Introduction: Power, Hegemony and the Universalization of Human Rights', in T. Evans (ed.) *Human Rights Fifty Years On: A Reappraisal*, Manchester: Manchester University Press.

—— (2001) *The Politics of Human Rights: A Global Perspective*, London: Pluto Press.

Evans, T. and Hancock, J. (1998) 'Doing Something without Doing Anything: International Human Rights Law and the Challenge of Globalisation', *The International Journal of Human Rights*, 2, 3: 1–21.

Ewick, P. and Silbey, S. S. (1995) 'Subversive Stories and Hegemonic Tales: Towards a Sociology of Narrative', *Law and Society Review*, 29, 2: 197–226.

Ewing, K. D. (2001) 'The Unbalanced Constitution', in T. Campbell, K. D. Ewing and A. Tomkins (eds) *Sceptical Essays on Human Rights*, Oxford: Oxford University Press.

Fanon, F. (1963) *The Wretched of the Earth*, trans. C. Farrington, London: Penguin Books.

Farmer, P. (2003) *Pathologies of Power: Health, Human Rights and the New War on the Poor*, Berkeley, CA: University of California Press.

—— (2004) 'An Anthropology of Structural Violence', *Current Anthropology*, 45, 3: 305–25.

Feitlowitz, M. (1998) *A Lexicon of Terror: Argentina and the Legacies of Torture*, Oxford: Oxford University Press.

Fellner, J. (2005) 'Torture in US Prisons', in K. Roth, M. Worden and A. Bernstein (eds) *Torture: Does it Make Us Safer? Is it Ever OK?*, New York: The New Press.

Fletcher, L. E. and Weinstein, H. M. (2002) 'Violence and Social Repair: Rethinking the Contribution of Justice to Reconciliation', *Human Rights Quarterly*, 24: 573–639.

Foucault, M. (1977) *Discipline and Punish: The Birth of the Prison*, London: Penguin.

Franke, K. M. (2006) 'Gendered Subjects of Transitional Justice', *Columbia Journal of Gender and Law*, 15, 3: 813–28.

Franks, E. (1996) 'Women and Resistance in East Timor: "The Centre, as They Say, Knows Itself by the Margins"', *Women's Studies International Forum*, 19, 1–2: 155–68.

Fraser, N. (1997) *Justice Interruptus: Critical Reflections on the 'Postsocialist' Condition*, London: Routledge.

—— (2000) 'Rethinking Recognition', *New Left Review*, 3: 107–20.

—— (2003) 'Social Justice in the Age of Identity Politics: Redistribution, Recognition, and Participation', in N. Fraser and A. Honneth (eds) *Redistribution or Recognition? A Political-Philosophical Exchange*, London: Verso.

—— (2005) 'Reframing Justice in a Globalizing World', *New Left Review*, 36: 69–88.

Freeman, M. (2002) *Human Rights: An Interdisciplinary Approach*, Cambridge: Polity Press.

Friedrichs, D. O. (2004) *Trusted Criminals: White Collar Crime in Contemporary Society*, 2nd edn. Belmont, CA: Wadsworth/Thomson.

Fukuyama, F. (2006) 'Introduction: Nation-Building and the Failure of Institutional Memory', in F. Fukuyama (ed.) *Nation-Building: Beyond Afghanistan and Iraq*, Baltimore, MD: John Hopkins University Press.

Galtung, J. (1994) *Human Rights in Another Key*, Cambridge: Polity Press.

Gault-Williams, M. (1990) 'Funu – Liberation War – Continues in East Timor', *Bulletin of Concerned Asian Scholars*, 22, 3: 21–31.

George, S. (1995) 'The Structure of Dominance in the International Geo-economic System and the Prospects for Human Rights Realization', in E. Eide and B. Hagtvet (eds) *Conditions for Civilized Politics: Political Regimes and Compliance with Human Rights*, Oslo: Scandinavian University Press.

Giddens, A. (1994) 'Living in a Post-Traditional Society', in U. Beck, A. Giddens and S. Lash (eds) *Reflexive Modernization: Politics, Tradition and Aesthetics in the Modern Social Order*, Cambridge: Polity Press.

Giroux, H. (2002) 'Global Capitalism and the Return of the Garrison State', *Arena Journal*, 19: 141–60.

—— (2004) *The Terror of Neoliberalism: Authoritarianism and the Eclipse of Democracy*, Boulder, CO: Paradigm Publishers.

Gledhill, J. (2003) 'Rights and the Poor', in R. A. Wilson and J. P. Mitchell (eds) *Human Rights in Global Perspective: Anthropological Studies of Rights, Claims and Entitlements*, London: Routledge.

Goldstone, A. (2004) 'UNTAET with Hindsight: The Peculiarities of Politics in an Incomplete State', *Global Governance*, 10, 1: 83–98.

Green, P. and Ward, T. (2000) 'State Crime, Human Rights, and the Limits of Criminology', *Social Justice*, 27, 1: 101–15.

—— (2004) *State Crime: Governments, Violence and Corruption*, London: Pluto Press.

Grenfell, D. (2004) 'Nation Building and the Politics of Oil in East Timor', *Arena Journal*, 22: 45–48.

—— (2006) *Reconstituting the Nation: Reconciliation and National Consciousness in Timor-Leste*, Occasional Series in Criminal Justice and International Studies, Melbourne: RMIT Publishing.

Gusmão, X. (2005a) *Address by H.E. The President of the Republic Kay Rala Xanana Gusmão on the Occasion of the Presentation of the Final Report of the Commission for Reception, Truth and Reconciliation (CAVR)*, Lahane Palace, 31 October 2005. Online. Available at http://www.etan.org/et2005/october/31/31xana.htm (accessed 25 November 2005)

—— (2005b) *Speech of His Excellency President Kay Rala Xanana Gusmão on the Occasion of the Handing Over of the Final Report of the CAVR to the National Parliament*, 28 November 2005. Online. Available at www.unmit.org/UNMISETW ebSite.nsf/e4899f58093d136749256f0a003f1073/2ca1c85976cca654492570c9003245f 3?OpenDocument (accessed 3 December 2005).

Guterres, A. (2005) *Address by Aniceto Guterres Lopes, CAVR Chair on the Presentation of the CAVR Report to the President of the Republic, Salao Nobre, Lahane*, 31 October 2005. Online. Available at www.etan.org/et2005/october/31/31anicet.htm (accessed 14 November 2005).

Haenel, F. (2003) 'The Effects of Social and Legal Circumstances on the Psychotherapeutic Treatment of Torture Survivors', *Torture*, 13, 2: 19–23.

Hamber, B. (1998) (ed.) *Past Imperfect: Dealing with the Past in Northern Ireland and Societies in Transition*, Derry: Incore.

—— (2006) '"Nunca Más" and the Politics of Person: Can Truth Telling Prevent the Recurrence of Violence', in T. Borer (ed.) *Telling the Truths: Truth Telling and Peace Building in Post-Conflict Societies*, Notre Dame, IN: Notre Dame Press.

Hamber, B. and Wilson, R. A. (2002) 'Symbolic Closure through Memory, Reparation and Revenge in Post-Conflict Societies', *Journal of Human Rights*, 1, 1: 35–53.

Hamber, B., Nageng, D. and O'Malley, G. (2000) '"Telling it Like it is ... ": Understanding the Truth and Reconciliation Commission from the Perspective of Survivors', *Psychology in Society*, 26: 18–42.

Hardy, C. (2002) 'An Act of Force: Male Rape Victims', *Torture*, 12, 1: 19–23.

Haritos-Fatouros, M. (2002) *The Psychological Origins of Institutionalized Torture*, London: Routledge.

Harris Rimmer, S. (2004) 'Untold Numbers: East Timorese Women and Transitional Justice', in S. Pickering and C. Lambert (eds) *Global Issues, Women and Justice*, Sydney: Institute of Criminology.

Harvard Law School (1997) *Truth Commissions: A Comparative Assessment (An Interdisciplinary Discussion Held at Harvard Law School in May 1996)*, Harvard, MA: Harvard Law School.

Harvey, L. (1990) *Critical Social Research*, London: Unwin Hyman.

Hasegawa, S. (2003) 'Strategies for Sustainable Human Capacity Development in Timor Leste: Achievements and Challenges', paper presented at the Unitar Hiroshima Inaugural Conference on Training and Human Capacity-Building in Post Conflict Countries, Hiroshima, 17–19 November 2003.

Hayden, P. and el-Ojeili, C. (2005) 'Confronting Globalization in the Twenty-first Century: An Introduction', in P. Hayden and C. el-Ojeili (eds) *Confronting Globalization: Humanity, Justice and the Renewal of Politics*, Basingstoke: Palgrave MacMillan.

Hayner, P. (1998) 'The Contribution of Truth Commissions', in B. Dunér (ed.) *An End to Torture*, London: Zed Books.

—— (2001) *Unspeakable Truths: Confronting State Terror and Atrocity*, London: Routledge.

Held, D., McGrew, A., Goldblatt, D. and Perraton, J. (1999) *Global Transformations: Politics, Economics and Culture*, Cambridge: Polity Press.

Herbst, P. (1992) 'From Helpless Victim to Empowered Survivor: Oral History as a Treatment for Survivors of Torture', *Women and Therapy*, 13: 141–54.

Herman, E. (1982) *The Real Terror Network: Terrorism in Fact and Propaganda*, Boston, MA: South End Press.

—— (2002) 'Foreword', in D. Chandler (2002) *From Kosovo to Kabul: Human Rights and International Intervention*, London: Pluto Press.

Hersh, S. (2004) *Chain of Command: The Road from 9/11 to Abu Ghraib*, Camberwell: Allen Lane.

Hirst, M. (2008) *Too Much Friendship, Too Little Truth: Monitoring Report on the Commission of Truth and Friendship in Indonesia and Timor-Leste*, New York: International Center for Transitional Justice.

Hirst, M. and Varney, H. (2005) *Justice Abandoned? An Assessment of the Serious Crimes Process in East Timor*, New York: International Center for Transitional Justice.

Hoffman, E. (2003) 'The Balm of Recognition: Rectifying Wrongs through the Generations', in N. Owen (ed.) *Human Rights, Human Wrongs: The Oxford Amnesty Lectures 2001*, Oxford: Oxford University Press.

Hogg, R. (2002) 'Criminology Beyond the Nation State: Global Conflicts, Human Rights and the 'New World Disorder'', in K. Carrington and R. Hogg (eds) *Critical Criminology: Issues, Debates, Challenges*, Cullompton: Willan Publishing.

Honneth, A. (2004) 'Recognition and Justice: Outline of a Plural Theory of Justice', *Acta Sociologica*, 47, 4: 351–64.

Hood, L. (2006) 'Security Sector Reform in East Timor, 1999–2004', *International Peacekeeping*, 13, 1: 60–77.

Hornblum, A. (1998) *Acres of Skin: Human Experiments at Holmesburg Prison*, New York: Routledge.

Huang, R. and Gunn, G. C. (2004) 'Reconciliation as State-Building in East Timor', *Lusotopie 2004*, 2004: 19–38.

Hudson, B. (1993) *Penal Policy and Social Justice*, London: MacMillan Press.

—— (2003) *Justice in the Risk Society: Challenging and Re-affirming Justice in Late Modernity*, London: Sage.

Huggins, M. K., Haritos-Fatouros, M. and Zimbardo, P. G. (2002) *Violence Workers: Police Torturers and Murderers Reconstruct Brazilian Atrocities*, Berkeley, CA: University of California Press.

Human Rights Watch (1994) *The Limits of Openness: Human Rights in Indonesia and East Timor*, New York: Human Rights Watch.

—— (1995) *Indonesia/ East Timor: Deteriorating Human Rights in East Timor*, New York: Human Rights Watch.

—— (2006) *Tortured Beginnings: Police Violence and the Beginnings of Impunity in East Timor*, New York: Human Rights Watch.

Humphrey, M. (2000) 'From Terror to Trauma: Commissioning Truth for National Reconciliation', *Social Identities*, 6, 1: 7–27.

—— (2002) *The Politics of Atrocity and Reconciliation: From Terror To Trauma*, London: Routledge.

—— (2003) 'From Victim to Victimhood: Truth Commissions and Trials as Rituals of Political Transition and Individual Healing', *The Australian Journal of Anthropology*, 14, 2: 171–87.

Hynes, M., Ward, J., Robertson, K. and Crouse, C. (2004) 'A Determination of the Prevalence of Gender-based Violence Among Conflict-Affected Populations in East Timor', *Disasters*, 28, 3: 294–321.

ICTJ, International Center for Transitional Justice (2006) *Briefing Paper: Dujail: Trial and Error? November 2006*, New York: ICTJ.

—— (2008) *CTF Submits Final Report*, 15 July 2008. Available at www.ictj.org/en/news/features/1856.html (accessed 19 July 2008).

Ignatieff, M. (2004) *The Lesser Evil: Political Ethics in an Age of Terror*, Princeton, NJ: Princeton University Press.

International Commission of Jurists (1992) *Tragedy in East Timor: Report on the Trials in Dili and Jakarta*, Geneva: International Commission of Jurists.

Ishizuka, K. (2004) 'Australia's Policy towards East Timor', *The Round Table*, 93, 374: 271–85.

Jakarta Post (2006) 'RI Dismisses Report on Timor Atrocities during Occupation', *The Jakarta Post*, 20 January 2006. Online. Available at www.etan.org/et2006/janu ary/14/20ri.htm (accessed 15 February 2006).

Jamieson, R. and McEvoy, K. (2005) 'State Crime by Proxy and Juridical Othering', *The British Journal of Criminology*, 45, 4: 504–27.

Jardine, M. (1997) 'Introduction', in C. Pinto and M. Jardine (1997) *East Timor's Unfinished Struggle: Inside the Timorese Resistance*, Boston, MA: South End Press.

—— (1999) *East Timor: Genocide in Paradise*, 2nd edn, Cambridge, MA: Odonian Press.

Järvinen, T. (2004) *Human Rights and Post-Conflict Transitional Justice in East Timor*, UPI Working Paper 47, Helsinki: Finnish Institute of International Affairs.

Jenkins, C. (2002) 'A Truth Commission for East Timor: Lessons from South Africa?', *Journal of Conflict and Security Law*, 7, 2: 233–51.

Jenkins, D. (1980) 'Death of a Dream of Freedom', *Far Eastern Economic Review*, 23: 30.

Jordan, J. (2004) *Word of a Woman? Police, Rape and Belief*, New York: Palgrave MacMillan.

JSMP (2004a) *The Future of the Serious Crimes Unit, January*, Dili: JSMP.

—— (2004b) *Unfulfilled Expectations: Community Views on CAVR's Community Reconciliation Process*, Dili: JSMP.

—— (2005a) *Justice Update 12/2005: The Special Panels for Serious Crimes hear their Final Case*, Dili: JSMP.

—— (2005b) *Overview of the Justice Sector: March 2005*, Dili: JSMP.

—— (2006) *Justice Update 15/2006: The Dissemination of 'Chega!': The Final Report of the CAVR*, Dili: JSMP.

—— (2007) *News Archive – May 2007*, Dili: JSMP.

Kappeler, S. (1986) *The Pornography of Representation*, Cambridge: Polity Press.

Kauzlarich, D., Matthews, R. A. and Miller, W. J. (2001) 'Towards a Victimology of State Crime', *Critical Criminology*, 10: 173–94.

Kauzlarich, D., Mullins, C. W. and Matthews, R. A. (2003) 'A Complicity Continuum of State Crime', *Contemporary Justice Review*, 6, 3: 241–54.

Kaye, M. (1997) 'The Role of Truth Commissions in the Search for Justice, Reconciliation and Democratisation: The Salvadorean and Honduran cases', *Journal of Latin American Studies*, 29: 693–716.

Kiernan, B. (2002) 'Cover-up and Denial of Genocide: Australia, the USA, East Timor and the Aborigines', *Critical Asian Studies*, 34, 2: 163–92.

King, D. Y. (1987) 'Human Rights Practices and the Indonesian Middle Class', *Bulletin of Concerned Asian Scholars*, 19, 1: 4–13.

Kingsbury, D. (2006) 'Timor-Leste's Way Forward: State and Nation Building', paper presented at Beyond the Crisis in Timor-Leste Seminar, Australian National University, Canberra, 9 June 2006.

Kingston, J. (2006a) 'Balancing Justice and Reconciliation in East Timor', *Critical Asian Studies*, 38, 3: 271–302.

—— (2006b) *East Timor's Search for Justice and Reconciliation*, New York: ICTJ.

Kira, I. (2004) 'Assessing and Responding to Secondary Traumatisation in the Survivors' Families', *Torture*, 14, 1: 38–45.

Klaehn, J. (2002) 'Corporate Hegemony: A Critical Assessment of the Globe and Mail's News Coverage of Near-Genocide in Occupied East Timor 1975–80', *Gazette: The International Journal for Communication Studies*, 64, 4: 301–21.

Kohen, A. (1981) 'Invitation to a Massacre in East Timor', *The Nation*, 7 February, 81, 232: 136–39.

Kois, L. M. (1998) 'Dance, Sister, Dance!', in Dunér B (ed.) *An End to Torture*, London: Zed Books.

Komnas HAM (2000) *Report of the Indonesian Commission of Investigation into Human Rights Violations in East Timor*, Jakarta: Komnas Ham.

Koumjian, N. (2004) 'Accomplishments and Limitations of One Hybrid Tribunal: Experience at East Timor', paper presented to the International Criminal Court's Office of the Prosecutor, The Hague, 14 October 2004.

Kristeva, J. (1982) *Powers of Horror: An Essay on Abjection*, trans. S. Leon Roudiez, New York: Columbia University Press.

Kritz, N. J. (ed.) (1995) *Transitional Justice: How Emerging Democracies Reckon with Former Regimes, Volumes I, II and III*, Washington, DC: United States Institute of Peace.

La'o Hamutuk (2000) *The La'o Hamutuk Bulletin*, 1, 4, December.

—— (2002a) *The La'o Hamutuk Bulletin*, 3, 1, February.

—— (2002b) *The La'o Hamutuk Bulletin*, 3, 7, October.

—— (2006) *La'o Hamutuk asks RDTL Parliament to Scrutinize CMATS Treaty*, 4 April 2006, Dili: La'o Hamutuk.

Langbein, J. H. (1976) *Torture and the Law of Proof: Europe and England in the Ancien Régime*, Chicago, IL: University of Chicago Press.

Laub, D. (1992) 'An Event Without a Witness: Truth, Testimony and Survival', in S. Felman and D. Laub (eds) *Testimony: Crises of Witnessing in Literature, Psychoanalysis, and History*, London: Routledge.

Lawler, S. (2002) 'Narrative in Social Research', in T. May (ed.) *Qualitative Research in Action*, London: Sage.

Lawyers Committee for Human Rights (1993) *Broken Laws, Broken Bodies: Torture and the Right to Redress in Indonesia*, New York: Lawyers Committee for Human Rights.

Le Touze, D., Silove, D. and Zwi, A. (2005) 'Can there be Healing without Justice? Lessons from the Commission for Reception, Truth and Reconciliation in East Timor', *Intervention*, 3, 3: 192–202.

Lea, H. C. (1878) *Superstition and Force*, 3rd edn, Philadelphia, PA: H. C. Lea.

Leebaw, B. A. (2008) 'The Irreconcilable Goals of Transitional Justice', *Human Rights Quarterly*, 30: 95–118.

Linton, S. (2002) 'New Approaches to International Justice in Cambodia and East Timor', *IRRC*, 84, 845: 93–119.

—— (2004) 'Unravelling the First Three Trials at Indonesia's Ad Hoc Court for Human Rights Violations in East Timor', *Leiden Journal of International Law*, 17: 303–61.

Lutz, E. (2006) 'Transitional Justice: Lessons Learned and the Road Ahead', in N. Roht-Arriaza and J. Mariezcurrena (eds) *Transitional Justice in the Twenty-First Century: Beyond Truth versus Justice*, Cambridge: Cambridge University Press.

Mackenzie, S. (2006) 'Systemic Crimes of the Powerful: Criminal Aspects of the Global Economy', *Social Justice*, 33, 1: 162–82.

MacMaster, N. (2004) 'Torture: From Algiers to Abu Ghraib', *Race and Class*, 46, 2: 1–21.

Malamud-Goti, J. (1990) 'Transitional Governments in the Breach: Why Punish State Criminals?', *Human Rights Quarterly*, 12, 1: 1–16.

Malloch, M. S. and Stanley, E. (2005) 'The Detention of Asylum Seekers in the UK: Representing Risk, Managing the Dangerous', *Punishment and Society*, 7, 1: 53–71.

Marshall, S. (2005) 'The East Timorese Judiciary: At the Threshold of Self-Suffi-ciency? Update', paper presented at Co-operating with Timor Leste Conference, Victoria University, Melbourne, 17–18 June 2005.

Martinkus, J. (2001) *A Dirty Little War*, Milsons Point: Random House Australia.

Mathiesen, T. (2004) *Silently Silenced: Essays on the Creation of Acquiesence in Modern Society*, Winchester: Waterside Press.

McColgan, A. (2000) *Women under the Law: The False Promise of Human Rights*, Harlow: Longman.

McCorquodale, R. and Fairbrother, R. (1999) 'Globalization and Human Rights', *Human Rights Quarterly*, 21, 3: 735–66.

McCosker, A. (2004) 'East Timor and the Politics of Bodily Pain: A Problematic Complicity', *Continuum: Journal of Media and Cultural Studies*, 18, 1: 63–79.

McCulloch, J. (2007) 'Transnational Crime as Productive Fiction', *Social Justice*, 34, 2: 19–32.

McDonald, C. (2001) 'Out of the Ashes – A New Criminal Justice System for East Timor', paper presented to the International Society for the Reform of the Crim-inal Law Conference, Canberra, 30 August 2001.

McGrew, A. G. (1998) 'Human Rights in a Global Age: Coming to Terms with Globalization', in T. Evans (ed.) *Human Rights Fifty Years On: A Reappraisal*, Manchester: Manchester University Press.

McRae, D. (2002) 'A Discourse on Separatists', *Indonesia*, 74: 37–58.

Méndez, J. E. (1997) 'In Defense of Transitional Justice', in A. J. McAdams (ed.) *Transitional Justice and the Rule of Law in New Democracies*, Notre Dame, IN: University of Notre Dame Press.

Mertus, J. (2000) 'Truth in a Box: The Limits of Justice through Judicial Mechan-isms', in I. Amadiuma and A. An-Na'im (eds) *The Politics of Memory, Truth, Healing and Social Justice*, London: Zed Books.

Miller, D. (1999) 'Knowing Your Rights: Implications of the Critical Legal Studies Critique of Rights for Indigenous Australians', *Australian Journal of Human Rights*. Online. Available at www.austlii.edu.au/au/journals/AJHR/1999/2.html (accessed 21 December 2005).

Minow, M. (1998) *Between Vengeance and Forgiveness: Facing History after Geno-cide and Mass Violence*, Boston, MA: Beacon Press.

Modvig, J., Pagaduan-Lopez, J., Rodenburg, J., Salud, C. M. D., Cabigon, R. V. and Panelo, C. I. A. (2000) 'Torture and Trauma in Post-Conflict East Timor', *The Lancet*, 18 November, 356: 1763.

Monk, P. M. (2001) 'Secret Intelligence and Escape Clauses: Australia and the Indo-nesian Annexation of East Timor, 1963–76', *Critical Asian Studies*, 33, 2: 181–208.

Morgan, R. (2000) 'The Utilitarian Justification of Torture: Denial, Desert and Dis-information', *Punishment and Society*, 2, 2: 181–96.

Motsemme, N. (2004) 'The Mute Always Speak: On Women's Silences at the Truth and Reconciliation Commission', *Current Sociology*, 52, 5: 909–32.

Moxham, B. (2004) *The World Bank's Land of Kiosks: 'Community Driven Develop-ment' in East Timor*. Online. Available at www.globalpolicy.org/socecon/bwi-wto/wbank/2004/1012easttimor.htm (accessed 5 February 2005).

Nagy, R. (2008) 'Transitional Justice as Global Project: Critical Reflections', *Third World Quarterly*, 29, 2: 275–89.

Nairn, A. (1997) 'Foreword', in C. Pinto and M. Jardine (1997) *East Timor's Unfin-ished Struggle: Inside the Timorese Resistance*, Boston: South End Press.

Neier, A. (1990) 'What Should Be Done about the Guilty?', *The New York Review of Books*, 37, 1: 32–35.

—— (1998) *War Crimes: Brutality, Genocide, Terror, and the Struggle for Justice*, New York: Times Books/Random House.

Neves, G. N. (2006) 'The Paradox of Aid in Timor-Leste', paper presented at the Cooperação International e a Construção do Estado no Timor-Leste Seminar, University of Brasilia, Brazil, 25–28 July 2006. Online. Available at www.laohamutuk.org/reports/06ParadoxOfAid.htm (accessed 15 August 2006).

Nevins, J. (2003) 'Restitution over Coffee: Truth, Reconciliation and Environmental Violence in East Timor', *Political Geography*, 22: 677–701.

—— (2005) *A Not-So-Distant Horror: Mass Violence in East Timor*, Ithaca, NY: Cornell University Press.

Ní Aoláin, F. (2006) 'Political Violence and Gender during Times of Transition', *Columbia Journal of Gender and Law*, 15, 3: 829–49.

Nixon, R. (2006) 'The Crisis of Governance in New Subsistence States', *Journal of Contemporary Asia*, 36, 1: 75–101.

Nusa, P. (1987) 'The Path of Suffering: The Report of a Political Prisoner on His Journey through Various Prison Camps in Indonesia', *Bulletin of Concerned Asian Scholars*, 19, 1: 15–23.

Nussbaum, M. (1999) 'Women and Equality: The Capabilities Approach', *International Labour Review*, 138, 3: 227–45.

—— (2006) *Frontiers of Justice: Disability, Nationality, Species Membership*, Cambridge, MA: The Belknap Press of Harvard University Press.

O'Neill, O. (1993) 'Justice, Gender, and International Boundaries', in M. Nussbaum and A. Sen (eds) *The Quality of Life*, Oxford: Clarendon Press.

Oosterveld, V. (2005) 'Prosecution of Gender-Based Crimes in International Law', in D. Mazurana, A. Raven-Roberts and J. Parpart (eds) *Gender, Conflict and Peacekeeping*, Oxford: Rowman and Littlefield.

Open Society and CIJ, Coalition for International Justice (2004) *Unfulfilled Promises: Achieving Justice for Crimes against Humanity in East Timor*, New York: Open Society and CIJ.

Orentlicher, D. F. (1995) 'Settling Accounts: The Duty to Prosecute Human Rights Violations of a Prior Regime', in N. J. Kritz (ed.) *Transitional Justice: How Emerging Democracies Reckon with Former Regimes*, Vol I: General Considerations, Washington, DC: United States Institute of Peace Press.

—— (2007) "Settling Accounts' Revisited: Reconciling Global Norms with Local Agency', *The International Journal of Transitional Justice*, 1: 10–22.

Orford, A. (2006) 'Commissioning the Truth', *Columbia Journal of Gender and Law*, 15, 3: 851–83.

Osiel, M. (2000) *Mass Atrocity, Collective Memory, and the Law*, New Brunswick, NJ: Transaction Publishers.

Otto, D. (1999) 'Everything is Dangerous: Some Poststructural Tools for Rethinking the Universal Knowledge Claims of Human Rights Law', *Australian Journal of Human Rights*. Online. Available at www.austlii.edu.au/au/journals/AJHR/1999/1.html (accessed 21 December 2005).

Paris, E. (2000) *Long Shadows: Truth, Lies and History*, New York: Bloomsbury.

Patrick, I. (2001) 'East Timor Emerging from Conflict: The Role of Local NGOs and International Assistance', *Disasters*, 25, 1: 48–66.

Pérez-Sales, P., Bacic, R.and Durán, T. (1998) *Muerte y Desaparición Forzada en la Auracanía: Una Aproximación Etnica*, Temuco: Universidad Católica de Temuco.

Peters, E. (1985) *Torture* (Expanded Edition), Philadephia, PA: University of Pennsylvania Press.

Peterson, V. S. and Parisi, L. (1998) 'Are Women Human? It's Not an Academic Question', in T. Evans (ed.) *Human Rights Fifty Years On: A Reappraisal*, Manchester: Manchester University Press.

Phelps, T. G. (2004) *Shattered Voices: Language, Violence, and the Work of Truth Commissions*, Philadelphia, PA: University of Pennsylvania Press.

Phythian, M. (2000) *The Politics of British Arms Sales Since 1964*, Manchester: Manchester University Press.

Pigou, P. (2003) *Crying without Tears: In Pursuit of Justice and Reconciliation in Timor-Leste: Community Perspectives and Expectations*, New York: International Center for Transitional Justice.

—— (2004) *The Community Reconciliation Process of the Commission for Reception, Truth and Reconciliation*, Dili: United Nations Development Programme.

Pilger, J. (1994) 'On Her Majesty's Blood Service', *New Statesman and Society*, 7, 290: 16–19.

—— (1998) *Hidden Agendas*, London: Vintage.

Pinto, C. (1997) 'Arrest and Torture', in C. Pinto and M. Jardine (1997) *East Timor's Unfinished Struggle: Inside the Timorese Resistance*, Boston, MA: South End Press.

Pogge, T. (2002) *World Poverty and Human Rights*, Cambridge: Polity Press.

—— (2005) 'Human Rights and Human Responsibilities', in A. Kuper (ed.) *Global Responsibilities: Who Must Deliver on Human Rights?*, London: Routledge.

Post-CAVR Technical Secretariat (2006) *Post-CAVR Update: September-October 2006*. Online. Available at www.cavr-timorleste.org/STP-CAVR.htm (accessed 5 December 2006).

Pouligny, B. (2006) *Peace Operations Seen from Below: UN Missions and Local People*, Bloomfield: Kumarian Press.

Powell, S. (2006) 'Xanana, SBY let Shame File Slide', *Weekend Australian*, 18 February 2006. Online. Available at www.etan.org/et2006/february/13–19/18xana.htm (accessed 13 March 2006).

Poynting, S., Noble, G., Tabar, P. and Collins, J. (2004) *Bin Laden in the Suburbs: Criminalising the Arab Other*, Sydney: Sydney Institute of Criminology.

Pratt, J. (2002) *Punishment and Civilization: Penal Tolerance and Intolerance in Modern Society*, London: Sage.

Rae, J. (2003) 'War Crimes Accountability: Justice and Reconciliation in Cambodia and East Timor?', *Global Change, Peace and Security*, 15, 2: 157–78.

Rapoza, P. (2005) 'The Serious Crimes Process in Timor-Leste: Accomplishments, Challenges and Lessons Learned', paper presented to the International Symposium on UN Peacekeeping Operations in Post-Conflict Timor-Leste, 28 April 2005.

Rasmussen, O. V., Amris, S., Blaauw, M. and Danielsen, L. (2005) 'Medical Physical Examination in Connection with Torture', *Torture*, 15, 1: 37–45.

Rawski, F. (2002) 'Truth-Seeking and Local Histories in East Timor', *Asia-Pacific Journal on Human Rights and the Law*, 1: 77–96.

—— (2005) 'World Bank Community-Driven Development Programming in Indonesia and East Timor: Implications for the Study of Global Administrative Law', *International Law and Politics*, 37: 919–51.

Redress (2003) *Reparation for Torture: A Survey of Law and Practice in 30 Selected Countries (Indonesia Country Report)*, London: Redress.

Rees, E. (2006) *Security Sector Reform (SSR) and Peace Operations: "Improvisation and Confusion" from the Field*, New York: United Nations Department of Peacekeeping Operations.

Rehman, J. (2003) *International Human Rights Law: A Practical Approach*, Harlow: Pearson Education.

Reiger, C. (2006) 'Hybrid Attempts at Accountability for Serious Crimes in Timor Leste', in N. Roht-Arriaza and J. Mariezcurrena (eds) *Transitional Justice in the Twenty-First Century: Beyond Truth versus Justice*, Cambridge: Cambridge University Press.

Reiger, C. and Wierda, M. (2006) *The Serious Crimes Process in Timor-Leste: In Retrospect*, New York: International Center for Transitional Justice.

Rejali, D. (1994) *Torture and Modernity: Self, Society and State in Modern Iran*, Boulder, CO: Westview.

—— (1999) 'Ordinary Betrayals: Conceptualizing Refugees who have been Tortured in the Global Village', *Human Rights Review*, July-Sep 2000: 8–25.

—— (2003) 'Modern Torture as a Civic Marker: Solving a Global Anxiety with a New Political Technology', *Journal of Human Rights*, 2, 2: 153–71.

—— (2004) 'A Long-Standing Trick of the Torturer's Art', *The Seattle Times*, 14 May 2004. Online. Available at http://seattletimes.nwsource.com (accessed 18 May 2004).

—— (2007) *Torture and Democracy*, Princeton, NJ: Princeton University Press.

Retboll, T. (1987) 'The East Timor Conflict and Western Response', *Bulletin of Concerned Asian Scholars*, 19, 1: 24–40.

Reus-Smit, C. (2001) 'Human Rights and the Social Construction of Sovereignty', *Review of International Studies*, 27: 519–38.

Rivera-Fuentes, C. and Birke, L. (2001) 'Talking With/In Pain: Reflections on Bodies under Torture', *Women's Studies International Forum*, 24, 6: 653–68.

Robben, A. (1995) 'The Politics of Truth and Emotion among Victims and Perpetrators of Violence', in C. Nordstrom and A. Robben (eds) *Fieldwork under Fire: Contemporary Studies of Violence and Survival*, Berkeley, CA: University of California Press.

Robinson, G. (2001) 'People's War: Militias in East Timor and Indonesia', *South East Asia Research*, 9, 3: 271–318.

—— (2002) 'If You Leave Us Here We Will Die', in N. Mills and K. Brunner (eds) *The New Killing Fields: Massacre and the Politics of Intervention*, New York: Basic Books.

Roht-Arriaza, N. (2006) 'The New Landscape of Transitional Justice', in N. Roht-Arriaza and J. Mariezcurrena (eds) *Transitional Justice in the Twenty-First Century: Beyond Truth versus Justice*, Cambridge: Cambridge University Press.

Rolston, B. (2000) *Unfinished Business: State Killings and the Quest for Truth*, Belfast: Beyond the Pale.

—— (2006) 'Dealing with the Past: Pro-State Paramilitaries, Truth and Transition in Northern Ireland', *Human Rights Quarterly*, 28, 3: 652–75.

Roper, S. D. and Barria, L. A. (2006) *Designing Criminal Tribunals: Sovereignty and International Concerns in the Protection of Human Rights*, Aldershot: Ashgate.

Rosenblum, N. L. (2002) 'Justice and the Experience of Injustice', in M. Minow with N. L. Rosenblum (ed.) *Breaking the Cycles of Hatred: Memory, Law, and Repair*, Princeton, NJ: Princeton University Press.

Rosenthal, G. (2003) 'The Healing Effects of Storytelling: On the Conditions of Curative Storytelling in the Context of Research and Counseling', *Qualitative Inquiry*, 9, 6: 915–33.

Ross, F. C. (2001) 'Speech and Silence: Women's Testimony in the First Five Weeks of Public Hearings of the South African Truth and Reconciliation Commission', in V. Das, A. Kleinman, M. Lock, M. Ramphele and P. Reynolds (eds) *Remaking a World: Violence, Social Suffering and Recovery*, Cambridge: University of California Press.

—— (2003a) *Bearing Witness: Women and the Truth and Reconciliation Commission in South Africa*, London: Pluto.

—— (2003b) 'On Having Voice and Being Heard: Some After-Effects of Testifying Before the South African Truth and Reconciliation Commission', *Anthropological Theory*, 3, 3: 325–41.

—— (2003c) 'Using Rights to Measure Wrongs: A Case Study of Method and Moral in the Work of the South African Truth and Reconciliation Commission', in R. A. Wilson and J. P. Mitchell (eds) *Human Rights in Global Perspective: Anthropological Studies of Rights, Claims and Entitlements*, London: Routledge.

Rothenberg, D. (2003) '"What We have Seen had been Terrible" Public Presentational Torture and the Communicative Logic of State Terror', *Albany Law Review*, 67, 2: 465–99.

Rowland, R. (1995) 'Human Rights Discourse and Women: Challenging the Rhetoric with Reality', *Australian and New Zealand Journal of Sociology*, 31, 2: 8–25.

Rusche, G. and Kirchheimer, O. (1968 [1939]) *Punishment and Social Structure*, New York: Russell and Russell.

Ruthven, M. (1978) *Torture: The Grand Conspiracy*, London: Weidenfeld and Nicolson.

Saldanha, E., Vong, M., Williams-van Klinken, C., Dhae, P., Piedade, S. and de Lima, I. (2004) *Survey on Public Perception of The East Timor National Police's Work*, Dili: Institute of Technology / Centre for Applied Research and Policy Studies.

Sarmento, T. A. (2005) *The Future of Serious Crimes*, Dili: JSMP.

Scarry, E. (1985) *The Body in Pain: The Making and Unmaking of the World*, Oxford: Oxford University Press.

Scheper-Hughes, N. (1992) *Death Without Weeping: The Violence of Everyday Life in Brazil*, Berkeley, CA: University of California Press.

—— (1996) 'Small Wars and Invisible Genocides', *Social Science and Medicine*, 43, 5: 889–900.

Schofield, C. (2005) 'A "Fair Go" for East Timor? Sharing the Resources of the Timor Sea', *Contemporary Southeast Asia*, 27, 2: 255–80.

Schwendinger, H. and Schwendinger, J. (1975) 'Defenders of Order or Guardians of Human Rights?', in I. Taylor, P. Walton and J. Young (eds) *Critical Criminology*, London: Routledge and Kegan Paul.

Scott, J. (1990) *Domination and the Arts of Resistance: Hidden Transcripts*, New Haven, CT: Yale University Press.

Seifert, R. (1993) 'War and Rape: A Preliminary Analysis', in A. Stiglmayer (ed.) *Mass Rape: The War against Women in Bosnia-Herzegovina*, Lincoln, NE: University of Nebraska Press.

Sen, A. (1985) *Commodities and Capabilities*, Oxford: Oxford University Press.

—— (1999) 'Human Rights and Economic Achievements', in J. R. Bauer and D. A. Bell (eds) *The East Asian Challenge for Human Rights*, Cambridge: Cambridge University Press.

Sherlock, S. (1996) 'Political Economy of the East Timor Conflict', *Asian Survey*, 36, 9: 835–51.

Sikkink, K. and Walling, C. B. (2006) 'Argentina's Contribution to Global Trends in Transitional Justice', in N. Roht-Arriaza and J. Mariezcurrena (eds) *Transitional Justice in the Twenty-First Century: Beyond Truth versus Justice,* Cambridge: Cambridge University Press.

—— (2007) 'The Impact of Human Rights Trials in Latin America', *Journal of Peace Research*, 44, 4: 427–45.

Silove, D., Manicavasagar, V., Baker, K., Mausiri, M., Soares, M., de Carvalho, F., Soares, A., Amiral, Z. F. (2004) 'Indices of Social Risk among First Attenders of an Emergency Mental Health Service in Post-Conflict East Timor: An Exploratory Investigation', *Australian and New Zealand Journal of Psychiatry*, 38: 929–32.

Silove, D., Zwi, A. and Le Touze, D. (2006) 'Do Truth Commissions Heal? The East Timor Experience', *The Lancet*, 367, 15 April: 1222–23.

Sim, J. (2003) 'Whose Side are We Not On? Researching Medical Power in Prisons', in S. Tombs and D. Whyte (eds) *Unmasking the Crimes of the Powerful: Scrutinizing States and Corporations*, New York: Peter Lang.

Sim, J., Scraton, P. and Gordon, P. (1987) 'Introduction: Crime, The State and Critical Analysis', in P. Scraton (ed.) *Law, Order and the Authoritarian State*, Milton Keynes: Open University Press.

Simons, G. (2000) *Indonesia: The Long Oppression*, London: MacMillan Press.

Simonsen, S. G. (2006) 'The Authoritarian Temptation in East Timor', *Asian Survey*, 46, 4: 575–96.

Simpson, G. (2002) 'Tell No Lies, Claim No Easy Victories: A Brief Evaluation of South Africa's Truth and Reconciliation Commission', in D. Posel and G. Simpson (eds) *Commissioning the Past: Understanding South Africa's Truth and Reconciliation Commission*, Johannesburg: Witwatersrand University Press.

Singer, P. W. (2005) *Children at War*, New York: Pantheon Books.

Sironi, F. and Branche, R. (2002) 'Torture and the Borders of Humanity', *International Social Science Journal*, 54, 174: 539–48.

Sivanandan, A. (2001) 'Poverty is the New Black', *Race and Class*, 43, 2: 1–5.

Skeggs, B. (2002) 'Techniques for Telling the Reflexive Self', in T. May (ed.) *Qualitative Research in Action*, London: Sage.

Slapper, G. and Tombs, S. (1999) *Corporate Crime*, Harlow: Pearson Education/ Longman.

Smart, C. (1989) *Feminism and the Power of the Law*, London: Routledge.

Sottas, E. (1998) 'Perpetrators of Torture', in B. Dunér (ed.) *An End to Torture*, London: Zed Books.

Stanley, E. (1996) *The Risks and Responsibilities of South Africa's Truthtelling*, unpublished thesis, Keele University, UK.

—— (2001) 'Evaluating the Truth and Reconciliation Commission', *Journal of Modern African Studies*, 39, 3: 525–46.

—— (2002) 'What Next? The Aftermath of Organised Truth Telling', *Race and Class*, 44, 1: 1–15.

—— (2004) 'Torture, Silence and Recognition', *Current Issues in Criminal Justice*, 16, 1: 5–25.

—— (2005a) *Torture and Transitional Justice in Timor-Leste: A Report for the Judicial System Monitoring Project*, Dili: JSMP.

—— (2005b) 'Truth Commissions and the Recognition of State Crime', *British Journal of Criminology*, 45, 4: 582–97.

—— (2007a) 'Towards a Criminology for Human Rights', in A. Barton, K. Corteen, D. Scott and D. Whyte (eds) *The Criminological Imagination: Readings in Critical Criminologies*, Cullompton: Willan.

—— (2007b) *Torture Survivors: Their Experiences of Violation, Truth and Justice*, Dili: JSMP.

—— (2007c) 'Transnational Crime and State-Building: The Case of Timor-Leste', *Social Justice*, 34, 2: 124–37.

—— (2008a) 'The Political Economy of Transitional Justice in Timor-Leste', in K. McEvoy and L. McGregor (eds) *Transitional Justice from Below: Grassroots Activism and the Struggle for Change*, London: Hart Publishing.

—— (2008b) 'Torture and Terror', in T. Anthony and C. Cunneen (eds) *The Critical Criminology Companion*, Sydney: Hawkins Press.

Stanley, E. and Marriott, A. (forthcoming, 2009) 'Timor-Leste', in D. Chu and H. Hayes (eds) *Crime and Punishment around the World: Asia/Pacific Volume*, Westport, CT: Greenwood Press.

Strejilevich, N. (2006) 'Testimony: Beyond the Language of Truth', *Human Rights Quarterly*, 28, 3: 701–13.

Suárez-Orozco, M. (1992) 'A Grammar of Terror: Psychocultural Responses to State Terrorism in Dirty War and Post-Dirty War Argentina', in C. Nordstrom and J. Martin (eds) *The Paths to Domination, Resistance and Terror*, Berkeley, CA: University of California Press.

—— (2004) 'The Treatment of Children in the 'Dirty War': Ideology, State Terrorism, and the Abuse of Children in Argentina', in N. Scheper-Hughes and P. Bourgois (eds) *Violence in War and Peace: An Anthology*, Oxford: Blackwood Publishing.

Sykes, G. and Matza, D. (1957) 'Techniques of Neutralization: A Theory of Delinquency', *American Sociological Review*, 22, 6: 664–70.

Taussig, M. (2002) 'Culture of Terror – Space of Death: Roger Casement's Putumayo Report and the Explanation of Torture', in A. L. Hinton (ed.) *Genocide: An Anthropological Reader*, Oxford: Blackwell.

Taylor, C. (1992) 'The Politics of Recognition', in A. Gutman (ed.) *Multiculturalism and 'The Politics of Recognition': An Essay by Charles Taylor*, Princeton, NJ: Princeton University Press.

Taylor, J. G. (1991) *Indonesia's Forgotten War: The Hidden History of East Timor*, London: Zed Books.

—— (2003) '"Encirclement and Annihilation" The Indonesian Occupation of East Timor', in R. Gellately and B. Kiernan (eds) *The Specter of Genocide: Mass Murder in Historical Perspective*, Cambridge: Cambridge University Press.

Taylor, J. (1994) 'Body Memories: Aide-memoires and the Collective Amnesia in the Wake of the Argentine Terror', in M. Gordon (ed.) *Body Politics: Disease, Desire and the Family*, Oxford: Westview Press.

Teitel, R. G. (2000) *Transitional Justice*, Oxford: Oxford University Press.

—— (2003) 'Transitional Justice Genealogy', *Harvard Human Rights Journal*, 16: 69–94.

Thomas, C. (1998) 'International Financial Institutions and Social and Economic Human Rights: An Exploration', in T. Evans (ed.) *Human Rights Fifty Years On: A Reappraisal*, Manchester: Manchester University Press.

Timor Sea Justice Campaign (2005) *Briefing Paper – 28 July 2005*. Online. Available at tsjc.asiapacificjustice.org/resources/greater_sunrise_briefing_sheet.pdf (accessed 4 August 2005).

Tolbert, D. with Solomon, A. (2006) 'United Nations Reform and Supporting the Rule of Law in Post-Conflict Societies', *Harvard Human Rights Journal*, 19: 29–62.

Tombs, S. and Whyte, D. (2003) 'Scrutinizing the Powerful: Crime, Contemporary Political Economy, and Critical Social Research', in S. Tombs and D. Whyte (eds) *Unmasking the Crimes of the Powerful: Scrutinizing States and Corporations*, New York: Peter Lang.

Trowbridge, E. (2002) 'Back Road Reckoning: Justice in East Timor', *Dissent*, Winter: 101–13.

Trumper, R. (1999) '"Healing" the Social Body: Silence, Terror, and (Re)Conciliation in Neoliberal Chile', *Alternatives*, 24: 1–37.

Turner, S. and Gorst-Unsworth, C. (1990) 'Psychological Sequelae of Torture: A Descriptive Model', *British Journal of Psychiatry*, 157: 475–80.

Tushnet, M. (1984) 'An Essay on Rights', *Texas Law Review*, 62, 8: 1363–1403.

UN (1999a) *Situation of Human Rights in East Timor*, Resolution 1999/S-4/1, 27 September 1999.

—— (1999b) *Situation of Human Rights in East Timor: Human Rights Situations and Reports of Special Rapporteurs and Representatives*, UN doc. A/54/660, 10 December 1999.

—— (2000a) *Report of the International Commission of Inquiry on East Timor to the Secretary-General*, UN doc. A/54/726, 31 January 2000.

—— (2000b) *Identical Letters Dated 31 January 2000 from the Secretary-General addressed to the President of the General Assembly, the President of the Security Council and the Chairperson of the Commission on Human Rights*, UN doc. A/54/726, 31 January 2000.

—— (2003) *Question of the Violation of Human Rights and Fundamental Freedoms in any Part of the World: Situation of Human Rights in Timor-Leste*, UN doc. E/CN.4/2003/37, 4 March 2003.

—— (2004) *The Rule of Law and Transitional Justice in Conflict and Post-Conflict Societies: Report of the Secretary-General*, UN doc. S/2004/616, 3 August 2004.

—— (2005a) *Report to the Secretary-General of the Commission of Experts to Review the Prosecution of Serious Violations of Human Rights in Timor-Leste (then East Timor) in 1999 (26 May 2005)*, UN doc. S/2005/458, Annex II, 15 July 2005.

—— (2005b) *Letter dated 14 July 2005 from the Secretary-General addressed to the President of the Security Council*, UN doc. S/2005/459, 15 July 2005.

—— (2005c) *Report of the UN High Commission for Human Rights on Technical Co-operation in the Field of Human Rights in Timor Leste*, UN doc. E/CN.4/2005/115, 22 March 2005.

—— (2006) *Report of the Secretary-General on Justice and Reconciliation for Timor-Leste*, UN doc. S/2006/580, 26 July 2006.

UN Special Rapporteur on Torture (1992) *Report of the Special Rapporteur on Torture on his visit to Indonesia and East Timor*, E/CN.4/1992/17/Add.1, 8 January 1992.

UNDP, UN Development Programme (2006) The Path out of Poverty: Integrated Rural Development – Timor-Leste Human Development Report, Dili: UNDP.

UNOTIL, UN Office in Timor-Leste (2006) *CAVR Report is not a UN Document*, 20 January 2006. Online. Available at www.unotil.org (accessed 13 March 2006).

UNTAET, UN Transitional Administration in East Timor (2000) *Regulation No 2000/15 On the Establishment of Panels with Exclusive Jurisdiction over Serious Criminal Offences*, UNTAET/REG/2000/15, 6 June 2000.

—— (2001) *Regulation No 2001/10, On the Establishment of the Commission for Reception, Truth and Reconciliation in East Timor*, UNTAET/REG/2001/10, 13 July 2001.

—— (2002) *Directive No. 2002/9 On Amending the Criteria for Determining Whether Offence Appropriately Dealt with in a Community Reconciliation Process*, UNTAET/DIR/2002/9, 18 May 2002.

van der Kroef, J. M. (1976–77) 'Indonesia's Political Prisoners', *Pacific Affairs*, 49, 4: 625–47.

Vidal-Naquet, P. (1963) *Torture: Cancer of Democracy, France and Algeria 1954–62*, Harmondsworth: Penguin.

Wandita, G., Campbell-Nelson, K. and Pereira, M. L. (2006) 'Learning to Engender Reparations in Timor-Leste: Reaching Out to Female Victims', in R. Rubio-Marín (ed.) *What Happened to the Women? Gender and Reparations for Human Rights Violations*, New York: Social Science Research Council.

Weschler, L. (1998) *A Miracle, A Universe: Settling Accounts with Torturers*, Chicago, IL: University of Chicago Press.

West, H. G. (2003) 'Voices Twice Silenced: Betrayal and Mourning at Colonialism's End in Mozambique', *Anthropological Theory*, 3, 3: 343–65.

Whyte, D. (2007) 'The Crimes of Neo-Liberal Rule in Occupied Iraq', *British Journal of Criminology*, 47, 2: 177–95.

Wilson, R. A. (2001) *The Politics of Truth and Reconciliation in South Africa: Legitimizing the Post-Apartheid State*, Cambridge: Cambridge University Press.

Woods, N. (2000) 'The Challenge to International Institutions', in N. Woods (ed.) *The Political Economy of Globalization*, New York: St Martins Press.

Wright, S. (1996) 'The New Trade in Technologies of Restraint and Electroshock', in D. Forrest (ed.) *A Glimpse of Hell: Reports on Torture Worldwide*, London: Cassell.

—— (2007) 'Preparing for Mass Refugee Flows: The Corporate Military Sector', in D. Cromwell and M. Levene (eds) *Clearing the Pathways to Survival – The State, Ourselves and Climate Change*, London: Pluto Press.

Young, I. (1990) *Justice and the Politics of Difference*, Princeton, NJ: Princeton University Press.

—— (1997) 'Unruly Categories: A Critique of Nancy Fraser's Dual Systems Theory', *New Left Review*, 222: 147–60.

Young, J. (1999) *The Exclusive Society: Social Exclusion, Crime and Difference in Late Modernity*, London: Sage.

Zifcak, S. (2004) *Restorative Justice in East Timor: An Evaluation of the Community Reconciliation Process of the CAVR*, Dili: Asia Foundation.

Index

Printed in the United States
by Baker & Taylor Publisher Services